Tax Dispute Resolution

Tax Dispute Resolution

A Commentary on the EU Council Directive 2017/1852

Edited by

Raul-Angelo Papotti

Wolters Kluwer

Published by:
Kluwer Law International B.V.
PO Box 316
2400 AH Alphen aan den Rijn
The Netherlands
E-mail: international-sales@wolterskluwer.com
Website: lrus.wolterskluwer.com

Sold and distributed by:
Wolters Kluwer Legal & Regulatory U.S.
7201 McKinney Circle
Frederick, MD 21704
United States of America
Email: customer.service@wolterskluwer.com

ISBN 978-94-035-2360-6

e-Book: ISBN 978-94-035-2361-3
web-PDF: ISBN 978-94-035-2362-0

Editor

Raul-Angelo Papotti is a partner and the head of tax and tax planning department of Chiomenti. As a qualified barrister and a certified tax expert in Italy, he advises Italian and international clients on tax law and tax planning, cross-border taxation and transfer pricing, M&A transactions, trusts and estate planning matters. He advises multinationals in pre-litigation and litigation concerning cross-border tax and transfer pricing matters. His clients include leading global investment banks, Italian and foreign multinationals, and prominent HNWIs, families and family offices. He is the author of many publications on international tax matters and is a frequent speaker at domestic and international congresses. He is also the co-author of a book on the Italian Patent Box regime, edited by EGEA.

Contributors

Nikolaj Bjørnholm concentrates his practice on tax controversy and international taxation. He is an experienced litigator and has appeared before the Supreme Court more than fifteen times since 2000. He is ranked as a leading tax lawyer in various directories. During his career, he has continuously published articles in both Danish and international tax journals. Further information is available at https://bjornholmlaw.com/en/.

Olivier Dauchez is a partner at Gide Loyrette Nouel. He has extensive experience in domestic and international tax law and cross-border disputes. He advises on international transactions: mergers and acquisitions, corporate reorganizations, real estate, structured finance, and project financing. He also advises on personal tax matters and is active in tax litigation for both individuals and companies, assisting in tax audits and litigation before tax courts. He is Chairman of the International Tax Committee of the French Tax Lawyers Association (IACF).

Joseph Duffy is a partner in the tax group at Matheson. With his more than twenty years' experience in corporate tax law, Joe advises on international restructurings, mergers and acquisitions, tax controversy and transfer pricing. Joe's clients include many of the leading multinational corporations established in Ireland, primarily in the pharmaceutical, technology, industrial and service sectors. Further information is available at https://www.matheson.com/our-people/profile/joe-duffy.

Alain Goebel is a partner in the tax law practice of Arendt & Medernach where he advises an international clientele on the tax and transfer pricing aspects of Luxembourg and cross-border transactions, in particular corporate reorganizations, acquisitions and financing structures. Further information is available at http://www.arendt.com.

Joan Hortalà is a partner in Cuatrecasas' tax practice and a former tax inspector at the Spanish Ministry of Finance and National Expert at the EU Commission. Mr. Hortalà advises corporate groups with a strong international profile. He specializes in international taxation and transfer pricing, enabling his clients to be taxed in line with their value chain. Additional information is available at https://www.cuatrecasas.com/lawyer/joan_hortala.html.

Stefan Mayer is a partner and head of the tax practice group of Gleiss Lutz. He advises clients on all aspects of domestic and international tax law, with a focus on transactions-related tax issues, in particular on M&A transactions and restructurings of distressed companies. His practice also includes advice on reorganizations as well as tax and succession planning. Further information is available at https://www.gleisslutz.com/en/lawyer/dr-stefan-mayer.html.

Natalie Reypens is specialized in corporate tax law, including (inter)national corporate restructuring, M&A, holdings and financing structures. She is an expert in transfer pricing. She assists multinationals in formulating transfer pricing policies. She also advises on the setting up and conversion of business models, restructurings and profit allocation to permanent establishments. Natalie prepares and assists in preparing transfer pricing documentation. She also handles audits, rulings and APAs and disputes through MAP and arbitration. Natalie also has experience in EU state aid. Further information can be found on the Loyens & Loeff website.

Harold Turot is a senior associate at the Paris office of Gide Loyrette Nouel. His practice mainly focuses on tax litigation, with a special emphasis on international tax law and criminal tax defence. He is a member of the International Fiscal Association (IFA), the French Tax Lawyers Association (IACF) and the Criminal Tax Law Association (IDPF2).

Mark Van Casteren is a tax partner in the Amsterdam offices of Loyens & Loeff. He heads the Amsterdam Pricing Team (focusing on transfer pricing, risk pricing, decision modelling and valuations). Mark studied Tax Law at the University of Amsterdam, Netherlands, and participated in an LLM tax programme at Emory University, Atlanta, Georgia. He has over twenty-eight years of experience in advising on international tax matters. Mark frequently lectures on transfer pricing and international tax. He is a member of the International Fiscal Association (IFA), the International Bar Association (IBA), the American Bar Association (ABA) and the Dutch Association of Tax Advisors (NOB).

Pedro Vidal Matos is a partner in the tax law practice of Cuatrecasas in Portugal. He focuses his practice on tax litigation, both administrative and judicial. He has been a member of the Portuguese Bar Association since 2002 and is a member of the Portuguese Tax Association and International Fiscal Association. He is a lecturer in the postgraduate programme on Taxation at the Portuguese Catholic University, Lisbon, Portugal. Mr. Vidal Matos obtained his Law degree from Nova University of Lisbon, Portugal (2002), completed a postgraduate degree in Company Law from University of Coimbra, Portugal (2004), a postgraduate degree in Taxation, from ISG – Business & Economics School, Lisbon, Portugal (2005), a postgraduate degree in Administrative and Tax Justice from University of Coimbra (2007), a Master's in Public Law from Nova

University of Lisbon (2009) and a Master's in Taxation from the Institute of Advanced Legal Studies of London University (2012), England. Further information and contact details are available at www.cuatrecasas.com.

Christian Wimpissinger is a partner in the tax team of Binder Grösswang with more than nineteen years of experience in advising on cross-border acquisitions and restructurings as well as on international tax law and accounting law (including IFRS). Christian is also an adjunct faculty member of the Graduate Program in Taxation of the University of Miami School of Law, Florida, United States, and an officer of the IBA's Taxes Committee. Further information is available at http://www.bindergroesswang.at.

Summary of Contents

Table of Contents

List of Abbreviations

ACD	Competent Luxemburg Authority (the so-called *Administration des contributions directes*)
AEAT	Spanish Tax Agency (the so-called *Agencia Estatal de Administración Tributaria*)
CCCTB	Common Consolidated Corporate Tax Base
DGT	Spanish General Directorate of Taxation (the so-called *Dirección General de Tributos*)
ECJ	European Court of Justice
EU	European Union
FFC	Austria Federal Fiscal Code
FFCA	Austrian Federal Finance Court Act
FPC	French Procedural Code
IRA	Italian Revenue Agency
MAP	Mutual Agreement Procedure
MLI	Multilateral Convention to Implement Tax Treaty Related Measures to Prevent Base Erosion and Profit Shifting
TCA	Ireland Taxes Consolidation Acts 1997
TEAC	Portuguese Central Economic-Administrative Tribunal

Acknowledgements

This book would have not been possible without the participation and contribution of all the authors and of many friends and clients around the world who took time to review earlier versions of the manuscript, share their views and ideas as well as their top-notch practical insights and real-life experiences.

Special thanks go to Andrea Alcara, Borja Pascual, Lukas Pechtl, Harold Turot, Pearse Walsh and Giuseppe Zorzi, who worked on the country chapters, and to Margherita Pittori for the editing.

To all my colleagues, partners and peers at Chiomenti and around the world: this book would not have been possible without you and your suggestions and inspiration and competence. I am blessed to have the company of great minds and great people.

Further, I thank Professor Stef van Weeghel for being an inspiration through almost twenty years and for the continuous interaction with him on many technical issues.

Special thanks go to the publishing team at Wolters Kluwer and in particular to Lisa Zoltowska for her constant guidance and patience.

On a more personal note, I would like to thank my wife Beatrice and my son Paolo Augusto. I am eternally grateful for all their love, support and understanding.

Introduction

Raul-Angelo Papotti

A. THE EU COUNCIL DIRECTIVE 2017/1852 OF 10 OCTOBER 2017 ON TAX DISPUTE RESOLUTION

Over the past few decades, there has been a progressive increase in the number of audit activities and tax assessments carried out by tax administrations, aiming at fighting cross-border tax evasion or avoidance or at scrutinizing the compliance of international transactions with transfer pricing regulations.

These activities have thus led to a growth of potential double taxation situations (the stock of MAPs lying with different tax authorities is increasing every year), the resolution of which necessarily requires the simultaneous involvement of the tax authorities in different States through the use of alternative dispute resolution mechanisms. Indeed, domestic measures – such as jurisdictional appeals or tax settlement procedures – inevitably leave some juridical double taxation on the table.

Traditionally, the resolution of international taxation disputes has been regulated on the basis of provisions drafted along the lines of Article 25 of the OECD Model Tax Convention on Income and on Capital (hereinafter the 'OECD Model Convention') on MAP, implemented within the single bilateral treaties against double taxation in force between the Contracting States (hereinafter the 'Tax Treaties').

Indeed, Article 25 of the OECD Model Convention provides that a MAP, independent from the ordinary legal remedies available under domestic laws, may allow the competent authorities of the Contracting States to resolve differences or difficulties regarding the interpretation or application of the relevant Tax Treaty on a mutually agreed basis.

However, since '*the integration of national economies and markets has increased substantially in recent years, putting a strain on the international tax rules which were designed more than a century ago'*,[1] national bodies and international organizations have started to elaborate and study new rules and legal framework, in order to grant the taxpayer(s) with a dispute resolution mechanism more effective than those currently available.

In this context, the OECD has elaborated BEPS Action 14 – Making Dispute Resolution Mechanism More Effective – following an intense discussion involving all G20 and OECD Countries as well as several international bodies. In the context of the BEPS project, on November 2016, over a hundred jurisdictions concluded negotiations on the Multilateral Convention to Implement Tax Treaty Related Measures to Prevent Base Erosion and Profit Shifting (hereinafter 'MLI') that will implement a series of tax treaty measures to update international tax rules and reduce tax avoidance opportunities for multinational enterprises. The MLI entered into force on 1 July 2018.

One of MLI's most important innovative aspects is the introduction of new and more effective measures to make MAPs more effective, including provisions on MAP arbitration. However, the implementation of more effective MAPs lies on the determination of each State to enter into the MLI, thus postponing the effective implementation of the principles here included in the next future when all the existing Tax Treaties will be updated according to the MLI.

In addition to the legal framework deriving from (updated) Tax Treaties, in the past, the European Union (EU) implemented special provisions concerning the elimination of double taxation in connection with the adjustment of profits of associated enterprises. In particular, Convention 90/463/EEC of 23 July 1990 (hereinafter the 'Arbitration Convention')[2] has been the most effective instrument available, for more than twenty-five years, to EU taxpayers to prevent double taxation issues arising from tax assessments carried out by national tax administration on transfer pricing and profit allocation matters.[3]

However, also the Arbitration Convention in the last years has suffered shortcomings in terms of scope, effectiveness and efficiency, mostly due to the circumstance that the Arbitration Convention was applicable only to transfer pricing and profit allocation issues and that the obligation of Member States to resolve disputes has not

1. OECD (2015), *Making Dispute Resolution Mechanisms More Effective, Action 14 – 2015 Final Report*, OECD/G20 Base Erosion and Profit Shifting Project, OECD Publishing, Paris. http://dx.doi.org/10.1787/9789264241633-en.
2. The Arbitration Convention has its origin in the commission's 1976 proposal for a directive to eliminate double taxation in the case of transfers of profits between associated enterprises in different Member States and the White Paper of 1985 on the completion of the Internal Market.
3. The Arbitration Convention was initially in force from 1 January 1995 until 31 December 1999 for a period of five years. Before the expiration of its first five-year application period, the Council adopted a Protocol to the Arbitration Convention that provided for an automatic extension of the Convention by periods of five years unless a Contracting State opposes. This Protocol of 25 May 1999 amended the Convention of 23 July 1990 on the elimination of double taxation in connection with the adjustment of profits of associated enterprises. In spite of its timely signature, this Protocol was only ratified by all fifteen Member States in 2004 and the Arbitration Convention re-entered into force, with retroactive effect from 1 January 2000, on 1 November 2004. With the enlargement of the EU, the Arbitration Convention was successively extended to the new Member States. On 30 December 2009, the EU Council published a revised code of conduct for implementation of the convention for transfer pricing disputes, and the EU Joint Transfer Pricing Forum recommended further amendments in a March 2015 report.

always been fully enforced, thus causing the taxpayer to not have any other recourse available in case the MAP procedure established according to the Arbitration Convention was prolonged or blocked.

Therefore, based on the opinion of the EU Commission, the mere implementation of OECD BEPS Action 14/15 would not constitute a sufficient action to improve existing dispute resolution mechanisms.[4] Furthermore, considering that the promotion of a one single market has always been one of the main missions within the EU, the ECOFIN Council adopted the new Council Directive 10 (EU) 2017/1852 of 10 October 2017 (hereinafter 'Directive 2017/1852') aiming at providing more certainty to the double taxation disputes resolution process, with a broader scope of application. Indeed, the scope of the new procedures set forth by Directive 2017/1852 is no longer limited to transfer pricing and allocation of profit issues only, but it rather extends to any dispute that leads to double taxation issues.[5] For instance, issues relating to the assessment of hidden permanent establishments, the beneficial ownership status in connection to dividends, interest and royalty payments and the qualification of the tax residence may benefit from the new procedures laid down by Directive 2017/1852.

In addition to a much wider scope, Directive 2017/1852 aims at ensuring effective resolution of disputes, since the monitoring exercise carried out as part of the application of the Arbitration Convention '*has revealed some important shortcomings, in particular as regards access to the procedure and as regards length and effective conclusion of the procedure*'.[6]

Furthermore, Directive 2017/1852 clearly recognizes that the implementation of a new effective and efficient MAP procedure is necessary in order to ensure the full respect of the right to a fair trial and the freedom to conduct a business, which are fundamental rights and principles recognized by the Charter of Fundamental Rights of the European Union.[7]

Directive 2017/1852 fits clearly in a new era of EU tax legislation, whose purpose is ensuring a comprehensive legal framework involving all the Member States. Indeed: (i) the new policy and rules on anti-abuse measures (Council Directive (EU) 2016/1164 of 12 July 2016 laying down rules against tax avoidance practices that directly affect the functioning of the Internal Market – so-called ATAD 1 – and Council Directive (EU) 2017/952 of 29 May 2017 amending Directive (EU) 2016/1164 as regards hybrid mismatches with third countries – so-called ATAD 2), (ii) the Common Consolidated

4. European Commission, Initiative on Improving Double Taxation Dispute Resolution Mechanisms (June 2016), available at http://ec.europa.eu/smart-regulation/roadmaps/docs/2016_taxud_007_improving_double_taxation_dispute_resolution_mechanisms_en.pdf.
5. T. Wiertsema, '*Council Directive on Double Taxation Dispute Resolution Mechanism: Resolving Companies' Areas of Concern?*', 19 Derivatives & Financial Instruments, 2017, No. 5.
6. *See* Preamble of Directive 2017/1852.
7. *See* Article 16 – Freedom to conduct a business – and Article 47 – Right to an effective remedy and to a fair trial – of the Charter of Fundamental Rights of the European Union (Official Journal C 326/2002). With respect to the interaction between the Fair Trail Protection and the provisions set forth by the Directive 2017/1852 *see* D. De Carolis, '*The EU Dispute Resolution Directive (2017/1852) and Fair Trial Protection under Article 47 of the EU Charter of Fundamental Rights*', European Taxation, 2018 (Volume 58), No. 11.

Corporate Tax Base (CCCTB) proposal[8] and (iii) the proposal of new rules to ensure that digital business activities are taxed in a fair and growth-friendly way in the EU,[9] all require an even more harmonized and coordinated implementation and application, leading to the risk of an increased number of double (or even multiple) taxation disputes. The introduction of Directive 2017/1852 will therefore grant the required legal environment to apply the new common rules as well as to allow the introduction of new EU-based tax legislation. The Covid emergency may also play a peculiar role in this further strengthening and harmonization of the EU's fiscal policy, with a deeper integration and an integrated scope of common action.

In this respect, it is worth noting that – although Directive 2017/1852 is still based on the traditional structure of international tax dispute resolution, where the process is basically controlled by the tax authorities of the States involved and no enforceable participation rights are granted to taxpayers[10] – a new innovative approach has been introduced, granting some authority to the national courts, which may be required to steer the procedure so to provide taxpayers with a legal enforceable remedy against the situation whereby a MAP remains stuck within the competent authorities.

As regards timing, according to Article 23 of Directive 2017/1852, the new MAP procedures apply to any complaint filed as from 1 July 2019 onwards with respect to disputes relating to income or capital earned in a fiscal year started on or after 1 January 2018. Noteworthily, the competent authorities concerned are in any case entitled to agree to the application of the new procedures also with respect to complaints that were submitted prior to 1 July 2019 or relates to previous tax years.

B. THE ARBITRATION CONVENTION: BRIEF DESCRIPTION, SHORTFALLS AND MAIN ISSUES

As anticipated, the scope of the Arbitration Convention is limited only to transfer pricing disputes and cases involving the attribution of profits to permanent establishments and, of course, only for cases involving different Member States.

The Arbitration Convention grants a binding arbitration phase where a dispute involving two or more Member States has not been resolved by competent authorities via the MAP initiated by the taxpayer within two years from the date on which the case was first submitted to one of the competent authorities. In this case – provided that the taxpayer waives any domestic remedy against the adjustment giving rise to double

8. *See* COM(2016) 685 final.
9. The so-called EU Digital Package was released on 21 March 2018, and it proposes a Council Directive laying down rules relating to the corporate taxation of a significant digital presence – COM(2018) 147 final – and a Council Directive on the common system of a digital services tax on revenues resulting from the provision of certain digital services – COM(2018) 148 final.
10. D. De Carolis, '*The EU Dispute Resolution Directive (2017/1852) and Fair Trial Protection under Article 47 of the EU Charter of Fundamental Rights*', European Taxation, 2018 (Volume 58), No. 11; the author underlines that Directive 2017/1852 is still based on the old idea of 'diplomatic protection' according to which only national States may act at international levels on behalf of their nationals who have been injured due to an infringement of public international law.

taxation[11] – the case is settled by an Advisory Commission composed of five members (including two independent persons of standing) during the arbitration phase.

Dispute resolution pursuant to the Arbitration Convention takes three different forms:

(1) Unilateral Relief (*see* Article 5 of the Arbitration Convention);
(2) MAP (*see* Article 6 of the Arbitration Convention); and
(3) Arbitration (*see* Articles 7-13 of the Arbitration Convention).

As said, the remedies granted according to the Arbitration Convention do not involve the taxpayer in any procedure whatsoever and the procedure is wholly under the competent authority's control. Furthermore, there was no clear procedural time frame for a resolution binding upon the parties.

In particular, the Unilateral Relief procedure requires a Contracting State to inform the taxpayer involved of its decision to make an adjustment to its profits, so that such taxpayer could inform the other enterprise(s) and the other Contracting State(s). If, based on this notification, the taxpayer(s) involved and the other Contracting State(s) agree to the adjustment, the case is not submitted to a MAP or arbitration.

The MAP is started with the presentation of the case before the competent authority within three years from the first serving of the action that resulted or is likely to result in double taxation.

The competent authority involved is obliged to commence the MAP, except if the complaint is not well founded, pursuant to Article 6 of the Arbitration Convention, or if the case determined the application of a severe penalty, pursuant to Article 8 of the Arbitration Convention, or, finally, if the competent authority is not allowed to derogate from judicial decisions and the enterprise did not waive domestic remedies, pursuant to Article 7 of the Arbitration Convention. In any case, similar to the provisions set forth by the OECD Model Convention, the two States are not bound to find an agreed solution to the dispute.

According to Article 7 of the Arbitration Convention, in case the competent authorities concerned failed to reach an agreement eliminating double taxation within two years from the date on which the case was first submitted, they would set up an Advisory Commission empowered to deliver its opinion on the elimination of the double taxation in question, within six months from the submission date. The decision should be implemented within six months of its delivery.

11. *See* Article 7 of the Arbitration Convention, according to which '*enterprises may have recourse to the remedies available to them under the domestic law of the Contracting States concerned; however, where the case has so been submitted to a court or tribunal, the term of two years referred to in the first subparagraph shall be computed from the date on which the judgment of the final court of appeal was given*' (para. No. 1) and '*where the domestic law of a Contracting State does not permit the competent authorities of that State to derogate from the decisions of their judicial bodies, paragraph 1 shall not apply unless the associated enterprise of that State has allowed the time provided for appeal to expire, or has withdrawn any such appeal before a decision has been delivered. This provision shall not affect the appeal if and in so far as it relates to matters other than those referred to in Article*' (para. No. 3).

The commission is composed of two representatives of each competent authority, as well as with an even number of independent persons to be appointed either by mutual agreement or by ballot. Several rules and procedures are set forth in order to grant that the members of the Advisory Commission can achieve an impartial conclusion.

The resolutions of the Advisory Commission are however not binding upon the competent authorities as the Arbitration Convention indeed allows a deviation from the decision of the Advisory Commission. Of course, the competent authorities remain free to find agreeable ways to eliminate double taxation through mutual agreement.

The final decision – or the agreement reached by the competent authorities after disregarding the even final resolution – is binding upon the taxpayer.

That said, in the context of the general consultation conducted by the EU in 2016, several issues related to the application of the Arbitration Convention have arisen. In particular, lack of legal certainty, lack of enforceable deadlines for reaching agreement, lack of a review or appeal procedure and inconsistency of the application of rules throughout the Member States, as well as taxpayers' inability to participate in the process raised major concerns on the effectiveness of the alternative dispute resolution mechanism at hand. Taxpayers also stressed that Arbitration Convention procedures (as well as the MAP under any applicable Tax Treaty) require excessive costs and compliance burdens, thus preventing individuals, micro, small and medium-sized enterprises from the access to the resolution procedures.[12]

Directive 2017/1852 aims to tackle and provide an answer to such issues.

C. DIRECTIVE 2017/1852: BRIEF DESCRIPTION OF THE NEW PROCEDURES

As already noted, one of the most important features of Directive 2017/1852 is its scope, which significantly broadens the scope of the Arbitration Convention. According to Article 1 of Directive 2017/1852, '*this Directive lays down rules on a mechanism to resolve disputes between Member States when those disputes arise from the interpretation and application of agreements and conventions that provide for the elimination of double taxation of income and, where applicable, capital. It also lays down the rights and obligations of the affected persons when such disputes arise*'.[13]

The scope of the Directive varies depending on which of the instruments it is applied to, them being a Tax Treaty, the MLI or the Arbitration Convention: Directive 2017/1852 is indeed an alternative to the dispute resolution mechanisms provided for by those instruments.[14]

12. In order to allow smaller taxpayer to benefit from Directive 2017/1852, a simplified procedure has been set out according to Article 17.
13. As with the Arbitration Convention, indirect taxes and penalties are out of scope of application of Directive 2017/1852.
14. According to Article 16(5) of Directive 2017/1852, once a complaint under the Directive has been submitted, all other proceedings under the agreements or conventions in question must be terminated ('*the submission of a complaint as provided under Article 3 shall put an end to any other ongoing proceedings under the mutual agreement procedure or dispute resolution procedure*

Moreover, Directive 2017/1852 provides certain exceptions for its application in cases where penalties are imposed due to '*tax fraud, wilful default and gross negligence*'; in addition, the new Directive 2017/1852 expressly allows the Member States to deny access on a case-by-case basis where a case does not involve double taxation.[15]

Nonetheless, the exception, which prevents the initiation of the procedure in case the required information is missing, is still operating. However, it is expressly provided that '*the competent authorities of each of the Member States concerned may request the information referred to in point (f) of paragraph 3 within 3 months from the receipt of the complaint. Further requests for information may be made during the mutual agreement procedure under Article 4 if the competent authorities consider this to be necessary*' (*see* Article 3(4) of Directive 2017/1852). Such provisions clearly aim at setting out a (very welcome) collaborative environment between the taxpayer and the competent authorities in order to grant an effective access (and – hopefully – actual positive results) to the procedure.

From a procedural point of view, the remedies set forth by Directive 2017/1852 are similar to those granted by the Arbitration Convention and are still hinged on a three-step procedure, as follows:

(1) complaint stage (*see* Articles 3-5 of Directive 2017/1852);
(2) MAP stage (*see* Article 4 of Directive 2017/1852); and
(3) dispute resolution stage (*see* Articles 5-15 of Directive 2017/1852).

This being said, the similarities somehow terminate. The complaint stage is indeed brand new, in very brief with a substantially complete replacement of the Unilateral Relief phase of the Arbitration Convention.

According to the principles set forth in the Preamble, where the Council expressly recognizes the need to grant an effective access to the procedure, the main focus of the complaint stage is ensuring taxpayers access to MAPs by providing detailed guidelines for the request on the one hand and legal remedies in the case of denial of access on the other hand. Moreover, as opposed to the Arbitration Convention, where most of the procedural rules were detailed within the Code of Conduct,[16] Directive 2017/1852 clearly sets out specific and autonomous provisions for all the procedural steps, requirements and data to be provided by the taxpayer (*see* Article 3(3) of Directive 2017/1852); a precise timeline for this stage is also set out, thereby increasing certainty and predictability for taxpayers and tax administrations alike, with clear time limits for the duration of the procedure.

As for the Arbitration Convention, the taxpayer may submit the complaint within three years from the first notification of action resulting in double taxation. However,

under an agreement or convention that is being interpreted or applied in relation to the relevant question in dispute. Such other ongoing proceedings concerning the relevant question in dispute shall come to an end with effect from the date of the first receipt of the complaint by any of the competent authorities of the Member States concerned').

15. Article 16(7), Directive 2017/1852.
16. The Code of Conduct, adopted by the European Council (2009/C 322/01), aims at the effective implementation of the Arbitration Convention.

in order to solve the issues deriving from the duration of the procedure and, most importantly, the effective access to the same procedure, according to Article 3(2) of Directive 2017/1852, '*each competent authority shall acknowledge receipt of the complaint within 2 months from the receipt of the complaint*'.

Moreover, and this is one of the most innovative features of the new Directive 2017/1852, the competent authorities are now required to decide on the acceptance of the complaint within six months from the receipt thereof, and the competent authorities shall inform the affected person and the competent authorities of the other Member States of their decision without delay (*see* Article 3(5) of Directive 2017/1852); the reasons for the rejection shall be provided to the taxpayer. A more stringent involvement of the taxpayer is indeed one of the most innovative aspects of Directive 2017/1852 compared to the framework previously applicable.

The effective protection of the right of access to the procedure is granted by Articles 5 and 6 of Directive 2017/1852, according to which the taxpayer is now entitled to the following remedies to ensure that valid complaints are not unjustifiably rejected.

In particular, the taxpayer can now file an appeal against the decision of the competent authorities of the Member States concerned, in accordance with national rules, where all the competent authorities of the Member States concerned have rejected the complaint.

On the other hand, and provided that no appeal is pending before any tax court:

- if the complaint submitted by the taxpayer was rejected by at least one, but not all of the competent authorities of Member States concerned; or
- if the competent authorities of the Member States concerned accepted the complaint that was submitted by the affected person but failed to reach an agreement on how to resolve the question in dispute by mutual agreement within the two-year period provided for in Article 4(1) of Directive 2017/1852; or
- if no appeal can be made against the decision or the taxpayer has formally renounced his right of appeal;

then the taxpayer is now entitled to request the setting up of an Advisory Commission to decide on the admissibility of the complaint.

The resolution on the acceptance of the complaint is to be adopted within six months from the date of the establishment of the Advisory Commission, and where the latter has confirmed that all of the requirements of the complaint set forth by Article 3 of Directive 2017/1852 have been satisfied, the MAP provided for in Article 4 of Directive 2017/1852 shall be initiated at the request of one of the competent authorities.[17]

17. It is worth noting that the two-year period provided for in Article 4 for the conclusion of the MAP shall start from the date of the notification of the decision taken by the Advisory Commission of the acceptance of the complaint.

In case none of the competent authorities has requested the initiation of the MAP within sixty days from the date of the notification of Advisory Commission's resolution, the latter shall provide an opinion on how to resolve the question in dispute[18] and the competent authorities concerned shall agree on how to resolve the question in dispute within six months from the notification of the opinion of the Advisory Commission.[19] In case no different agreement is reached, the opinion will be binding and final.

As mentioned, the complaint stage is followed by the MAP stage, whose rules and procedures are set forth by Article 4 of Directive 2017/1852. Similar to the MAP stage under the Arbitration Convention, pursuant to the MAP stage of Directive 2017/1852, the competent authorities of the Member States concerned shall endeavour (but without binding effect) to resolve the question in dispute by mutual agreement within two years; this term can eventually be extended by up to one year at the request of a competent authority.

Should an agreement be reached, the competent authority of each of the Member States concerned shall, without delay, notify the agreement to the taxpayer. This decision is binding on the tax authority and enforceable by the taxpayer, subject to the latter accepting the decision and renouncing the right to any other remedy.

On the contrary, in case an agreement is not reached, the taxpayer is entitled to request the set-up of the Advisory Commission that, similar to the case where a complaint has been denied, will endeavour in order to resolve the dispute through the delivery of another opinion. Also in this case the competent authorities concerned shall agree on how to resolve the question in dispute within six months from the notification of the opinion of the Advisory Commission. If no different agreement is reached between the competent authorities, the opinion so released by the Advisory Commission will be binding and final.

As an alternative to the Advisory Commission, the competent authorities of the Member States concerned may agree to set up an Alternative Dispute Resolution Commission; the Alternative Dispute Resolution Commission, subject to the agreement of the competent authorities of the Member States, may be established with a permanent nature.

The Alternative Dispute Resolution Commission will also have to render a final opinion on the subject matter, but it may differ from the Advisory Commission in terms of its composition and, most notably, it may also apply – upon agreement between competent authorities – other means of resolution than the independent opinion

18. As per Article 6(2), Directive 2017/1852.
19. *See* Article 15 – Final Decision – Directive 2017/1852; in particular, according to para. No. 2 '*the competent authorities may take a decision which deviates from the opinion of the Advisory Commission or Alternative Dispute Resolution Commission. However, if they fail to reach an agreement as to how to resolve the question in dispute, they shall be bound by that opinion*'. The final decision so reached shall be implemented upon the condition that the taxpayer accepting the final decision and renouncing its right to any domestic remedy within sixty days from the date when the final decision was notified.

process applied by the Advisory Commission (where the opinion is reached by a simple majority of the commission members with the chair deciding in case of a draw), such as, the so-called baseball arbitration, or final offer arbitration, where the decision is limited to choosing one of either of the competent authorities' proposals on the dispute, thus naturally promoting the parties to elaborate well-balanced proposals.[20]

That said, one of the aspects having the utmost importance in the framework of Directive 2017/1852 is the chance for the taxpayer to involve national courts to unblock procedures.

In particular, the right to request a decision of a national court with respect to the rejection of a complaint and, most importantly, the chance to apply to a competent court (or to any other body or persons so designated in their national law for carrying out of such function) to set up the Advisory Commission[21] will clearly implement the principles of effectiveness and reasonable duration of the procedure whose absence in the previous legislative framework led to the introduction of the new Directive 2017/1852.

Finally, and this may represent one of the points of weakness of Directive 2017/1852, no substantial innovation compared to the framework existing under the Arbitration Convention has been set forth with respect to the potential interaction between the new international procedures and the domestic legal proceedings that may be initiated by the taxpayer.

Indeed, since the taxpayer is entitled (and in most cases required) to start a domestic legal proceeding, it might have been appropriate to include some specific coordination provisions or principles also with respect to the rules to be specifically implemented at a domestic level, in order to facilitate the coexistence between the two procedures until the taxpayer resolves which path is more suitable for his case. In this respect, Directive 2017/1852 only provides certain restrictions to the new international dispute resolution mechanism in the event a domestic judicial proceeding has been started by the taxpayer.

In particular, if domestic legal proceedings are pursued, the term for acceptance of the Complaint (for initiating the MAP stage) will only commence on the date of the final decision of the relevant court or upon the expiry of the term for initiating such proceedings. A resolution reached under the MAP will only become binding to the taxpayer (subject to his consent) upon termination of the (already) initiated domestic legal proceedings or upon the waiving rights to such proceedings (if not yet commenced). If a Member State's domestic law does not allow the competent authority to derogate from a court decision, Directive 2017/1852 provides that the MAP will be terminated if the court decision is rendered before an agreement is reached during the MAP stage.

Furthermore, terms for access to arbitration are also extended for the duration of the domestic legal proceedings and the Advisory Commission's opinion will only become binding subject to the same requirements as provided for the MAP stage. In

20. *See* Article 10, Directive 2017/1852.
21. *See* Article 7, Directive 2017/1852.

addition, where Member States' domestic laws do not allow the competent authorities to derogate from court decisions, then: (i) access to arbitration is denied if a court has rendered a decision before the request for access to arbitration is made and (ii) the arbitration stage is terminated if a court decision is rendered after the request to access arbitration and before the opinion of the Advisory Commission.

CHAPTER 1

Austria

Christian Wimpissinger

A. IMPLEMENTING MEASURES ADOPTED BY AUSTRIA WITH RESPECT TO DIRECTIVE 2017/1852

The Austrian EU Tax Dispute Resolution Act (i.e., the Austria's act implementing Directive 2017/1852) applies to dispute resolution complaints relating to income or assets generated during a tax period beginning on or after 1 January 2018 (while such act formally entered into force on 1 September 2019). In addition to the new act, it was necessary to modify existing domestic laws as well, in particular, the Federal Fiscal Code (FFC) and the Federal Finance Court Act (FFCA).

Even though Competent Authorities of Member States concerned may agree to apply Directive 2017/1852 for any complaint submitted for any earlier tax period (Article 23 Directive 2017/1852), the affected taxpayers will not be able to do so on their own, because Austria formally made no use of this option. If another Member State's law provides for the option to apply Directive 2017/1852 to earlier cases, the decision whether to do so is in the hands of the Member States concerned.[1]

Since the Directive sets 1 July 2019 as the implementation deadline, the EU Commission has initiated infringement proceedings against Austria.[2] A consequence is probably not to be expected due to the fact that Directive 2017/1852 was transposed only two months late and is implemented at the time of the decision of the procedure.

1. *Kubik* in Steuer- und Wirtschaftskartei (SWK) 25/2019, pp. 1018, 1021.
2. https://ec.europa.eu/atwork/applying-eu-law/infringements-proceedings/infringement_decisions/index.cfm?lang_code = EN&typeOfSearch = false&active_only = 1&noncom = 0&r_dossier = &decision_date_from = &decision_date_to = &EM = AT&DG = TAXU&title = &submit = Search (accessed 4 December 2019).

B. GENERAL PROVISIONS

B.1. Subject Matter and Scope

Pursuant to section 2(1) of the Austrian EU-TDRA, this Federal Law lays down the procedures for settling disputes between Austria and another Member State or several other Member States arising from the interpretation and application of agreements or conventions (according to section 3(1)(1)). Disputes with third countries are therefore excluded.

From an Austrian perspective, it is another alternative to the already existing procedures for international tax dispute resolutions. Taxpayers have previously been able to initiate a two-stage dispute resolution procedure – MAP and then arbitration – in selected double tax conventions[3] and under the Arbitration Convention for specific issues in order to resolve international tax disputes.[4]

Moreover, the OECD has set out a minimum standard for MAP and a scheme implementing this mechanism. The MLI now contains both the provisions of the minimum standard for MAP and, as an optional provision, the introduction of a mandatory and legally binding arbitration procedure that follows the unsuccessful implementation of a MAP.[5]

The Austrian EU-TDRA also contains a two-stage procedure: on the one hand the MAP (sections 22 to 31) and on the other hand the arbitration proceedings (sections 32 to 52).

Even though Austria has a track record of being one of the most active countries in the field of international dispute resolution,[6] the scope of the Austrian EU-TDRA means that in the future more cases within the EU will be accessible to an international dispute resolution, in particular, to the (obligatory) arbitrational settlement. Prior to the introduction of an arbitration clause in the OECD Model Convention (2008), Austria had already negotiated arbitration clauses with Tax Treaties partners. Notwithstanding the MLI, thirteen Tax Treaties executed by Austria contain arbitration clauses.[7] Some of these arbitration clauses deviate considerably from the OECD Model Convention, as the negotiations for their introduction had already begun before the introduction of Article 25(5) OECD Model Convention in 2008.

3. From an Austrian point of view, it is the DTC with the following thirteen countries: Armenia, Azerbaijan, Bahrain, Bosnia and Herzegovina, Chile, Germany, Japan, Kosovo, Macedonia, Mongolia, San Marino, Switzerland and United Kingdom; Federal Ministry of Finance BMF-010221/0237-IV/8/2019 of 24 July 2019.
4. *Kubik* in SWK 25/2019, pp. 1018, 1019.
5. Article 16 MLI; Article 18 to 26 MLI; *Kubik* in SWK 25/2019, p. 1018.
6. *Turcan in Kubik/Schmidjell-Dommes/Staringer* (Hrsg), The EU Tax Dispute Resolution Act, p. 19; OECD, Making Dispute Resolution More Effective – MAP Peer Review Report, Austria (Stage 1) (2017) 9: '*[Austria] has a relatively large MAP inventory, with a considerable number of new cases submitted each year.*'
7. *Turcan in Kubik/Schmidjell-Dommes/Staringer* (Hrsg), The EU Tax Dispute Resolution Act, p. 19.

A special position within Austria's bilateral arbitration clauses is occupied by the provision in Article 25(5) Tax Treaty executed between Austria and Germany, which provides for recourse to the ECJ as an arbitrator and which first applied in 2017.[8]

The fact that the ECJ has accepted its jurisdiction as an arbitral tribunal appears positive for the taxpayers because it provides them with an important instrument for eliminating international tax conflicts in their relations with Germany if - as in the present case due to differences of interpretation - no agreement can be reached between the two countries in the MAP. It was not disputed between the two states that the income from participation certificates was interest within the meaning of Article 11 and not dividends within the meaning of Article 10 Tax Treaty executed between Austria and Germany, but it was not clear in which country the taxation may take place. In the case itself, the ECJ ruled that this interest is taxed only in the State of residence of the beneficial owner.[9]

Austria's positive attitude towards international dispute resolution can also be seen in the fact that on 22 September 2017 Austria was the first state to ratify the MLI signed on 7 June 2017 and one of only thirty states to opt for the applicability of the MLI arbitration clause.[10]

The dispute resolution mechanisms in the EU instruments and those in Tax Treaties can, in principle, be applied in parallel. As a result, generally, within the EU a dispute can be resolved by several intergovernmental solutions.[11] Only transfer pricing cases and cases concerning the allocation of income to permanent establishments within the EU could be settled under the Arbitration Convention by MAP and an arbitrational procedure. Therefore, the relevance the dispute resolution procedure regulated in the Arbitration Convention will have in the future remains to be seen.[12]

B.2. Definitions

Section 3(1) of the Austrian EU-TDRA provides the following definitions:[13]

- 'Agreements or Conventions' means international treaties providing for the elimination of double taxation of income and, where appropriate, capital. In particular, Tax Treaties and the Arbitration Convention, last amended by the Agreement on the Accession of the Czech Republic, the Republic of Estonia, the Republic of Cyprus, the Republic of Latvia, the Republic of Lithuania, the Republic of Hungary, the Republic of Malta, the Republic of Poland, the Republic of Slovenia and the Slovak Republic to the convention on the

8. *Turcan in Kubik/Schmidjell-Dommes/Staringer* (Hrsg), The EU Tax Dispute Resolution Act, p. 20; ECJ 12 September 2017, *Austria/Germany*, C-648/15.
9. *Frank* in GES - Zeitschrift für Gesellschaftsrecht und angrenzendes Steuerrecht 2018, p. 36.
10. *Turcan in Kubik/Schmidjell-Dommes/Staringer* (Hrsg), The EU Tax Dispute Resolution Act, p. 20.
11. *Turcan in Kubik/Schmidjell-Dommes/Staringer* (Hrsg), The EU Tax Dispute Resolution Act, p. 21.
12. *Kubik* in SWK 25/2019, p. 1020.
13. The definitions reported in this paragraph are used also for the purposes of this chapter.

elimination of double taxation in connection with the adjustment of profits of associated enterprise, OJ C 160, 30.6.2005, p. 1;

- 'Concerned Member State' means a Member State of the EU, which is named by the Affected Person in the dispute resolution complaint and is a Contracting State to Agreements or Conventions, as defined above;
- 'Smaller Undertakings' means:
  - (i) a corporation; or
  - (ii) a partnership in which no partner with unlimited liability is a natural person, who does not exceed at least two of the following size characteristics as at the balance sheet date:
- EUR 20,000,000.00 balance sheet total,
- EUR 40,000,000.00 net turnover,
- 250 employees on average during a financial year,

and which is not part of a group whose parent company is required to prepare a consolidated financial statement and a group management report (section 246(1)(2) of the Austrian Commercial Code – the 'UGB');

- 'Austrian Competent Authority' means the Federal Minister of Finance or its authorized representative;
- 'Competent Court' means, from the Austrian perspective, the Federal Finance Court and, from the perspective of another Member State, the court, tribunal or other body which has been designated as such by the Member State concerned.

C. COMPLAINT TO START A MAP

C.1. Filing a Complaint to Start a MAP

The structure of the Austrian EU-TDRA proceeding can be roughly divided into three phases

(1) dispute resolution complaint;
(2) MAP;
(3) arbitration proceedings.

Depending on how the questions to be resolved in the respective phases are decided, the next steps lead or do not lead to another phase.

Pursuant to section 8(1) of the Austrian EU-TDRA, any Affected Person shall be entitled to submit a dispute resolution complaint on a Question in Dispute to each of the Competent Authorities of each of the Concerned Member States simultaneously.

The provision that the dispute resolution complaint must be submitted at the same time and with the same information with all Competent Authorities concerned contrasts with the previously possible procedures (DBA, MLI, Arbitration Convention).[14] Therefore, in proceedings under the *Austrian EU-TDRA*, the Affected Person must examine which Competent Authorities are to be specifically addressed in their case in order to file the complaint with all of them.

Paragraph 2 states that the submission of the dispute resolution complaint to the Austrian Competent Authority must be made via '*FinanzOnline*', the Austrian online filing platform.[15] Only in those cases in which the electronic submission is impossible due to a lack of technical capabilities (such as a lack of IT infrastructure or because of a lack of delivery options abroad) or a lack of eligibility (such as withdrawal of eligibility), the submission has to be made using the official form.[16]

Paragraph 4 contains a special provision, which applies in various parts of the law in order to simplify the process for certain people. By way of derogation from paragraph 1, an individual resident in Austria or a Smaller Undertaking resident in Austria (section 3(1)(5) of the Austrian EU-TDRA) shall be entitled to submit the dispute resolution complaint only to the Austrian Competent Authority (outbound case). The residency is determined according to the respective Tax Treaty.[17] The Austrian Competent Authority shall notify the Competent Authorities of all the other Concerned Member States at the same time within two months of the submission of the dispute resolution complaint. Once this notification has been made, the Affected Person's complaint will be deemed to have been submitted with the Competent Authorities of all the Member States concerned at the time of this notification. However, an individual or a Smaller Undertaking may also make use of the general provision in paragraph 1. But if the special provision is invoked, the time limit for the review of the dispute resolution complaint (section 16) does not begin until the notification of the Austrian Competent Authority to the Competent Authorities of all other Concerned Member States has been made, potentially an extension of up to two months.[18]

For the opposite case to paragraph 4, paragraph 6 provides if the Austrian Competent Authority receives notification from the Competent Authority of another Concerned Member State about the submission of a dispute resolution complaint by a natural person established in that other Member State or a Smaller Undertaking established in that other Member State (inbound case), the dispute resolution complaint shall be deemed to be submitted to the Austrian Competent Authority one at the time of this notification.[19]

Section 9(1) of the Austrian EU-TDRA specifies the necessary content of a dispute resolution complaint.

14. *Kubik* in SWK 25/2019, pp. 1018, 1019.
15. FinanzOnline is a e-government service in Austria. It is free of charge and available 365 days a year, 24 hours a day. FinanzOnline facilitates the access to the Austrian tax administration for citizens and businesses as well as for the public administration.
16. AB 644 BlgNR 26. GP, p. 9.
17. AB 644 BlgNR 26. GP, p. 9.
18. AB 644 BlgNR 26. GP, p. 9.
19. AB 644 BlgNR 26. GP, pp. 9 f.

Pursuant to section 10(1) of the Austrian EU-TDRA, the dispute resolution complaint can be submitted from the receipt of the first notification of the action resulting in, or that will result in, the Question in Dispute. However, it must be submitted at the latest within three years after notification (section 97 of the FFC) of the notice relevant for the Question in Dispute.

Paragraph 2 substantiates the actions referred to in Article 3(1) of Directive 2017/1852 from an Austrian point of view. In addition to executions with a declaratory character (so-called *Erledigungen mit Bescheidcharakter*), even executions with a non-declaratory character (so-called *Erledigungen ohne Bescheidcharakter*) may be considered as actions within the meaning of this paragraph.

The Affected Person can submit a dispute resolution complaint regardless of whether it could have or has submitted other remedies available by virtue of domestic law. It can submit a dispute resolution complaint even if the action relevant to the Question in Dispute has already become effective.

Since the existence of a Question in Dispute is one of the admission requirements for a dispute resolution complaint (section 15(2)(3) of the Austrian EU-TDRA), the Affected Person concerned is well advised to explain this point in detail in its complaint. In addition, information must be provided on pending legal remedies, legal proceedings, and already initiated MAPs or dispute resolution proceedings. The filing of the dispute resolution complaint causes the automatic termination of already running MAPs or dispute resolution proceedings pending on the same Question in Dispute and for the same period of time, which were based on a Tax Treaty or on the Arbitration Convention (section 13(1) of the Austrian EU-TDRA). This must be observed by the Affected Person before the dispute resolution complaint is filed.[20]

Pursuant to section 11 of the Austrian EU-TDRA, the Austrian Competent Authority shall confirm to the Affected Person that it has received the dispute resolution complaint within two months.

In accordance with section 12 of the Austrian EU-TDRA, the Austrian Competent Authority shall notify the Competent Authorities of the other Member States concerned within two months of receiving the dispute resolution complaint and notify the Competent Authorities of the other Member States concerned about the language or languages they are using for their communication during the MAP and the arbitration procedure. In accordance with section 4 of the Austrian EU-TDRA, the communication with the Austrian Competent Authority is in German or English.

Pursuant to section 13(1) of the Austrian EU-TDRA, by filing a dispute resolution complaint according to section 8, any ongoing MAP or dispute resolution procedure initiated by the Affected Person in the same Question in Dispute for the same period shall be terminated by virtue of an agreement or convention. The initiated MAP or arbitration procedure ends *ex lege*. Concerned this is a MAP initiated pursuant to a Tax Treaty or the Arbitration Convention.[21]

By section 14(1) of the Austrian EU-TDRA the Austrian Competent Authority may, within three months after receipt of the dispute resolution complaint, request the

20. *Kubik* in SWK 25/2019, pp. 1018, 1020.
21. AB 644 BlgNR 26. GP, p. 11.

Affected Person to provide additional information considered necessary to undertake the substantive examination of the disputed case. The Affected Person may refuse to provide the requested additional information in so far as it would entail the disclosure of protection of trade, business, industrial or professional secret or trade processes and would be in breach of Austrian law. In this case, the Affected Person must inform the Austrian Competent Authority of the reasons for the refusal.

D. THE RESOLUTION OF THE QUESTION IN DISPUTE UNDER THE MAP

Pursuant to section 15 of the Austrian EU-TDRA, the Austrian Competent Authority must decide by notice on the admission or rejection of the filed dispute resolution complaint. The cases in which rejection has to be made are also listed there. Generally, the examination must be completed within six months of the receipt of the dispute resolution complaint by the Austrian Competent Authority.

Noteworthy is section 16(5) of the Austrian EU-TDRA, which provides that if the Affected Person submitted a domestic remedy in Austria or another Concerned Member State on the same Question in Dispute, the deadline shall commence from the date on which a judgment delivered in those proceedings has become final or on which those proceedings have otherwise been definitively concluded or where the proceedings have been suspended. Therefore, in a Question in Dispute that may be resolved under the Austrian EU-TDRA, the Affected Person has to carefully plan the parallel submission of national remedies against the background of the deadline.[22]

D.1. MAP

According to section 22 of the Austrian EU-TDRA, the Austrian Competent Authority must make an effort to resolve the Question in Dispute in a MAP if the dispute resolution complaint was accepted by the Competent Authority of all the Member States concerned. The procedure of the MAP is not regulated separately in the Austrian EU-TDRA, but the internal administrative procedures previously provided for MAPs will apply.[23]

Pursuant to section 24 of the Austrian EU-TDRA, an agreement in the MAP should be sought within two years of the date of the last notification on the acceptance of the dispute resolution complaint (section 22 of the Austrian EU-TDRA). If the Advisory Commission accepted the dispute resolution complaint and another Member State notified to initiate a MAP, the day of the notification of the acceptance is relevant. The two-year period may be extended by a maximum of one year if the Austrian

22. *Kubik* in SWK 25/2019, pp. 1018, 1021 f.
23. *Kubik* in SWK 25/2019, pp. 1018, 1022.

Competent Authority requests in writing and justifies to the other Competent Authority. A pending domestic appeal in turn inhibits the start of the deadline until a final decision, an otherwise final conclusion or a suspension of the domestic proceedings.[24]

D.2. Appeal of the Taxpayer Against the Decision Rejecting the Complaint

The Affected Person can appeal against a rejection of the dispute resolution complaint either by a complaint according to sections 243 *et seq*. FFC or by application for approval of the dispute resolution complaint by the Advisory Commission (Arbitration) (sections 17 to 21 of the Austrian EU-TDRA).[25] If the dispute resolution complaint is approved by the Advisory Commission and the relevant Competent Authorities do not declare that they want to conduct a MAP, the procedure automatically enters the arbitration stage (section 47(2) of the Austrian EU-TDRA, which provides a separate deadline for the submission of an independent opinion for this case, the so-called arbitration award).[26]

D.3. Termination of the Dispute Resolution Procedure

A MAP may end due to a decision or other terminations. A decision requires a settlement of the Competent Authorities of the Member States concerned in the MAP (section 26 of the Austrian EU-TDRA) within the deadline of section 24 of the Austrian EU-TDRA and the settlement must be communicated to the Affected Person immediately. Section 27 of the Austrian EU-TDRA states that at the latest sixty days after the date on which the settlement was communicated to the Affected Person, it must have provided the following to all Competent Authorities concerned:

- the approval to the settlement;
- proof of the waiver of the complaint against the notice pursuant to section 48(2) of the FFC, with which the agreement (section 26 of the Austrian EU-TDRA) is to be decided;
- evidence of a waiver of all remedies available under the law of another Member State concerned in proceedings relating to the same Question in Dispute; and
- where applicable, evidence of measures taken to close proceedings under the law of another Concerned Member State concerning the same Question in Dispute.

The Austrian Competent Authority must reach an agreement with the Competent Authority of the other Member State(s) concerned that the requirements in section 27 of the Austrian EU-TDRA were fulfilled and must subsequently send the notice pursuant to section 48(2) of the FFC to the Affected Person (section 28 of the Austrian

24. *Kubik* in SWK 25/2019, pp. 1018, 1022.
25. *Vock/Spanblöchl*, Overview of the EU-TDRA, Recht der Wirtschaft (RdW) 2019/154, p. 193.
26. *Kubik* in SWK 25/2019, pp. 1018, 1022.

EU-TDRA). The agreement solution is then to be implemented in accordance with section 295(2a) of the FFC regardless of the domestic statute of limitations or legal effect of the original administrative decision.[27] Due to the provision of the new section 118 (9) (c) of the FFC in the course of the amendments to the FFC to implement Directive 2017/1852, a notice can be revoked if it contradicts the agreement in the MAP or the final decision in the arbitration procedure.[28]

Other terminations can be by time lapse (section 29 of the Austrian EU-TDRA), abortion (section 30 of the Austrian EU-TDRA), or omission of the Question in Dispute (section 31 of the Austrian EU-TDRA). Section 29 of the Austrian EU-TDRA applies to those cases in which the two- or up to three-year deadline has elapsed without agreement. Section 30 of the Austrian EU-TDRA applies to cases in which it is clear even before the deadline of the MAP that an agreement is excluded and, therefore, in order to avoid the Affected Person having to await the deadline until an arbitration tribunal can be called. The provision in section 31 of the Austrian EU-TDRA is confined to those cases where the Federal Finance Court has explicitly ruled on the Question in Dispute, which is also the subject of the dispute resolution complaint. Since it is not possible for the Austrian Competent Authority in such cases to deviate from a decision of the Federal Finance Court, the MAP must be terminated in these cases.[29]

E. DISPUTE RESOLUTION PROCEDURE

E.1. Request of Appointment of the Advisory Commission

If there is no solution to the Question in Dispute between the Austrian Competent Authority and the other Competent Authorities in the MAP (sections 29 and 30 of the Austrian EU-TDRA), the Affected Person may file a written application for the establishment of an arbitration tribunal (section 32 of the Austrian EU-TDRA).[30] The application must be filed within fifty days from the day following the date on which the Affected Person received the notification in accordance with section 29 or 30 of the Austrian EU-TDRA.

Unlike the content of the dispute resolution complaint, the Austrian EU-TDRA does not provide prerequisites for the content of the application in accordance with section 32 of the Austrian EU-TDRA. However, it must also be submitted via '*FinanzOnline*' and special regulations (section 32(4) and (6) of the Austrian EU-TDRA) apply in turn to natural persons and Smaller Undertakings.[31]

The application is not admissible if:

- the Question in Dispute has been omitted (section 34 of the Austrian EU-TDRA);

27. *Spanblöchl/Turcan* in Tax and Business Review (SWI) 2019, 187, The new EU-TDRA, p. 192.
28. *Spanblöchl* in Zeitschrift für Steuerstrafrecht und Steuerverfahren (ZSS) 2019, pp. 5, 8.
29. AB 644 BlgNR 26. GP, p. 18.
30. *Kubik* in SWK 25/2019, pp. 1018, 1022.
31. *Kubik* in SWK 25/2019, pp. 1018, 1022.

- a penalty or a legal entity's fine (so-called *Verbandsgeldbuße*) has been imposed on the Affected Person in respect of a financial criminal offence committed intentionally or through gross negligence, in the five years preceding the filing of the dispute resolution complaint, for such offence committed in the last seven years prior to the filing (section 35 of the Austrian EU-TDRA);
- the Question in Dispute is not a question of double taxation (section 36 of the Austrian EU-TDRA).

Pursuant to section 37 of the Austrian EU-TDRA, the Affected Person has no access to an arbitration tribunal if there is a reason for an inadmissibility (section 33(2) of the Austrian EU-TDRA) either from an Austrian point of view or from the point of view of that Member State.

Arbitration enables two possible procedures: (i) the procedure before the Advisory Commission or (ii) the procedure before the Alternative Dispute Resolution Commission.

E.2. Appointment of the Advisory Commission

The Advisory Commission is composed of:

- a chairperson;
- one representative or two representatives from each Competent Authority of each Concerned Member State; and
- one independent person or two independent persons (sections 5 to 7 of the Austrian EU-TDRA), designated by each Competent Authority of each Member State concerned (section 72 of the Austrian EU-TDRA).

The deadline for setting up the Advisory Commission is 120 days (section 39 of the Austrian EU-TDRA), assuming that no grounds for inadmissibility apply. In the Austrian EU-TDRA, the Affected Person has numerous options against delaying the proceedings at this stage of the procedure (i.e., sections 40(8), 42, 43 and 58(4) of the Austrian EU-TDRA).[32]

Within a period of six months, the Advisory Commission issues a written independent opinion on how to resolve the Question in Dispute, with an extension of up to three months being possible (section 46 in conjunction with section 47 of the Austrian EU-TDRA).

The way for the Advisory Commission to the independent opinion results implicitly from section 52(1) of the Austrian EU-TDRA, according to which the Commission for Alternative Dispute Resolution may adopt '*any kind of the procedure of the binding dispute resolution, including the procedure of final offer (last best offer)*', in deviation from the procedure for the Advisory Commission. Thus, the Advisory Commission will mostly have to give a reasoned independent opinion, unless the

32. *Kubik* in SWK 25/2019, p. 1023.

underlying double tax convention or the Arbitration Convention provides something different via the reference in section 3(2) of the Austrian EU-TDRA.[33]

E.3. Alternative Dispute Resolution Commission

As an alternative to the Advisory Commission, a Commission for Alternative Dispute Resolution can be set up, if the Austrian Competent Authority has agreed with the Competent Authorities of the other Member States concerned in accordance with section 38(2) of the Austrian EU-TDRA that the request for the establishment of an arbitration tribunal will be complied by setting up a Commission for Alternative Dispute Resolution.

The deadline for the setting up is as well 120 days as for the Advisory Commission (section 50 of the Austrian EU-TDRA).

The Austrian Competent Authority has to agree with the Competent Authorities of the other Member States concerned on the following elements of the establishment (section 49(2) of the Austrian EU-TDRA):

- the form;
- the composition;
- the rules for the appointment of the independent persons including any reasons for rejection;
- the procedure for submitting the opinion; and
- the rules of functioning.

F. COMMON PROCEDURAL PROVISION

F.1. Procedural Rules of the Advisory Commission or Alternative Dispute Resolution Commission

The Affected Person does not have access to the correspondingly extensive options for preventing the delay in proceedings, such as the procedure for setting up an Advisory Commission, which is to be seen as the weak point of Directive 2017/1852 and thus also of the Austrian EU-TDRA.

The Austrian Competent Authority and the Competent Authorities of the other Member States concerned must agree within six months of the day following the submission of the opinion that either the Question in Dispute be resolved in accordance with the opinion of the arbitration tribunal or how the Question in Dispute can be resolved differently from the opinion of the arbitration tribunal (section 58(1) of the Austrian EU-TDRA).

If the Austrian Competent Authority has not reached an agreement with the Competent Authorities of the other Member States concerned or has not reached it

33. *Kubik* in SWK 25/2019, p. 1023.

within the deadline, it is bound by the opinion of the arbitration tribunal (section 58(2) of the Austrian EU-TDRA).

F.2. Final Decision of the Competent Authorities

Pursuant to section 58(3) of the Austrian EU-TDRA the solution to the Question in Dispute is the final decision. The Austrian Competent Authority must notify the Affected Person concerned of the final decision immediately, but at the latest within thirty days. The final decision does not constitute a precedent.

At the latest sixty days after the date on which the final decision has been transmitted to the Affected Person, the Affected Person must have sent the following to the Austrian Competent Authority and the Competent Authorities of the other Member States concerned (section 59 of the Austrian EU-TDRA):

- consent to the final decision;
- proof of the waiver of the complaint against the decision in accordance with section 48(2) of the FFC, with which the final decision is to be established;
- evidence of the waiver of all legal remedies that could be brought under the law of another Member State concerned in proceedings relating to the same Question in Dispute;
- where appropriate, evidence of measures taken to terminate proceedings under the law of another Member State concerned concerning the same Question in Dispute; and
- an explanation of whether the publication of the final decision is approved.

If all of these prerequisites are met, the final decision is recorded in an assessment notice in accordance with section 48(2) of the FFC and implemented pursuant to section 295(2a) of the FFC.[34]

F.3. Publicity

If the publication of the final decision is approved, the full text of the decision can be published by the EU Commission; otherwise only a summary will be published (sections 63 to 65 of the Austrian EU-TDRA).

F.4. Information, Evidence and Hearings

In accordance with section 70 of the Austrian EU-TDRA, the Affected Person has no party position within the meaning of section 78 of the FFC both in the MAP and in the arbitration proceedings. In particular, no access to files is granted due to the fact that section 90 of the FFC is not applicable.

34. *Kubik* in SWK 25/2019, p. 1024.

The Affected Person is entitled to provide the arbitration tribunal with any information, evidence or documents that may be relevant to the decision on the relevant Question in Dispute or to appear in person before the arbitration tribunal or to send an authorized representative (section 55(1) and (2) of the Austrian EU-TDRA). The prerequisite for this is that the Affected Person has previously obtained the consent of the Competent Authorities of all the Member States concerned. The declaration of consent must be sent to the arbitration tribunal. If the Affected Person is summoned by the arbitration tribunal, it is obliged to appear in person or has the right to be represented by an authorized representative (section 53(1) of the Austrian EU-TDRA).

G. CONCLUSION

Some call it an oversupply of procedures available as of today for resolving international tax dispute referring to the MLI, the Austrian EU-TDRA, generally the MAPs under double tax conventions, and the Arbitration Convention.[35] The positive aspect: taxpayers may in the future have some room to manoeuvre and choose the procedure they consider appropriate for their purposes.

From the taxpayer's point of view, the Austrian EU-TDRA procedure, which is not as transparent as some might have wished for and in which the taxpayer generally has no party position, could be seen critically. In particular, in cases in which the Competent Authorities agree that a Commission for Alternative Dispute Resolution is to be set up and for which a different type of binding dispute resolution procedure applies pursuant to section 52 of the Austrian EU-TDRA, the outcome of the proceedings might not be predictable for the taxpayers.[36]

Nevertheless, in contrast to the procedures under a double tax convention or the Arbitration Convention, in which the taxpayer only has the right to suggest initiating a MAP, it does have an actively enforceable entitlement to initiate such a procedure under the Austrian EU-TDRA. In contrast to a procedure under the Arbitration Convention or a double tax convention, the taxpayer can file an appeal if the initiation of a MAP under the Austrian EU-TDRA did not lead anywhere or if it was rejected. In addition, if the MAP has ended without an agreement, the taxpayer has the right to initiate an arbitration proceeding.[37] The mandatory procedural step of an arbitration, in case a MAP, is often seen as 'pressure' for the Competent Authorities. Knowing that a decision will be made in the end by an (at least so some extent) independent body of the Competent Authorities could motivate to solve the procedure within the framework of the MAP.[38]

With respect to the new arbitration procedures under the Austrian EU-TDRA, it should be noted that, on the one hand, the mere fact that a dispute resolution mechanism for interstate double taxation disputes is now being created throughout the EU is, without doubt, a step in the right direction and potentially a grand step.

35. *Kubik* in SWK 25/2019, p. 1025.
36. *Bernegger*, Zeitschrift für Steuerstrafrecht und Steuerverfahren (ZSS) 2019, pp. 12, 19.
37. *Rzeszut/Turpin*, Steuerexpress 2019/256.
38. *Kubik* in SWK 25/2019, pp. 1018, 1024 f.

Generally, the entire MAP and arbitration procedure becomes a framework that is more legally founded and should, therefore, be welcomed in light of the rule of law, even if this makes the procedure considerably more demanding from a technical point of view. However, this will not prevent taxpayers threatened by double taxation from engaging in arbitration proceedings, especially as this will open up nothing less than an additional opportunity to avoid double taxation.[39]

On the other hand, the arbitration procedure of the Austrian EU-TDRA based on Directive 2017/1852 is structurally conservative in its design. Conceptually a mere escalation stage of the MAP, which developed to be a pure government-to-government procedure often remaining non-transparent for the taxpayer. The entire procedure continues to remain in the corner of the administration, rather than in the corner of courts. Although the taxpayer is entitled to initiate the procedure, it is then almost a foreign body in the procedure, which is largely controlled by the Competent Authorities. It would have been exciting if the Directive had had the courage not to leave this procedure 'in the hands' of the Competent Authorities, but on the contrary to deliberately 'take it out of their hands' at one point or another.[40]

39. *Staringer* in *Kubik/Schmidjell-Dommes/Staringer* (Hrsg), The EU Tax Dispute Resolution Act, p. 48.
40. *Staringer* in *Kubik/Schmidjell-Dommes/Staringer* (Hrsg), The EU Tax Dispute Resolution Act, p. 48.

CHAPTER 2

Belgium

Natalie Reypens

A. IMPLEMENTING MEASURES ADOPTED BY BELGIUM WITH RESPECT TO DIRECTIVE 2017/1852

Directive 2017/1852 was implemented into Belgian law by the Law of 2 May 2019[1] (hereinafter the 'Law of 2 May 2019').

The Law of 2 May 2019 has remained largely faithful to the structure and terms of the Directive. This law applies to any complaint introduced with effect from 1 July 2019 concerning disputes over revenue or capital received during a taxable period beginning on or after 1 January 2018.[2]

B. GENERAL PROVISIONS

B.1. Subject Matter and Scope

The scope of the Law of 2 May 2019 does not differ from the one provided by Directive 2017/1852. The Law of 2 May 2019 provides for rules on a mechanism to resolve disputes between Member States which arise from the interpretation and application of agreements and conventions that provide for the elimination of double taxation of income and, where applicable, capital.[3]

---

1. Loi transposant la Directive (UE) 2017/1852 du Conseil du 10 octobre 2017 concernant les mécanismes de règlement des différends fiscaux dans l'Union européenne/Wet tot omzetting van de Richtlijn (EU) 2017/1852 van de Raad van 10 oktober 2017 betreffende mechanismen ter beslechting van belastinggeschillen in de Europese Unie, Moniteur belge, 17 May 2019, 47285.
2. Article 26 of the Law of 2 May 2019.
3. Article 1(3) of the Law of 2 May 2019.

The Directive applies to all taxpayers who are subject to tax on income tax or capital. The matter giving rise to such disputes is referred to as a 'Question in Dispute'.

In accordance with Directive 2017/1852, the dispute resolution mechanism provides for a three-step procedure:

(1) the complaint stage including the possibility to resolve the Question in Dispute on a unilateral basis;
(2) the MAP stage; and
(3) the dispute resolution stage itself by the Advisory Commission or the Alternative Dispute Resolution Commission.

B.2. Definitions

Article 2 of the Law of 2 May 2019 provides for the following definitions:

- 'Belgian Competent Authority' means the Competent Authority appointed by the King per decree;
- 'Competent court' means the court or the president of the Court of First Instance, sitting in summary proceedings, who sits at the Court of Appeal of the jurisdiction of the tax authorities that have taken the contested decision. In case the procedure is handled in German, only the Court of First Instance of Eupen is competent. The King can designate, within the jurisdiction of the Court of Appeal another court or president of the court than the one referred to above, who takes knowledge of disputes related to the application of this law;
- 'Large enterprise' means an enterprise which, on the balance sheet date, exceeds at least two of the following criteria:
  (i) EUR 20,000,000.00 balance sheet total;
  (ii) EUR 40,000,000.00 net turnover;
  (iii) 250 employees on average during a financial year;
- 'Large Group' means a group of parent companies and subsidiaries which are reported in a consolidation, which, on a consolidated basis and on the balance sheet date, exceed at least two of the following thresholds:
  (i) EUR 20,000,000.00 balance sheet total;
  (ii) EUR 40,000,000.00 net turnover;
  (iii) 250 employees on average during a financial year.

The definition of large enterprise and large group is inspired by Directive 2013/34/EU of the EU Parliament and of the Council of 26 June 2013 on the annual financial statements, consolidated financial statements and related reports of certain types of undertakings.

C. COMPLAINT TO START A MAP

C.1. Filing of a Complaint

Any Affected Person shall be entitled to submit a complaint on a Question in Dispute[4] to the Belgian Competent Authority, requesting the resolution thereof. The complaint shall be submitted within three years from the receipt of the first notification of the action resulting in, or that will result in, the Question in Dispute, regardless of whether the Affected Person has recourse to the available remedies.

The Affected Person shall simultaneously submit the complaint with the same information to each Competent Authority of the other Member States concerned and shall indicate in the complaint which other Member States are concerned. The complaint should be filed in at least one of the Belgian official languages or in English.[5]

Within two months from the receipt of the complaint, the Belgian Competent Authority shall:

- acknowledge receipt of the complaint;[6] and
- inform the competent authorities of the other Member States concerned of the receipt of the complaint.[7] The Belgian Competent Authority shall inform the competent authorities of the other Member States concerned at that time also about the preferred language or languages its intends to use for its communications during the relevant proceedings.

The complaint shall only be accepted if the Affected Person making the complaint provides the competent authorities of each of the Member States concerned with the following information, as listed in Article 3(4) of the Law of 2 May 2019:

- the name, address and tax identification number and all other information relevant for identification of the Affected Person that filed the complaint and all other persons concerned;
- the tax periods concerned;
- further information on the relevant facts and circumstances of the case and supporting documentation if any, as listed in detail in Article 3(4) of the Law of 2 May 2019;
- reference to the applicable domestic legislation and the agreements and conventions as referred to above;
- additional information, and supporting documentation if any, on the details of any appeals of litigation, a commitment of the Affected Person to respond to appropriate requests, the final tax assessment decision, and information on a

4. In this chapter, 'Question in Dispute' means in particular the issue which gave rise to the dispute as referred to in Article 1(3) of the Law of 2 May 2019.
5. Article 3(1) of the Law of 2 May 2019.
6. Article 3(2) of the Law of 2 May 2019.
7. Article 3(3) of the Law of 2 May 2019.

complaint filed under other (MAP) proceedings, as listed in detail in this Article.
- any specific additional information that is considered necessary to undertake the substantive consideration of the particular case.

This list of information is identical to the list of information as provided for in Article 3 of Directive 2017/1852.

C.2. Subsequent Actions of the Competent Authority in the Complaint Stage

Within three months from the receipt of the complaint, the Belgian Competent Authority may request any specific additional information that is considered necessary to undertake the substantive consideration of the particular case. Further requests for information may be made during the MAP if the competent authorities consider this to be necessary. The two types of request may not lead to the disclosure of trade, business, industrial or professional secret or trade processes. An Affected Person that receives such request shall reply within three months of receiving the request. A copy of this reply shall also be sent simultaneously to the competent authorities of the other Member States concerned.[8]

The Belgian Competent Authority shall take a decision on the acceptance or rejection of the complaint within six months of the receipt thereof or within six months of the receipt of the specific additional information, whichever is later. The Belgian Competent Authority shall inform the Affected Person and the competent authorities of the other Member States of its decision without delay[9] (*see also* section D.1 below).

Within the period of six months from the receipt of a complaint, or within six months of the receipt of the specific additional information, whichever is later, the Belgian Competent Authority may decide to resolve the Question in Dispute on a unilateral basis, without involving the other competent authorities of the Member States concerned. In such case, the Belgian Competent Authority shall notify the Affected Person and the other competent authorities of the Member States concerned without delay, following which the proceedings under this Directive shall be terminated.

C.3. Withdrawal of a Complaint

An Affected Person that wishes to withdraw a complaint shall simultaneously submit a written notification of withdrawal to the Belgian Competent Authority and to each of the competent authorities of the Member States concerned. Such notification shall terminate all proceedings. The Belgian Competent Authority who receives such a

8. Article 3(5) of the Law of 2 May 2019.
9. Article 3(6) of the Law of 2 May 2019.

notification shall inform the other competent authorities of the Member States concerned of the termination of proceedings without delay.[10]

If for any reason a Question in Dispute ceases to exist, all proceedings under the complaint shall terminate with immediate effect, and the competent authorities of the Member States concerned shall inform the Affected Person of this state of affairs and of the general reasons therefore without delay.[11]

D. THE RESOLUTION OF THE QUESTION IN DISPUTE UNDER THE MAP

D.1. Decision of the Competent Authority with Reference to the Complaint

In accordance with Article 5 of the Law of 2 May 2019, the Belgian competent Authority may decide to reject a complaint within the six months period provided here above if:

- the complaint lacks information required (including any information requested that was not submitted within the deadline);
- there is no Question in Dispute; or
- the complaint was not submitted within the three-year period.

When informing the Affected Person, the Competent Authority shall provide the general reasons for its rejection.

Where Belgian Competent Authority has not taken a decision on the complaint within the relevant six-month period, the complaint shall be deemed to be accepted by that Competent Authority.

The Affected Person shall be entitled to appeal against the decision of the Belgian Competent Authority in accordance with the petition rules under Articles 1385*decies* and 1385*undecies* JC (Court of First Instance) where all competent authorities of the Member States concerned have also rejected the complaint.

An Affected Person who exercises this appeal right shall be barred from making a petition:

- while the decision is still under appeal according to the laws of the Member State concerned;
- where the rejection decision can still be further appealed under the appeal procedure of the Member States concerned; or
- when a rejection decision has been confirmed under the appeal procedure in the first point above but it is not possible to derogate from the decision of the relevant court or other judicial bodies in any of the Member States concerned.

Where the appeal right has been exercised, the decision of the relevant court or other judicial body shall be considered for the purposes of appointing of an Advisory Commission (*see* below section E.1).

10. Article 3(7) of the Law of 2 May 2019.
11. Article 3(8) of the Law of 2 May 2019.

D.2. MAP

Where the complaint is accepted by the Belgian Competent Authority and by the other competent authorities of the Member States concerned, they shall endeavour to resolve the Question in Dispute by mutual agreement within two years, starting from the last notification of a decision of one of the Member States on the acceptance of the complaint.[12] The period of two years may be extended by up to one year at the request of a Competent Authority of a Member State concerned to all of the other competent authorities of the Member States concerned if the requesting Competent Authority provides written justification.

Once the Belgian Competent Authority has reached an agreement with the other competent authorities of the Member States as to how to resolve the Question in Dispute within the period provided for here above, the Belgian Competent Authority shall, without delay, notify this agreement to the Affected Person, as a decision that is binding on the authority and enforceable by the Affected Person, subject to the Affected Person accepting the decision and renouncing the right to any other remedy, where applicable.[13]

Where proceedings regarding such other remedies have already commenced, the decision shall only become binding and enforceable once the Affected Person has provided evidence to the Belgian Competent Authority that action has been taken to terminate those proceedings. Such evidence shall be provided not later than sixty days from the date on which such decision was notified to the Affected Person. The Law of 2 May 2019 does not mention that '*the decision shall then be implemented without delay, irrespective of any time limits prescribed by the national law of the Member States concerned*' as is the case in Article 4.2 of Directive 2017/1852.

Where the competent authorities of the Member States concerned have not reached an agreement on how to resolve the Question in Dispute within the period provided here above, the Competent Authority of each of the Member States concerned shall inform the Affected Person indicating the general reasons for the failure to reach agreement.[14]

E. DISPUTE RESOLUTION PROCEDURE

E.1. Appointment of the Advisory Commission

Upon a request made by the Affected Person to the competent authorities of the Member States concerned, an Advisory Commission shall be set up by such competent authorities, in accordance with Article 6 of the Law of 2 May 2019, where:

- the complaint submitted by such Affected Person was rejected by at least one, but not all of the competent authorities of Member States concerned; or

12. Article 4(1) of the Law of 2 May 2019.
13. Article 4(2) of the Law of 2 May 2019.
14. Article 4(3) of the Law of 2 May 2019.

- the competent authorities of the Member States concerned had accepted the complaint that was submitted by the Affected Person but failed to reach an agreement on how to resolve the Question in Dispute by mutual agreement within the two-year time limit.

The Affected Person may only make such a request if, in accordance with any applicable national rules against a rejection, no appeal can be made, no appeal is pending, or the Affected Person has formally renounced his right of appeal. The request shall include a declaration to this effect.

The Affected Person shall make the request to set up an Advisory Commission in writing, not later than fifty days from the date of receipt of the notification or fifty days from the date of delivery of the decision by the relevant court or judicial body, as the case may be.

The Advisory Commission shall be set up not later than 120 days from the receipt of such request, and once set up, its chair shall inform the Affected Person thereof without delay. If the Advisory Commission is not set up within 120 days, the Affected Person can initiate a summary proceeding with the president of the competent court, in accordance with Article 7 of the Law of 2 May 2019.

In accordance with Article 8 of the Law of 2 May 2019, the Advisory Commission shall be composed of:

- a chairman;
- one representative of each of the involved competent authorities. Where agreed by the competent authorities, the number of such representatives may be increased to two for each of the competent authorities;
- one independent person of standing appointed by each Competent Authority from a specific list as referred to in Article 9 of the Law of 2 May 2019. Where agreed by the competent authorities, the number of such persons appointed may be increased to two for each Competent Authority.

The Belgian competent authorities and the other competent authorities shall agree upon the rules for the appointment of the independent persons of standing as mentioned above. Also, a replacement shall be appointed for cases where the independent persons of standing are prevented from performing their duties.[15] If the rules for the appointment of the independent persons of standing have not been agreed, they shall be appointed by drawing lots.[16]

Except where the independent persons of standing have been appointed by the competent court in accordance with Article 7(1) of the Law of 2 May 2019, the Competent Authority of each Member State may reject the appointment of an independent person of standing for any reason agreed in advance with the concerned competent authorities or for one of the following reasons:

15. Article 8(2) of the Law of 2 May 2019.
16. Article 8(3) of the Law of 2 May 2019.

- that person belongs to one of the tax administrations concerned or performs functions on behalf of one of those administrations or has been in that situation at any time during the preceding three years;
- at any time during the last five years preceding the date of his appointment, that person has or has had a significant holding or voting right or is or has been employed or advised by an Affected Person;
- that person does not offer adequate objectivity for the resolution of the dispute;
- that person is employed by an undertaking which provides tax advice, or otherwise provides tax advice on a professional basis, or has been in that situation at any time during a period of at least three years before his appointment.[17]

Upon request of a Competent Authority of a Member State concerned, a person of standing or his substitute shall disclose any interest, relationship or other matter which might affect the independency or impartiality of that person or which might reasonably give rise to a suspicion of bias in the procedure. An independent person who is a member of the Advisory Commission must not, for a period of twelve months from the date of delivery of the decision of the Advisory Commission, be in a situation which would have led a Competent Authority to object to his appointment if he had been in that situation at the time of his appointment to the Advisory Commission.[18]

The representatives of the Competent Authority and the independent persons of standing appointed in accordance with Article 8(1) of the Law of 2 May 2019 shall appoint a chairman from the list of persons of standing provided by Article 9.[19]

E.2. List of Independent Persons of Standing

This list shall consist of all independent persons of standing and their substitutes appointed by the Member States.

The King appoints at least three persons who are qualified and independent, and are capable of acting impartially and with integrity. The notification of the rules for appointment and their profile will be published in the Belgian Official Gazette.[20]

E.3. Alternative Dispute Resolution by the Advisory Commission

In the case mentioned above where the complaint was rejected, the Advisory Commission shall adopt a decision on the acceptance of the complaint within six months from the date of its establishment. It shall notify the competent authorities of its decision within thirty days of the adoption thereof.[21]

17. Article 8(4) of the Law of 2 May 2019.
18. Article 8(5) of the Law of 2 May 2019.
19. Article 8(6) of the Law of 2 May 2019.
20. Article 9(1) of the Law of 2 May 2019.
21. Article 6(2) of the Law of 2 May 2019.

Where the Advisory Commission has confirmed that all of the requirements for a valid complaint have been satisfied, the MAP shall be initiated at the request of one of the competent authorities. When the Belgian Competent Authority decides to start the MAP, it shall notify the Advisory Commission, the other competent authorities concerned and the Affected Person of that request. The two-year period for the MAP to achieve shall start from the date of the notification of the decision taken by the Advisory Commission of the acceptance of the complaint. Where none of the competent authorities has requested initiation of the MAP within sixty days of the date of the notification of the decision of the Advisory Commission, the Advisory Commission shall provide an opinion on how to resolve the Question in Dispute within the six-month period. In such a case, for the six-month period, the Advisory Commission shall be deemed to have been set up on the date on which that the first sixty-day period expired.

Where the competent authorities of the Member States concerned had accepted the complaint that was submitted by the Affected Person but failed to reach an agreement on how to resolve the Question in Dispute by mutual agreement within the two-year time limit, the Advisory Commission shall deliver an opinion on how to resolve the Question in Dispute within the six-month period.

E.4. The Alternative Dispute Resolution Commission

The Belgian Competent Authority and the competent authorities of the Member States concerned may agree to set up an Alternative Dispute Resolution Commission instead of an Advisory Commission to deliver an opinion on how to resolve the Question in Dispute.[22] The Belgian Competent Authority and the competent authorities of the Member States may also agree to set up an Alternative Dispute Resolution Commission in the form of a committee that is of a permanent nature (i.e., Standing Committee).

Except for the rules regarding the independence of its members, the Alternative Dispute Resolution Commission may differ regarding its composition and form from the Advisory Commission.[23] An Alternative Dispute Resolution Commission may apply, where appropriate, any dispute resolution processes or technique to solve the Question in Dispute in a binding manner.

As an alternative to the type of dispute resolution process applied by the Advisory Commission, any other type of dispute resolution process, including the 'final offer' arbitration process (otherwise known as 'last best offer' arbitration), can be agreed by the competent authorities of the Member States and applied by the Alternative Dispute Resolution Commission.[24]

The competent authorities of the Member States concerned shall agree on the Rules of Functioning.[25]

22. Article 10(1) of the Law of 2 May 2019.
23. Article 10(2) of the Law of 2 May 2019.
24. Article 10(2) of the Law of 2 May 2019.
25. Article 10(3) of the Law of 2 May 2019.

The rules concerning costs of proceedings and the information, evidence and hearings shall apply to the Alternative Dispute Resolution Commission unless otherwise agreed to in the Rules of Functioning.[26]

F. COMMON PROCEDURAL PROVISIONS

F.1. Rules of Functioning for the Advisory Commission

The Belgian Competent Authority shall, within the 120-day period, notify the Affected Person with the following:[27]

- the Rules of Functioning for the Advisory Commission or Alternative Dispute Resolution Commission;
- the date by which the opinion on the resolution of the Question in Dispute shall be adopted;
- references to any applicable legal provisions in national law of the Member States and to any applicable agreements or conventions.

The Rules of Functioning shall provide in particular:[28]

(i) the description and the characteristics of the Question in Dispute;
(ii) the terms of reference on which the competent authorities of the Member States agree as regards the legal and factual questions to be resolved;
(iii) the form of the dispute resolution body, which shall be either an Advisory Commission or an Alternative Dispute Resolution Commission, as well as the type of process for any Alternative Dispute Resolution, if the process differs from the independent opinion process applied by an Advisory Commission;
(iv) the time frame for the dispute resolution procedure;
(v) the composition of the Advisory Commission or Alternative Dispute Resolution Commission (including the number and names of the members, details of their competence and qualifications, and disclosing any conflicts of interest of the members);
(vi) the rules governing the participation of the Affected Person(s) and third parties in the proceedings, exchanges of memoranda, information and evidence, the costs, the type of dispute resolution process to be used, and any other relevant procedural or organizational matters;
(vii) the logistical arrangements for the Advisory Commission's proceedings and delivery of its opinion.

If an Advisory Commission is set up to deliver an opinion, only the information referred to points (i), (iv), (v) and (vi) shall be set out in the Rules of Functioning.

26. Article 10(4) of the Law of 2 May 2019.
27. Article 11(1) of the Law of 2 May 2019.
28. Article 11(2) of the Law of 2 May 2019.

The Rules of Functioning shall be signed between the competent authorities of the Member States involved in the dispute.

In cases where the Rules of Functioning are incomplete or were not notified to the Affected Person, the standard Rules of Functioning established by the Commission shall apply.[29]

F.2. Costs of Proceedings

With some exceptions, and unless the competent authorities of the Member States concerned have agreed otherwise, the following costs shall be shared equally among the Member States:[30]

- the expenses of the independent persons of standing, which are to be an amount equivalent to the average of the usual amount reimbursed to high-ranking civil servants of the Member States concerned; and
- the fees of the independent persons, where applicable, which are to be limited to EUR 1,000 per person per day for every day on which the Advisory Commission or Alternative Dispute Resolution Commission meets.

Costs that are incurred by the Affected Person shall not be borne by Member States.

By way of exception, where the Affected Person has made:

(i) a notification of withdrawal of complaint; or

(ii) a request following a rejection made and the Advisory Commission has decided that the relevant competent authorities were correct in rejecting the complaint; and, where the competent authorities of the Member States concerned agree, all the costs referred to in the paragraphs above shall be borne by the Affected Person.[31]

F.3. Information, Evidence and Hearings

Where the Belgian Competent Authority and the other competent authorities of the Member States concerned agree, the Affected Person(s) concerned may provide the Advisory Commission or Alternative Dispute Resolution Commission with any information, evidence or documents that may be relevant for the decision.[32]

The Affected Person(s) and the competent authorities of the Member States concerned shall provide any information, evidence or documents upon request by the Advisory Commission or Alternative Dispute Resolution Commission. However, the

29. Article 11(3) of the Law of 2 May 2019. Specific other rules apply where the competent authorities have not notified the Rules of Functioning to the Affected Person (Article 11(4) of the Law of 2 May 2019).
30. Article 12(1) of the Law of 2 May 2019.
31. Article 12(2) of the Law of 2 May 2019.
32. Article 13(1) of the Law of 2 May 2019.

Belgian Competent Authority may refuse to provide information to the Advisory Commission in any of the following cases:

- obtaining the information requires carrying out administrative measures that are against national law;
- the information cannot be obtained under the national law of the Member State concerned;
- the information concerns trade secrets, business secrets, industrial secrets, professional secrets or trade processes;
- the disclosure of the information is contrary to public policy.

Affected Persons, at their request and with the consent of the competent authorities of the Member States concerned, may appear or be represented before an Advisory Commission or Alternative Dispute Resolution Commission.[33]

F.4. The Opinion of the Advisory Commission or Alternative Dispute Resolution Commission

An Advisory Commission or Alternative Dispute Resolution Commission shall deliver its opinion to the Belgian Competent Authority and the other competent authorities of the Member States concerned no later than six months after the date on which it was set up.[34]

Where the Advisory Commission or Alternative Dispute Resolution Commission considers that the Question in Dispute is such that it would need more than six months to deliver an opinion, this period may be extended by three months.

The Advisory Commission or Alternative Dispute Resolution Commission shall inform the competent authorities of the Member States concerned and the Affected Persons of any such extension.

The Advisory Commission or Alternative Dispute Resolution Commission shall base its opinion on the provisions of the applicable agreement or convention as well as on any applicable national rules.[35]

The Advisory Commission or Alternative Dispute Resolution Commission shall adopt its opinion by a simple majority of its members.[36] Where a majority cannot be reached, the vote of the chair shall determine the final opinion.

The chair shall communicate the opinion of the Advisory Commission or Alternative Dispute Resolution Commission to the Belgian Competent Authority and the other competent authorities concerned.

33. Article 13(2) of the Law of 2 May 2019.
34. Article 14(1) of the Law of 2 May 2019.
35. Article 14(2) of the Law of 2 May 2019.
36. Article 14(3) of the Law of 2 May 2019.

F.5. Decision of the Competent Authorities Following the Dispute Resolution Procedure

The Belgian Competent Authority and the other competent authorities concerned shall agree on how to resolve the Question in Dispute within six months of the notification of the opinion of the Advisory Commission or Alternative Dispute Resolution Commission.[37]

The Belgian Competent Authority in accord with the other competent authorities may take a decision which deviates from the opinion of the Advisory Commission or Alternative Dispute Resolution Commission.[38]

However, if they fail to reach an agreement as to how to resolve the Question in Dispute, they shall be bound by the opinion of the Advisory Commission or Alternative Dispute Resolution Commission.

The Belgian Competent Authority shall notify the final decision on the resolution of the Question in Dispute to the Affected Person within thirty days.[39]

In the absence of such notification within thirty days of the decision having been taken, the Affected Person may initiate summary proceedings (so-called *action en référé – kortgeding*) in order to obtain the final decision. Except where the relevant Belgian court decides that there was lack of independence of the Advisory Commission or Alternative Dispute Resolution Commission, the final decision shall be implemented (under the national law of the Member States concerned which as a result of the final decision shall amend their taxation, irrespective of any time limits prescribed by the national law).

The final decision of competent authorities shall be binding on the Member States concerned and shall not constitute a precedent.[40]

The final decision shall be implemented subject to the Affected Person(s) accepting the final decision and renouncing the right to any domestic remedy within sixty days from the date when the final decision was notified, where applicable.

Where the final decision has not been implemented, the Affected Person shall apply to the Court of First Instance in accordance with the petition rules under Articles 1385*decies* and 1385*undecies* JC in order to enforce implementation thereof.

F.6. Interaction with Belgian Proceedings and Derogations

The fact that a tax assessment has become final or a decision made by the General Counsellor has become final shall not prevent the Affected Persons from having recourse to the procedures provided for in the Law of 2 May 2019.[41]

The submission of the Question in Dispute to the MAP or to the dispute resolution procedure shall not prevent the Belgian State from imposing administrative penalties or

37. Article 15(1) of the Law of 2 May 2019
38. Article 15(2) of the Law of 2 May 2019.
39. Article 15(3) of the Law of 2 May 2019.
40. Article 15(4) of the Law of 2 May 2019.
41. Article 16(1) of the Law of 2 May 2019.

initiating proceedings for administrative penalties or initiating or continuing judicial proceedings in relation to the same matters.[42]

Affected Persons may have recourse to the remedies available to them under the national law of the Member States concerned. However, where the Affected Person has commenced proceedings to seek such a remedy, the terms of periods referred to in Articles 3(5) and 4(1) of the Law of 2 May 2019 respectively shall commence from the date on which a judgment delivered in those proceedings has become final or on which those proceedings have otherwise been definitively concluded or where the proceedings have been suspended.[43]

Where a final decision on a Question in Dispute has been rendered by the relevant court, the Belgian Competent Authority notifies the other competent authorities of the Member States concerned of the decision of the relevant court, and:[44]

- the MAP under Article 4 of the Law of 2 May 2019 on that Question in Dispute is to be terminated as from the date of such notification;
- the provisions of Article 6(1) of the Law of 2 May 2019 do no longer apply if the Question in Dispute had remained unresolved during the whole of the MAP under Article 4 of the Law of 2 May 2019;
- the dispute resolution process under Article 6 of the Law of 2 May 2019 is to be terminated if the decision of the relevant court was rendered at any time after an Affected Person has made a request under Article 6(1) of the Law of 2 May 2019 but before the Advisory Commission or the Alternative Dispute Resolution Commission has delivered its opinion to the competent authorities of the Member States concerned in accordance with Article 14 of the Law of 2 May 2019. In such a case, the Competent Authority of the relevant Member State concerned is to inform the other competent authorities of the Member States concerned and the Advisory Commission or the Alternative Dispute Resolution Commission of the effect of the decision of the relevant court.

The submission of a complaint as provided under Article 3 shall put an end to any other ongoing proceedings under the MAP or dispute resolution procedure under an agreement or convention that is applied in relation to the relevant Question in Dispute. Such other ongoing proceedings concerning the relevant Question in Dispute shall come to an end with effect from the date of the first receipt of the complaint by any of the competent authorities of the Member States concerned.[45]

The person concerned may not initiate the dispute resolution procedure under Article 6 of the Law of 2 May 2019 in cases where penalties were imposed in Belgium in relation to the adjusted income or capital for tax fraud. Where judicial or administrative proceedings were commenced that could potentially lead to such penalties, and these proceedings are being conducted simultaneously with any of the proceedings referred to in this Law of 2 May 2019, the Belgian Competent Authority may stay the

42. Article 16(2) of the Law of 2 May 2019
43. Article 16(3) of the Law of 2 May 2019.
44. Article 16(4) of the Law of 2 May 2019.
45. Article 16(5) of the Law of 2 May 2019.

proceedings under this Law of 2 May 2019 as from the date of acceptance of the complaint until the date of the final outcome of those proceedings.[46]

The person concerned may not initiate the dispute resolution procedure under Article 6 of the Law of 2 May 2019 on a case-by-case basis where a Question in Dispute does not involve double taxation. In such a case, the Belgian Competent Authority shall inform the Affected Person and the competent authorities of the other Member States concerned without delay.[47]

F.7. Special Provisions for Individuals and Smaller Undertakings

Where the Affected Person is either: (i) a Belgian tax resident individual or (ii) a corporation resident in Belgium (not being a large undertaking or a corporation that does form part of a large group, both as defined in Directive 2013/34/EU of the European Parliament and of the Council[48]), the Affected Person may submit the complaints, replies to a request for additional information, withdrawals and requests (respectively 'communications'), only to the Belgian Competent Authority.[49]

The Belgian Competent Authority shall notify the competent authorities of all the other Member States concerned at the same time and within two months of receipt of such communications.

Once such a notification has been made, the Affected Person shall be deemed to have submitted the communication to all the Member States concerned as of the date of such notification.

In the case of additional information received, the Belgian Competent Authority shall transmit a copy to the competent authorities of all the other Member States concerned at the same time. Once this submission has been made, it shall be deemed that additional information has been received by all the Member States concerned as at the date of such receipt of information.

F.8. Publicity

Advisory Commissions and Alternative Dispute Resolution Commissions shall issue their opinions in writing.[50]

The Belgian Competent Authority and the other competent authorities may agree to publish the final decisions in their entirety, subject to the consent of each of the Affected Person concerned.[51]

---

46. Article 16(6) of the Law of 2 May 2019.
47. Article 16(7) of the Law of 2 May 2019.
48. Directive 2013/34/EU of the European Parliament and of the Council of 26 June 2013 on the annual financial statements, consolidated financial statements and related reports of certain types of undertakings, amending Directive 2006/43/EC of the European Parliament and of the Council and repealing Council Directives 78/660/EEC and 83/349/EEC (OJ L 182, 29.6.2013, p. 19).
49. Article 17(1) of the Law of 2 May 2019.
50. Article 18(1) of the Law of 2 May 2019.
51. Article 18(2) of the Law of 2 May 2019.

Where the competent authorities or Affected Person concerned does not consent to publishing the final decision in its entirety, the competent authorities shall publish an abstract of the final decision (Article 18(3)). That abstract shall contain a description of the issue and the subject matter, the date, the tax periods involved, the legal basis, the industry sector, and a short description of the final outcome. It shall also include a description of the method of arbitration used.

The Belgian Competent Authority shall send the information to be published to the Affected Person before its publication. No later than sixty days from the receipt of such information, the Affected Person may request the Belgian Competent Authority not to publish information that concerns any trade, business, industrial or professional secret or trade process, or that is contrary to public policy.

The Belgian Competent Authority shall notify the information to be published to the Commission without delay[52]

F.9. Obligation of Secrecy

The members of an Advisory Commission or an Alternative Dispute Resolution shall be subject to obligations of secrecy in relation to information they receive in their capacity as members of an Advisory Commission or Alternative Dispute Resolution Commission.[53]

Affected Persons and, where applicable, their representatives shall undertake to treat any information (including knowledge of documents) that they receive during such proceedings as secret.[54] The Affected Person and his representatives shall make a declaration to this effect to the competent authorities of the Member States concerned when so requested during the proceedings. The Member States shall adopt appropriate sanctions for any breach of secrecy obligations.

Any breach of secrecy shall be punished under Article 458 of the Criminal Code.[55]

52. Article 18(3) of the Law of 2 May 2019.
53. Article 19 of the Law of 2 May 2019.
54. Article 20 of the Law of 2 May 2019.
55. Article 20 of the Law of 2 May 2019.

CHAPTER 3

Denmark

Nikolaj Bjørnholm

A. IMPLEMENTING MEASURES ADOPTED BY DENMARK WITH RESPECT TO DIRECTIVE 2017/1852

Denmark has implemented Directive 2017/1852 of 2017 simply by an amendment to the act on the implementation of the Arbitration Convention stating that Directive 2017/1852 is also applicable in Denmark.

The implementation was adopted as section 2 to act No. 1726 of 27 December 2018 and became effective as of 30 June 2019 (hereinafter 'Implementation Act').

Besides stating that Directive 2017/1852 is applicable in Denmark, the Implementation Act contains only three additional implementing measures.

From the Implementation Act it follows that the competent court, cf. Articles 7, 11 and 15 of Directive 2017/1852 is the city court (so-called *byret*) to which the affected person belongs.

It further follows that the independent persons of standing of the Advisory Commission or the Alternative Dispute Resolution Commission and the affected person and his/her representative are subject to the confidentiality provisions of sections 152 and 152 of the Danish Penal Code.

Finally, the Implementation Act grants the Minister of Taxation the authority to lay down more detailed regulations by statutory order (so-called *bekendtgørelse*). To date, the Minister of Taxation has only issued one statutory order, which is very brief.

By statutory order number 685 of 2 July 2019, the Minister of Taxation determined, effective from 15 July 2019, that the Danish Tax Authority, which is an agency under the Ministry of Taxation (so-called *skatteforvaltningen*), is the competent authority with respect to the Arbitration Convention and Directive 2017/1852. Further, the order states that a question eligible under Directive 2017/1852 cannot be brought before the Advisory Commission or Alternative Dispute Resolution Commission in case the question has been determined by the Danish courts.

B. GENERAL PROVISIONS

B.1. Subject Matter and Scope

Article 1 of Directive 2017/1852 is directly applicable and no specific regulation or guidance has been provided by the Danish Tax Authorities.

The guidance published by Danish Tax Authority and revised biannually (*'Den Juridiske Vejledning'*) contains a paragraph discussing the relationship to the Arbitration Convention and Tax Treaties concluded by Denmark with other Member States. Denmark has no arbitration clauses in the Tax Treaties concluded with other Member States. The Arbitration Convention is still in force. The guidance states that the arbitration provisions of Directive 2017/1852 prevail. The link to the guidance is as follows: https://skat.dk/skat.aspx?oid=2293005.

B.2. Definitions

Article 2 of Directive 2017/1852 is directly applicable.

The Danish Tax Authority (so-called *skatteforvaltningen*) has been designated 'competent authority' by the Minister of Taxation, cf. statutory order number 685 of 2 July 2019, section 1.

The city court (so-called byret) to which the affected person belongs has been designated 'competent court', cf. the Implementation Act, section 2(2).

Denmark has currently twenty-four city courts. The Danish judicial system has three levels of judicial courts: (i) the city courts, (ii) the high courts, and (iii) the Supreme Court. A civil case, including a tax case, is initiated at the city (district) court (so-called *byret*). The ordinary courts handle any matter of criminal and civil law and thus the judges are generalists with little experience in tax.

A ruling by the first instance of the ordinary courts may be appealed within four weeks to the second and last instance. An appeal from a city court lies with the Danish high court (so-called *landsretten*). The Supreme Court (so-called *Højesteret*) is a Court of Appeal and last instance for judgments made by the high courts.

As a general rule, a judgment may only be appealed once. Thus, if a case has originated in the city court, the high court will be the last instance for judicial proceedings.

The parties may request that the city court refer a civil case to the high court (so-called *landsretten*) for first instance court proceedings if the case is of general public importance or concerns a principle matter of law, and in such case, the high court's judgment may always be appealed to the Supreme Court. A referral to the high court was made in the first-ever Danish (and possibly EU) court case on the Arbitration Convention discussed in section E.2 below.

If a case is a matter of general public interest, the Board of Appeal (so-called *Procesbevillingsnævnet*) may grant leave for appeal to the Supreme Court even if the case has already been heard in two instances.

C. COMPLAINT TO START A MAP

C.1. Filing a Complaint to Start a MAP

Article 3 of Directive 2017/1852 is directly applicable.

The complaint to the Danish competent authority shall be submitted to:

Skattestyrelsen,
Store Selskaber - Kompetent Myndighed,
Sluseholmen 8B,
2450 København SV,
or by mail to HovedpostkasseJura@SKTST.dk.

The head of the competent authority is Mr. Bo Darling Larsen.

The three-year deadline from the receipt of the first notification of the action resulting in, or that will result in, the Question in Dispute is under Danish law interpreted as from the final assessment (decision) made by the Danish Tax Authority any demand for payment made by the Danish Tax Authority or if brought before the courts by the Ministry of Taxation in case a complaint has been decided upon in favour of the affected person at the administrative appeal level (in Danish '*afgørelse, kendelse eller betalingsanmodning eller det tidspunkt, hvor Skatteministeriets stævning indgives til retten*').

The Implementing Act states that the competent authority determines which languages are acceptable. Such determination has not been made, but in general the competent authority accepts complaints in English, Danish, Swedish and Norwegian.

The guidance published by Danish Tax Authority and revised biannually ('*Den Juridiske Vejledning*') contains a general discussion in Danish of the three phases, which basically repeats the content of Directive 2017/1852. The link to the guidance is as follows: https://skat.dk/skat.aspx?oid=2293005.

D. THE RESOLUTION OF THE QUESTION IN DISPUTE UNDER THE MAP

D.1. Decision of the Competent Authority with Reference to the Complaint

Article 5 of Directive 2017/1852 is directly applicable, and no specific regulation or guidance has been provided by the Danish Tax Authorities.

D.2. MAP

Article 4 of Directive 2017/1852 is directly applicable, and no specific regulation or guidance has been provided by the Danish Tax Authorities.

E. DISPUTE RESOLUTION PROCEDURE

E.1. Appointment of the Advisory Commission

Article 6 of Directive 2017/1852 is directly applicable, and no specific regulation or guidance has been provided by the Danish Tax Authorities.

It follows from the Implementation Act that the independent persons of standing of the Advisory Commission or the Alternative Dispute Resolution Commission and the affected person and his / her representative are subject to the confidentiality provisions of sections 152 and 152 e of the Danish Penal Code. Breach of section 152 is subject to fine or imprisonment up to six months.

Article 8 of Directive 2017/1852 is directly applicable, and no specific regulation or guidance has been provided by the Danish Tax Authorities.

When individuals and smaller undertakings are involved, Article 17 of Directive 2017/1852 is directly applicable and no specific regulation or guidance has been provided by the Danish Tax Authorities.

E.2. Appointment of the Advisory Commission Made by a Competent Court

Article 7 of Directive 2017/1852 is directly applicable.

From section 2 to act number 1726 of 27 December 2018, it follows that the competent court, cf. Directive 2017/1852 Articles 7, 11 and 15, is the city court (so-called *byret*) to which the affected person belongs. This is parallel to the venue principle applicable to a taxpayer wishing to bring an administrative decision before the Danish courts, cf. section 240(2) of the Danish Administration of Justice Act (so-called *retsplejeloven*).

As mentioned in section A.2. above, Denmark has currently twenty-four city courts. The Danish judicial system has three levels of judicial courts: 1) the city courts, 2) the high courts, and 3) the Supreme Court. A civil case, including a tax case, is initiated at the city (district) court (so-called *byret*). The ordinary courts handle any matter of criminal and civil law and thus the judges are generalists with little experience in tax.

A ruling by the first instance of the ordinary courts may be appealed within four weeks to the second and last instance. An appeal from a city court lies with the Danish high court (so-called *landsretten*). The Supreme Court (so-called *Højesteret*) is a Court of Appeal and last instance for judgments made by the high courts.

As a general rule, a judgment may only be appealed once. Thus, if a case has originated in the city court, the high court will be the last instance for judicial proceedings.

The parties may request that the city court refer a civil case to the high court (so-called *landsretten*) for first instance court proceedings if the case is of general public importance or concerns a principle matter of law, and in such case, the high court's judgment may always be appealed to the Supreme Court. A referral to the high court was, for example, made in the first-ever Danish (and possibly EU) court case on the Arbitration Convention. The issue in the case was whether or not the taxpayer's MAP request had been rightly denied by the Danish Tax Authorities on the grounds that it failed to state certain particulars, which, according to the taxpayer, were not required under either the Arbitration Convention itself or the Code of Conduct. The Court agreed with the taxpayer.[1]

If a case is a matter of general public interest, the Board of Appeal (so-called *Procesbevillingsnævnet*) may grant leave for appeal to the Supreme Court even if the case has already been heard in two instances.

E.3. List of the Independent Persons of Standing

Article 9 of Directive 2017/1852 is directly applicable, and no specific regulation or guidance has been provided by the Danish Tax Authorities. The list of independent persons is under preparation (August 2020) and has not yet been published.

E.4. Alternative Dispute Resolution Commission

Article 10 of Directive 2017/1852 is directly applicable, and no specific regulation or guidance has been provided by the Danish Tax Authorities.

F. COMMON PROCEDURAL PROVISIONS

F.1. Rules of Functioning for the Advisory Commission or Alternative Dispute Resolution Commission

Article 11 of Directive 2017/1852 is directly applicable, and no specific regulation or guidance has been provided by the Danish Tax Authorities.

For competent court (Article 11(4) of Directive 2017/1852), reference is made to Article 7 above.

F.2. Costs of Proceedings

Article 12 of Directive 2017/1852 is directly applicable, and no specific regulation or guidance has been provided by the Danish Tax Authorities.

1. The court case is discussed by the author of this chapter in an article published by IBFD in European Taxation, December 2016, pp. 534ff.

F.3. Resolution of the Controversy by the Advisory Commission or the Alternative Dispute Resolution Commission

As to the information, evidence and hearing that could be provided by the affected person, Article 13 of Directive 2017/1852 is directly applicable and no specific regulation or guidance has been provided by the Danish Tax Authorities.

As to the opinion that can be issued by the Advisory Commission or Alternative Dispute Resolution Commission, Article 14 of Directive 2017/1852 is directly applicable and no specific regulation or guidance has been provided by the Danish Tax Authorities.

F.4. Decision of the Competent Authorities Following the Dispute Resolution Procedure

Article 15 of Directive 2017/1852 is directly applicable, and no specific regulation or guidance has been provided by the Danish Tax Authorities.

For competent court (Article 15(4)), reference is made to Article 7 above.

As to the interaction of the decision of the Competent Authorities following the dispute resolution procedure with national proceeding, Article 16 of Directive 2017/1852 is directly applicable.

Under Danish law, the competent authority cannot derogate from a court's decision in the same matter. The so-called *travaux préparatoires* to the Implementation Act suggest that the Danish competent authority remains (as with the Arbitration Convention) unable to derogate from decisions rendered by the courts. Unlike the Arbitration Convention, the mere fact that legal proceedings before the courts are pending will not automatically prevent MAP or arbitration. If legal proceedings before the courts are initiated, MAP or arbitration may continue provided that the court proceedings are suspended / stayed meanwhile. Such suspension may be granted by the court upon request from the parties. The Minister of Taxation has stated that the Minister of Taxation would support such request for suspension or request it if the court case is initiated by the Minister of Taxation. Should a court decision be rendered during MAP or arbitration, the MAP or arbitration will come to an end.

Accordingly, section 2(2) of the statutory order number 685 of 2 July 2019 issued by the Minister of Taxation states, effective from 15 July 2019, that a question eligible under Directive 2017/1852 cannot be brought before the Advisory Commission or Alternative Dispute Resolution Commission in case the question has been ruled upon by the Danish courts.

F.5. Publicity

Article 18 of Directive 2017/1852 is directly applicable, and no specific regulation or guidance has been provided by the Danish Tax Authorities.

G. FINAL AND TRANSITORY PROVISIONS

G.1. Role of the Commission and Administrative Support

Article 19 of Directive 2017/1852 is directly applicable, and no specific regulation or guidance has been provided by the Danish Tax Authorities.

G.2. Committee Procedure

Article 20 of Directive 2017/1852 is directly applicable, and no specific regulation or guidance has been provided by the Danish Tax Authorities.

G.3. Review

Article 21 of Directive 2017/1852 is directly applicable, and no specific regulation or guidance has been provided by the Danish Tax Authorities.

G.4. Transposition

Article 22 of Directive 2017/1852 is directly applicable, and no specific regulation or guidance has been provided by the Danish Tax Authorities.

G.5. Entry into Force

Article 23 of Directive 2017/1852 is directly applicable, and no specific regulation or guidance has been provided by the Danish Tax Authorities.

G.6. Addressees

Article 24 of Directive 2017/1852 is directly applicable, and no specific regulation or guidance has been provided by the Danish Tax Authorities.

CHAPTER 4
France

Olivier Dauchez & Harold Turot

A. IMPLEMENTING MEASURES ADOPTED BY FRANCE IN RESPECT OF DIRECTIVE 2017/1852

The hair of the dog that bit you: quite ironically, the methods and procedures to respond to double taxation are not single, nor double, but multiple.

Directive 2017/1852 has been quickly implemented into French law by Article 130 of the Finance Law for 2019 No. 2018-1317 of 28 December 2018, under the new Articles L. 251 B to L. 251 ZH of the French Procedural Code (FPC). The implementation rules have been specified by a subsequent Decree No. 2019-616 dated of 21 June 2019 (hereinafter the 'Implementing Decree'), under the new Articles R. 251 D-1 to R. 251 ZF-1 of the FPC.[1]

1. In addition to implementation in recent years of measures to prevent tax avoidance and evasion and enhance transparency in tax matters, more efficient dispute resolution has emerged as another key requirement in improving legal certainty for taxpayers. Among the various measures which have been proposed, the EU has implemented thirty years ago a specific mechanism, the Arbitration Convention, which had previously constituted the EU's sole instrument on dispute resolution, but only applies to transfer pricing cases. The MLI also addresses this aspect under Articles 16 to 26. However, only twenty or so States have agreed to adopt its provisions on arbitration (Part VI – Articles 18 to 26). This is where Directive 2017/1852 comes in. A lot is at stake: just from a French perspective, 885 MAPs were under process as of 2018, according to the statistics released by the OECD on 16 September 2019. And that is before implementation of the BEPS and ATAD measures. Once they take effect, these figures are likely to shoot up. The fourth recital of Directive 2017/1852 acknowledges as much, albeit in the following diplomatic terms: '*Improvements to dispute resolution mechanisms are also necessary to respond to the risk that the number of double or multiple taxation disputes will increase, with potentially high amounts being at stake, because tax administrations have established more regular and focused audit practices.*'

   The rapidity with which Directive 2017/1852 was adopted, less than one year after the Commission's proposal, is a clear sign of both the importance of this issue for Member States and the EU's new role in the field of tax legislation.

These measures entered into force in France as from 1 July 2019, in accordance with Directive 2017/1852. They apply to all complaints submitted to the French tax authorities as from 1 July 2019 in respect of tax years commencing on or after 1 January 2018.

Directive 2017/1852 has not left to Member States a very wide margin of appreciation in the transposition of these rules. However, when making the choices which were left open by Directive 2017/1852, France has mainly adopted a strict and narrow approach which may unfortunately impediment the access to the procedure.

The big question is therefore not only how effective will Directive 2017/1852 itself be in tackling the challenges of resolution of double taxation disputes but also how the implementing choices made in France will impact this mechanism's efficiency. In an attempt to answer these questions, we will consider the scope and the terms of its dispute resolution mechanism of Directive 2017/1852 provisions as currently implemented into French law.

Directive 2017/1852 aims to strengthen the procedural framework so as to ease all potential bottlenecks. However, the measures implemented in France in order to achieve this may jeopardize the efficiency of this procedure.

B. GENERAL PROVISIONS

B.1. Subject Matter and Scope

The general principle is that only cases involving actual double taxation are eligible for the dispute resolution procedure of Directive 2017/1852.

The scope of this new double taxation dispute resolution procedure, following Directive 2017/1852 in this aspect, is however broader than the one of previous mechanisms, in that it applies to a more extensive range of disputes, taxpayers and taxes.

Directive 2017/1852 applies to '*disputes [that] arise from the interpretation and application of agreements and conventions that provide for the elimination of double taxation of income and, where applicable, capital*'. Directive 2017/1852 therefore covers any and all disputes that may arise from the interpretation or application of Tax Treaties; this of course includes not only transfer pricing disputes but also matters of residence, existence of permanent establishments, deductibility of expenses, application of withholding taxes, etc.

Only cases involving actual double taxation are eligible for the dispute resolution procedure of Directive 2017/1852. The definition of 'double taxation' provided by Directive 2017/1852 is implemented verbatim into French law under L. 251 C of the FPC as meaning either:

- an additional tax charge;
- an increase in tax liabilities;
- the cancellation or reduction of losses that could be used to offset taxable profits.

The French implementation of Directive 2017/1852 has however tightened a little the scope of disputes covered, Article L. 251 B of the FPC providing that only disputes '*resulting in a taxation not compliant with these agreements and conventions*' that provide for the elimination of double taxation are covered by the mechanism. This additional requirement of unconformity was not provided for under Article 1 of Directive 2017/1852. In theory, it may seem redundant: a complaint introduced to eliminate a double taxation would obviously have no chance to succeed if the taxation is compliant with the Tax Treaty. However, in practice, it may give rise to a certain number of discussions, depending on the interpretation of the Tax Treaties by the tax authorities, and be a source of uncertainty in the implementation of the procedure.

Directive 2017/1852 procedure applies to '*any person, including an individual, that is a resident of a Member State* [...]'. This opens up the EU's dispute resolution procedure to a significantly wider range of taxpayers, in that both individual and corporate EU-resident taxpayers are now eligible. It is implemented into French law under Article L. 251 D of the FPC which specifies that the taxpayer must be '*resident of France or of another Member State within the meaning of the applicable tax treaty between France and this other Member Stat*es'. This requirement may give rise to the first difficulties, given the very strict interpretation by French courts of this requirement when construing Tax Treaties, if, for instance, the taxpayer is not fully subject to tax in France or another Member State but still suffers from double taxation.

The permanent establishment is here again an issue at stake: unlike under the Arbitration Convention, permanent establishments are not specifically cited in the provisions detailing the mechanism's scope.

Disputes involving relations between a permanent establishment and either its parent or another company were definitely covered by the Arbitration Convention, but it is important to ascertain whether they also fall within the scope of Directive 2017/1852. The draft directive from 2016 was clearly intended to cover permanent establishments: its definition of 'taxpayer' included '*any person or permanent establishment subject to income taxes [...]*'. Although this definition was not retained in the final Directive 2017/1852, its removal does not appear to reflect any intention to exclude permanent establishments from the benefit of the mechanism. Indeed, the seventh recital of Directive 2017/1852 stipulates that '*[t]he improved dispute resolution mechanism should build on existing systems in the Union, including the Union Arbitration Convention. However, the scope of this Directive should be wider than that of the Union Arbitration Convention, which is limited to disputes over transfer pricing and the attribution of profits to permanent establishments. This Directive should apply to all taxpayers that are subject to taxes on income and capital covered by bilateral tax treaties and the Union Arbitration Convention*'. Based on this reference to the Arbitration Convention and the fact that the latter specifically provides that its arbitration procedure is open to permanent establishments, it seems reasonable to deduce that permanent establishments similarly fall within the scope of Directive 2017/1852.

Given that Directive 2017/1852 extends the scope of the EU's dispute resolution mechanism to encompass individual as well as corporate taxpayers, it necessarily covers a broader range of taxes than the Arbitration Convention. Thus, in addition to disputes involving corporate income taxes, the mechanism also applies to personal income tax and wealth tax disputes (including inheritance or gift taxes if those taxes are covered by the applicable Tax Treaty). The French implementation corresponds to Directive 2017/1852 in that regard.

C. COMPLAINT TO START A MAP

C.1. Filing a Complaint to Start a MAP

One of the issues identified by the EU Commission's impact study on the Arbitration Convention was the implicit or explicit denial of access to the procedure for certain claims. Directive 2017/1852 mechanism aims to resolve this issue by broadening taxpayer's access to the dispute resolution procedure, introducing stricter rules of implementation for both taxpayers and competent authorities alike, especially as regards time frames, and offering taxpayers rights of appeal if they are denied access to the procedure.

As to the broader access to the procedure, Directive 2017/1852 provides for the simultaneous submission of complaints to two (or more) competent authorities: '*The affected person shall simultaneously submit the complaint with the same information to each competent authority, and shall indicate in the complaint which other Member States are concerned.*' This is in line with Action 14 of the BEPS plan, which seeks to '*improve the resolution of tax-related disputes*' and pursuant to which taxpayers may, and indeed must, submit their complaint to the competent authorities of each of the Member States concerned. Conversely, under the Arbitration Convention, taxpayers could in principle only submit complaints to the competent authority of the Member State in which the affected person is resident or has its permanent establishment.

The French transposition achieves a satisfactory and balanced result in that respect by implementing into Article L. 251 D of the FPC the rules of Directive 2017/1852 which provide that individuals and undertakings that are not large undertakings and do not form part of a large group – as these terms are defined in Directive 2013/34/EU on the annual financial statements, consolidated financial statements and related reports of certain types of undertakings – i.e., primarily micro-entities and small- and medium-sized enterprises, do not need to submit their complaints and any additional information requested to both competent authorities but only to the competent authority of the Member State in which they are resident. In those cases, the French tax authorities must handle themselves all the communications to be done with the other concerned tax authorities.

At least there is now a clear rule, answering the ever-returning question of whether or not the second competent authority should be informed.

However, as mentioned above, Directive 2017/1852 permits stricter rules of implementation. In this respect, the process applicable under Directive 2017/1852 as implemented into French law is as follows.

As under the Arbitration Convention, taxpayers have three years as from receipt of the first 'administrative measure' which may trigger double taxation.

Regarding the Arbitration Convention, the French tax authorities' guidelines had stipulated that, for cases involving reassessments on which the taxpayer was invited to submit its observations, the notice in question was the reassessment proposal.

Regarding the Directive, the Implementing Decree specifies (FPC, Article R. 251 D-2) that the 'administrative measure' referred to under Article L. 251 D can be a:

- reassessment proposal; or
- tax reassessment based on the automatic taxation procedure; or
- tax collection in case of withholding tax.

As to the procedure for submitting a complaint:

- according to Directive 2017/1852, affected persons must submit their complaint in the official language of each authority's Member State or else another language that the Member State in question accepts; this requirement of complaint drafted in French has been transposed by the Implementing Decree;
- the terms regarding the content of the complaint specified by the Implementing Decree (FPC, Article R. 251 D-2) are basically the same as under Article 3 of the Directive; i.e., complaints must include:
    - (i) the name(s), address(es), tax identification number(s) and any other information necessary for identification of the affected person(s) who presented the complaint to the competent authorities and of any other person concerned;
    - (ii) the taxes and tax periods concerned;
    - (iii) details of the relevant facts and circumstances of the case;
    - (iv) copy of the documents issued by the French tax authorities and by the other Member State in question, as well as any other supporting document;
    - (v) an explanation of why the affected person considers that there is a question in dispute and a presentation of the national rules or international agreement or convention on the basis of which the complaint is submitted;
    - (vi) details of any appeals and litigation initiated in such respect and copies of any decision issued in such respect;
    - (vii) information on any other complaint submitted under another MAP or dispute resolution procedure and a declaration acknowledging that initiating this procedure ends these previous initiated ones.

Surprisingly enough, the French list does not reproduce the requirement for a commitment from the affected person to respond as completely and quickly as possible to any requests made by the competent authority.

D. THE RESOLUTION OF THE QUESTION IN DISPUTE UNDER THE MAP

D.1. Decision of the Competent Authority with Reference to the Complaint

As to the handling of the complaint, the competent authorities have two months from receipt of the complaint in which to acknowledge receipt and, if necessary, inform the other competent authority involved. They also have three months as from receipt of the complaint in which to request any additional information from the taxpayer concerned. The taxpayer has three months as from any such request in which to provide the competent authorities with the additional information in question. All information provided must be sent simultaneously to both competent authorities concerned: this was of course already generally accepted as best practice in dispute resolution procedures, but Directive 2017/1852 makes it mandatory. These rules are implemented under Article R. 251 D-3 of the FPC, unless the taxpayer falls within the exception provided for under Article L. 251 D.

D.2. MAP

The French authorities must accept or reject the complaint within six months from its submission or else from the taxpayer's response to their requests for additional information (FPC, Article L. 251 E).

The six-month delay is postponed in the event the taxpayer files a tax complaint under Article L. 190 of the FPC until the outcome of this complaint (FPC, Article L. 251 E III).

During such six-month period, either authority may decide to resolve the question in dispute on a unilateral basis. In such cases, the relevant competent authority must notify the other competent authority and the taxpayer of its decision. Any such unilateral action will terminate the dispute resolution proceedings.

Complaints that are accepted proceed to the MAP stage. Directive 2017/1852 also stipulates that if the competent authority fails to take any decision on a complaint, '*the complaint shall be deemed to be accepted by that competent authority*'. This provision for tacit acceptance, which plays in favour of taxpayers, should encourage the competent authorities to respect the six-month deadline so as to ensure that they need to only consider further those complaints with due merit.

The mutual agreement phase remains the phase during which the French tax authorities and the competent authorities of the other Member States concerned attempt to agree on how to resolve the dispute. With a view to enabling them to do so, the Directive extends the duration of this phase and clarifies the date from which it starts to run. Note, however, that if serious penalties are (or may be) imposed on the income or capital in question, access to the MAP may be denied or any ongoing proceedings stayed.

The duration of the mutual agreement phase is in principle two years (i.e., the same as under the Arbitration Convention), but either competent authority can now request its extension to three years, provided it supplies written justification (FPC, Article L. 251 G). If the taxpayer files a tax complaint under Article L. 190 of the FPC, the time limit is postponed until the outcome of this complaint (FPC, Article L. 251 J).

This change is in line with the BEPS measures, which have prompted the OECD to amend the MAP clause in its Model Convention, granting competent authorities a period of three years in which to resolve disputes. It also reflects past experience: the two-year deadline (which under the Arbitration Convention is fixed unless the taxpayer concerned agrees to an extension) was not often met. Under the combined effect of this new extension right, practical experience and France's election under the MLI, it seems likely that proceedings will now often last for three years, especially given that the condition of written justification will probably be more or less a formality (indeed, it is not clear what would happen if the second competent authority disagrees with the justification given).

The Directive also clarifies the date from which the mutual agreement phase begins to run. Whereas the revised Code of Conduct for the Arbitration Convention stipulates that the two-year period runs as from the later of either the date of the tax assessment notice (or equivalent) or the date on which the competent authority receives the request and the minimum information required, the Directive, duly implemented in that respect, defines just one start point: the last notification of a decision of one of the Member States on the acceptance of the complaint (FPC, Article L. 251 G). This should clear up the issue of differing interpretations between competent authorities and establish a more efficient standard practice with a view to resolving disputes more quickly.

The Directive has left to the Member States the possibility to provide that the competent authorities may still deny a taxpayer access to the MAP if it comes to light that it is subject to any sanctions 'for tax fraud, wilful default and gross negligence' in respect of the income or capital in connection with which the MAP is sought.

Similarly, if any judicial or administrative proceedings that could potentially lead to such penalties are ongoing, the competent authorities may stay the proceedings under the Directive pending their conclusion. The wording of Directive 2017/1852 on this point is similar to that of the Arbitration Convention; unfortunately, the drafters have chosen not to follow the recommendation from the revised Code of Conduct for the Arbitration Convention, according to which access should only be denied in exceptional cases.

France has chosen to implement both these rules: under Article L. 251 J of the FPC, the MAP is stayed when the judicial or administrative proceedings can potentially lead to the confirmation of penalties provided for under:

- Article 1728, 1, b of the FTC: 40% penalty for default in filing a declaration or a deed thirty days after receipt of a formal notice;
- Article 1728, 1, c of the FTC: 80% penalty in the event of hidden activity;
- Article 1729 of the FTC: 40% penalty for wilful default, 80% in the event of abuse of right as set forth under Article L. 64 of the FPC or 40% when the taxpayer was neither the principal initiator nor the principal beneficiary of the abuse, 80% penalty for fraud;

- Article 1732, a of the FTC: 100% penalty in the event of opposition to the tax audit;
- Article 1758, first paragraph of the FTC: 40% penalty for default in filing foreign assets;
- Article 1758, last paragraph of the FTC: 80% in the event of presumptive taxation based on outward signs of lifestyle.

The same penalties are listed under Article L. 251 M of the FPC providing that the procedure before the advisory commission cannot be initiated where any of the aforementioned penalties has been applied and has become final.

These limitations may substantially impediment the resort to the dispute resolution procedure, in light of the very common use of these penalties by the French tax authorities; it is indeed quite rare nowadays to see a tax reassessment notice without application of at least the 40% penalty for wilful default and the French courts have broadly enforced the application of this penalty. The French parliamentary work specifies that this implementation choice has been driven by the French tax authorities' intention to give access to this dispute resolution procedure only to 'taxpayers acting in good faith'.

D.3. Appeal of the Taxpayer Against the Decision Rejecting the Complaint

Directive 2017/1852 sets out the grounds on which the competent authority of a Member State may reject a taxpayer's complaint. Complaints can only be validly rejected on the specific grounds listed in Directive 2017/1852, namely: lack of information, absence of a question in dispute, or failure to submit the complaint within the three-year period. This limitative list of grounds for rejections has not been implemented into French law, Article L. 251 E of the FPC merely stating that the rejection must take the form of a reasoned decision. Directive 2017/1852 provisions should nevertheless be applicable in that respect.

One of the most significant developments of Directive 2017/1852 is the right for taxpayers to contest the rejection of their complaints; under Directive 2017/1852, taxpayers can now refer the matter to a second body. The procedure for such appeals depends on whether the complaint has been rejected by all competent authorities or just one of them:

- if all competent authorities concerned deny access to the MAP, the taxpayer now has the right to appeal this decision '*in accordance with national rules*'. This means that taxpayers can contest the rejection of a complaint before their national courts: under French law, the French appeal procedure will take the form of an ordinary complaint before the judge having jurisdiction, administrative or judicial, as provided under the general rules set out by Article L. 199 of the FPC (FPC, Article L. 251 F). In view of the average duration of proceedings in France, the appeal procedure should have allowed for an expedited ruling, so as to avoid dragging out what will already be a lengthy dispute resolution process. This is especially crucial in light of the fact that the

French authorities neither suspend collection of taxes pending dispute resolution nor pay interest on any taxes subsequently refunded;

- if just one of the competent authorities concerned or one of the national courts rejects the taxpayer's complaint, the taxpayer can request that an advisory commission rules on its admissibility (FPC, Article L. 251 K, 1°). Under the Arbitration Convention, the advisory commission's role was limited to the arbitration stage of proceedings. The Directive thus grants it a new prerogative: ruling on appeals when a taxpayer contests the rejection of its complaint by one of the two competent authorities involved. In the event of such an appeal, the advisory commission is set up in the same way as for the mutual agreement stage. The advisory commission must be set up within 120 days as from receipt of the taxpayer's request provided for under Article L. 251 K of the FPC (FPC, Article L. 251 L) and render its ruling within six months as from the date it is set up (FPC, Article L. 251 N, I).

Directive 2017/1852 stipulates under Article 7 (3) that, if the competent authorities fail to set up the advisory commission in due time, the taxpayer may apply to the competent court or national appointing body to set up the advisory commission in their stead and that, in such cases, the applicable procedure will be '*the same as the procedure under national rules in matters of civil and commercial arbitration that applies when courts or national appointing bodies appoint arbitrators because parties have failed to agree in this respect*'. The competent authority that initially failed to set up the advisory commission will then be entitled to appeal the decision of the court or national appointing body, provided it has the right to do so under the relevant national law. However, Article 7(3) of the Directive has not been implemented into French law and, if applicable, this new appeal procedure is left without precision: would Articles 1450 *et seq.* of the Civil Procedure Code, governing civil and commercial arbitration in France, and Articles 1504 *et seq.* governing international arbitration be applicable? And would the President of the Paris *Tribunal Judiciaire* (District Court) acting as the 'supporting judge' be the competent court? These issues remain unclear.

E. DISPUTE RESOLUTION PROCEDURE

E.1. Request of Appointment of the Advisory Commission

Under the Directive, the time frames for each phase may be extended if necessary in light of the particularities of the disputes submitted. Moreover, the competent authorities can now choose between a new ad hoc commission or the advisory commission in the arbitration phase.

When the competent authorities are unable to resolve the dispute before them within the time frame allowed for the MAP, they must inform the taxpayer, detailing the points on which they have been unable to agree. The taxpayer may then request that the dispute be submitted to arbitration (FPC, Article L. 251 I).

Directive 2017/1852 offers various avenues for dispute resolution in the arbitration phase. Taxpayers' cases may now be handled either by an advisory commission or by a new ad hoc body: the alternative dispute resolution commission. This new commission has been introduced as a way to offer greater flexibility in handling disputes that have not been resolved through the MAP as well as to ensure the timely resolution of disputes during the arbitration phase. The advisory commission or alternative dispute resolution commission is in principle required to issue an opinion within six months, but the Directive allows them to extend this deadline by a further three months if they deem it necessary (FPC, Article L. 251 Y). In such cases, the commission in question must inform the taxpayer of the extension.

Taxpayers can request the advisory commission to be set up in two cases:

- as indicated above, if just one of the competent authorities concerned or one of the national courts rejects the taxpayer's complaint (FPC, Article L. 251 K, 1°);
- if the competent authorities indicate to the taxpayer that they have failed to resolve the dispute through the MAP in which to request that an advisory commission be set up (FPC, Article L. 251 K, 2°).

Pursuant to Article R. 251 K-1 of the FPC, taxpayers have then fifty days to file a written request to set up the advisory commission as from the:

- receipt of the notice of rejection of the taxpayer's request for opening the MAP, provided for under Article L. 251 E;
- date on which a decision is delivered by the court on the appeal provided for under Article L. 251 F (right to appeal open when all tax authorities have denied access to the MAP);
- date of notification of the decision provided for under Article L. 251 I, when the French tax authorities and the other concerned Member State's tax authorities have not been able to reach an agreement as to how to resolve the question in dispute.

E.2. Appointment of the Advisory Commission

The advisory commission must be set up within 120 days as from receipt of the taxpayer's request (FPC, Article L. 251 L).

The advisory commission comprises:

- a chair;
- one (or two) representative of each competent authority concerned; and
- one (or two) independent person of standing appointed by each Member State (FPC, Article L. 251 P).

These representatives and independent persons of standing appoint the chair; unless they agree otherwise, the chair of the advisory commission will be a judge (FPC, Article L. 251 S). A substitute is also appointed for each independent person of standing. The Implementing Decree also specifies that at least three persons on the list of independent persons of standing to be provided to the EU Commission are designated by the Budget Minister (FPC, Article R. 251 P-1).

There are strict rules on who can be appointed as an independent person of standing – the following appointments can be objected by the tax authorities:

- any person who has belonged to or worked on behalf of one of the tax administrations concerned at any time over the past three years (FPC, Article L. 251 Q II, 1°);
- any person who holds or has held any voting right in or is or has been an employee of or adviser to any person involved in the dispute, at any time during the last five years prior to the date of his or her appointment (FPC, Article L. 251 Q II, 2°);
- any person who does not present enough guarantee of his or her impartiality regarding the resolution of the dispute at hand (FPC, Article L. 251 Q II, 3°);
- any person who is or has been an employee of an enterprise that provides tax advice or who otherwise gives or has given tax advice on a professional basis at any time over the past three years, at least, prior to the date of his or her appointment (FPC, Article L. 251 Q II, 4°).

So as to ensure the complete impartiality and integrity of the independent persons of standing, it is also provided that '*[f]or a period of 12 months after the decision of the advisory commission was delivered, an independent person of standing who is part of the advisory commission shall not be in a situation that would have given cause to a competent authority to object to his appointment*' (FPC, Article L. 251 Q IV).

Lastly, the sentence of Article L. 251 S of the FPC providing that the chair of the advisory commission shall in principle be a judge is another step in the advisory commission's transformation into a more court-like body.

Pursuant to Article L. 251 T of the FPC, the functioning rules of the advisory commission must be notified by the French tax authorities to the taxpayer with the following elements specified by the Implementing Decree (FPC, Article R. 251 T-1):

- the limit date by which the opinion on the dispute resolution must be delivered and the means of delivery of this opinion;
- the applicable regulatory or legal provisions, agreement or convention;
- the description and the main features of the dispute;
- the mandate on which the concerned tax authorities agree with respect to the legal and factual issues to be resolved;
- the structure of the dispute resolution body;
- the timeline of the dispute resolution procedure;
- the number of members, their names, details about their qualification and experience, as well as communication of the conflict of interest about them;
- the rules on the taxpayer's and third parties' participation to the procedure, the exchanges of notes, information or evidence, the costs, the applicable method to resolve the dispute and any other procedural or organizational issue that the French tax authorities deem necessary.

E.3. Appointment of the Advisory Commission Made by a Competent Court

If it is not set up within this time, the taxpayer may apply to the competent court or national appointing body to set up the advisory commission and thus to appoint the independent persons of standing who are to be its members. In France, it will be the President of the Paris *Tribunal Judiciaire* pursuant to Article L. 251 R of the FPC. Article L. 251 Z provides that the advisory commission must base its opinion on the provisions of the applicable agreement or convention as well as on any applicable national rules.

E.4. Alternative Dispute Resolution Commission

Pursuant to the Directive 2017/1852 stipulations, Article L. 251 ZD of the FPC provides that the French authorities and the other Member States' competent authorities may decide to set up an alternative dispute resolution commission. It is also provided that the competent authorities may decide that this alternative dispute resolution commission can depart from the rules applicable to the advisory commission, such as the requirement to base its opinion on the provisions of the applicable agreement or convention as well as on any applicable national rules.

This ad hoc body and the way in which it operates reflect the EU Commission's desire to offer competent authorities greater flexibility so as to allow them to resolve disputes as efficiently as possible. The competent authorities have a great deal of freedom in deciding how the alternative dispute resolution commission should be set up and operate. As a result, the alternative dispute resolution commission may differ significantly from the advisory commission in its make-up and functioning. The independent persons of standing appointed to make up an alternative dispute resolution commission must nonetheless satisfy the conditions of independence and impartiality, in the same way as for the advisory commission.

The competent authorities also have the option of setting up an alternative dispute resolution commission on a more permanent basis, as a 'standing committee', provided they both agree. What makes this ad hoc body particularly interesting is that it can '*apply [...] any dispute resolution processes or technique to solve the question in dispute in a binding manner*'. The Directive cites the technique of 'final offer' arbitration (also known as 'last best offer' arbitration) as one example. This opens the door to a range of alternative dispute resolution methods, such as collaborative practice, participatory proceedings, mediation or conciliation. These methods are typically used in civil disputes and would therefore probably need to be adjusted for application to matters of tax law.

However, the precise details of functioning of this permanent standing committee having not yet been discussed at the EU level, France has not implemented the Directive's provision in that respect.

F. COMMON PROCEDURAL PROVISION

F.1. Enforcement of a Decision Taken under the MAP or Dispute Resolution Procedure

When the competent authorities reach an agreement as to how to resolve the question in dispute during the mutual agreement phase, their decision is binding on them and enforceable by the taxpayer, provided the latter accepts the decision and withdraws from all other ongoing proceedings for remedies, particularly domestic judicial proceedings. The taxpayer must provide evidence that it has taken action to terminate any such proceedings within sixty days from the date on which the competent authorities notify it of their decision (FPC, Article R. 251 H-1).

The advisory commission and alternative dispute resolution commission both adopt opinions by a simple majority of their members (FPC, Article L. 251 Z). All opinions are delivered in writing (FPC, Article R. 251 Y-1). Precise details on the requisite content of opinions would be helpful: Directive 2017/1852 specifies only that they must be based on the provisions of the applicable agreement or convention as well as on any applicable domestic rules. In drafting opinions, the advisory commission and alternative dispute resolution commission could look to the revised Code of Conduct for the Arbitration Convention, which stipulates that opinions should in particular include the relevant information on the complaint (i.e., the names and addresses of the enterprises involved, identification of the competent authorities involved, a description of the facts and circumstances of the dispute and a clear statement of what is claimed), the names of the members of the advisory commission, a short summary of the proceedings, and details of the arguments and methods on which the decision in the opinion is based.

Article L. 251 ZA of the FPC provides that the advisory commission must deliver its opinion to the competent authorities, which will then have six months in which to take a final decision. The competent authorities may deviate from the advisory commission's opinion, provided they are able to agree on an alternative resolution (as under the Arbitration Convention). In the same way as for decisions issued further to the MAP, the decision delivered by the competent authorities in this context is binding on them and enforceable by the taxpayer, provided the latter accepts the decision and withdraws from all other ongoing domestic proceedings, supplying the competent authorities with evidence that it has done so within sixty days from the date on which they notify it of their decision (FPC, Article L. 251 ZC). This stipulation that the taxpayer must accept the competent authorities' decision in order for it to be binding marks a difference between the Directive and the 2015 proposal for revision of the Code of Conduct, which does not require the taxpayer's consent to the competent authorities' decision. In practice, however, as noted in the proposed revision of the Code of Conduct, the taxpayer should generally be satisfied provided the double taxation has been resolved.

The Member States concerned are required to implement the competent authorities' decision (which concerns solely the taxable basis in question) under their national law, amending the disputed taxation according to the applicable domestic rules. French implementation is very terse in that respect, merely providing that the final decision, once notified and accepted, modifies accordingly the taxpayer's taxation (FPC, Article L. 251 ZC II). However, the Directive stipulates that, if the competent authorities fail to notify the taxpayer of their final decision within thirty days of taking it, or if the relevant Member State fails to implement the final decision, the taxpayer may appeal in accordance with the applicable national rules in its Member State of residence in order to obtain the final decision or enforce its implementation, as the case may be.

The Directive stipulates that the competent authorities may publish final decisions provided the taxpayer agrees. However, even if the competent authorities or the taxpayer do not agree to publication of the final decision in its entirety, the Directive provides that an abstract must still be published, containing 'a description of the issue and the subject matter, the date, the tax periods involved, the legal basis, the industry sector, [...] a short description of the final outcome [and] a description of the method of arbitration used'. Under French law, the publication takes the form of an automatic transmission to the EU Commission of an abstract of the final decision for publication purposes (FPC, Article L. 251 ZF, clarified by Article R. 251 ZF-1). The Implementing Decree merely adds that, before being transmitted to the EU Commission, the abstract must be communicated to the taxpayer who has sixty days to request that information covered by commercial and industrial secret or contrary to public order not be published (FPC, Article R. 251 ZF, II).

F.2. Interaction Between Directive 2017/1852 and the National Proceedings

As under the Arbitration Convention, the Directive stipulates that the instigation of proceedings under national law, or even a final ruling under national law, will not prevent a taxpayer from availing itself of the remedies offered under the Directive. Indeed, a court judgment does not always suffice to resolve a situation of double taxation. Taxpayers may therefore simultaneously submit a dispute to the competent authorities under the Directive and to the French courts under the domestic appeal procedure (see, above, section D.2, FPC, Article L. 251 E III) or file a complaint to the French courts during the MAP (see, above, section D.2, Article L. 251 J), both resulting in a postponement of delays.

However, the MAP will be terminated if the French court seized by the taxpayer's complaint delivers a ruling which becomes final after the filing of request by the taxpayer to set up the advisory commission but before the delivery of the advisory commission's opinion (FPC, Article L. 251 ZH).

F.3. Interaction Between Directive 2017/1852 and the Tax Treaty Proceedings

Article L. 251 ZG of the FPC governs the interaction between the various dispute resolution procedures available under Directive 2017/1852, the Arbitration Convention and Tax Treaties. In accordance with Directive 2017/1852, it provides that the opening of proceedings under Directive 2017/1852 procedure will put an end to any other ongoing proceedings in relation to the same matter pursuant to an agreement or convention, as from the date on which the complaint is first received by one of the Member States and that such opening will prevent the taxpayer from resorting to any other mutual agreement or dispute resolution procedures provided for under an agreement or convention entered into by France.

Although, strictly speaking, this provision does not prevent taxpayers from submitting disputes to the resolution procedures available under Tax Treaties, it could nonetheless result in a change in practice: previously, French taxpayers tended to submit complaints under both the treaty provisions and the Arbitration Convention, based on the French tax authorities' guidelines, so as to ensure that the double taxation issue would be resolved and to avoid the risk of time-barring in certain countries which take a particularly strict view in terms of limitation periods.

CHAPTER 5

Germany

Stefan Mayer

A. IMPLEMENTING MEASURES ADOPTED BY GERMANY IN RESPECT OF DIRECTIVE 2017/1852

By means of the 'Law to implement the Council Directive (EU) 2017/1852 of 10 October 2017 on Tax Dispute Resolution Mechanisms in the European Union' ('*Gesetz zur Umsetzung der Richtlinie (EU) 2017/1852 des Rates vom 10. Oktober 2017 über Verfahren zur Beilegung von Besteuerungsstreitigkeiten in der Europäischen Union*') as of 10 December 2019 (hereinafter 'TDRM Law'), Germany has transposed Directive 2017/1852 into domestic law. The TDRM Law shall apply with retroactive effect for any complaint submitted from 1 July 2019 and relating to a tax year commencing on or after 1 January 2018.

The TDRM Law provides a proceeding to resolve disputes between Member States arising from the interpretation and application of Tax Treaties or the Arbitration Convention. Such proceeding is an addition to the dispute resolution mechanisms existing in a Tax Treaty or in the Arbitration Convention, such as the MAP (*see* Article 25 of the OECD Model Convention) or the mandatory binding arbitration as implemented into many Tax Treaties by the MLI. However, any complaint submitted under the TDRM Law shall terminate any ongoing proceedings under these dispute resolution mechanisms (and further proceedings shall become inadmissible).[1]

The TDRM Law largely represents a faithful transposition of Directive 2017/1852 into German law. The interaction between the proceedings foreseen by Directive 2017/1852 and national proceedings is mostly solved in favour of a Directive-friendly way. Although Germany has used the possibility to deny access to the dispute

1. Section 4 para. 4 TDRM Law.

resolution mechanism foreseen by Directive 2017/1852 in cases the taxpayer has (potentially) violated tax law the approach is rather moderate in this respect.

The German legislator decided to transpose Directive 2017/1852 into domestic law by means of a stand-alone act rather than implementing the respective rules in the German General Fiscal Code (‘*Abgabenordnung*’) or the German Code of Procedures for Fiscal Courts (‘*Finanzgerichtsordnung*’). The structure of the TDRM Law does not entirely follow the scheme of Directive 2017/1852 but is instead built up in the chronological order of a proceeding.[2]

The TDRM Law is divided into eight chapters. While Chapter 1 and Chapter 8 deal with general rules, Chapter 2 through Chapter 7 mirror the chronological order of a proceeding: Chapter 2 governs rules on how to raise a complaint, Chapter 3 covers the MAP, Chapter 4 and Chapter 5 deal with the dispute resolution mechanism, and Chapter 7 defines the possibility to set up the alternative dispute resolution commission. Furthermore, some special provisions for individuals and smaller undertakings are defined in Chapter 6.

B. GENERAL SECTION

B.1. Subject Matter and Scope

The TDRM Law provides rules to resolve disputes between Germany and one or several Member States.[3] The TDRM Law implements the scope of Article 1 of Directive 2017/1852 into German law and further clarifies that also a Dispute involving more than two parties (Germany and more than one other Member State) is within the scope of the TDRM Law. The procedure under the TDRM Law is part of the ordinary administrative proceeding applicable to tax matters; i.e., the German General Fiscal Code (‘*Abgabenordnung*’) is applicable to such procedure.[4] German tax authorities are not prevented from initiating or continuing any administrative, criminal or court proceedings once a Dispute Resolution Complaint (as defined in section B.2. below) is filed during an ongoing procedure under the TDRM Law.[5] However, the submission of a Dispute Resolution Complaint ends ex officio any ongoing proceedings under the MAP or dispute resolution procedure under an Agreement or Convention (as defined in section B.2. below) in relation to the relevant Question in Dispute (as defined in section B.2. below).[6]

B.2. Definitions

Section 2 of the TDRM Law provides the following definitions:

2. *See* the explanatory notes to the TDRM Law (*Bundestagdrucksache* No. 19/12112, p. 26).
3. Section 1 para. 1 TDRM Law.
4. Explanatory notes to the TDRM Law (*Bundestagdrucksache* No. 19/12112, p. 31).
5. Section 1 para. 2 TDRM Law.
6. Section 4 para. 4 TDRM Law.

- 'Agreement' means a Tax Treaty between Germany and a further Member State that provides for the elimination of double taxation of income and capital;
- 'Convention' means the Arbitration Convention (i.e., the Convention on the elimination of double taxation in connection with the adjustment of profits of associated enterprises (90/463/EEC)) as well as future conventions to be named by law;
- 'Dispute' means legal disagreements arising from the interpretation of Conventions and Agreements; the content of such Dispute constitutes a 'Question in Dispute';
- 'Double Taxation' means the imposition of taxes covered by an Agreement or Convention by Germany and one or several other Member State(s) in respect of the same taxable income or capital, if such imposition gives rise to: (i) an additional tax charge, (ii) an increase in tax liability or (iii) the cancellation or reduction of losses that could be used to offset taxable profits;
- 'Competent Authority of Germany' means the German Federal Ministry of Finance ('*Bundesfinanzministerium*') or any authority to which the German Federal Ministry of Finance delegates its competence; in case of the TDRM Law, the German Federal Ministry of Finance delegates its competence to the German Federal Central Office of Taxation ('*Bundeszentralamt für Steuern*');
- 'Competent Authority of another Member State' means the authority named by such other Member State;
- 'Competent Court of Germany' means the German fiscal court being competent for proceedings against the German Federal Central Office of Taxation according to the German Code of Procedures for Fiscal Courts ('*Finanzgerichtsordnung*'); this is currently the Lower Tax Court of Cologne;
- 'Competent Court of another Member State' means the court named by such other Member State;
- 'Affected Person' means a person or enterprise that: (i) is (treated) resident in a Member State pursuant to an Agreement and (ii) whose taxation is affected by the Question in Dispute.

Terms not defined in the TDRM Law shall, unless the context requires otherwise, have the meaning ascribed to them in the respective Agreement or Convention on the date of receipt of the first notification of the action that has or may have given rise to the Question in Dispute.[7]

7. Section 2 para. 2 TDRM Law.

C. COMPLAINT TO START A MAP

C.1. Filing a Complaint to Start a MAP

Chapter 2 of the TDRM Law (sections 4 to 12) stipulates provisions for the procedure from the submission of a Dispute Resolution Complaint until the decision on the acceptance or rejection of such Dispute Resolution Complaint.

Section 4 paragraph 1 TDRM Law defines a complaint on a Question in Dispute as 'Dispute Resolution Complaint' ('*Streitbeilegungsbeschwerde*'). This term, which is not specifically used by Directive 2017/1852, constitutes a key term of the TDRM Law being used in most chapters. The details of the submission of the Dispute Resolution Complaint comply with the requirements of Directive 2017/1852. The Dispute Resolution Complaint has to be filed with both the German Federal Central Office of Taxation and the Competent Authority(s) of each of the Member States concerned within three years after the receipt of first notification of the action/measure having resulted, or that will result, in the Question in Dispute.[8] In this context, the TDRM Law clarifies that the three-year limitation period for the Dispute Resolution Complaint shall apply regardless of whether or not the underlying action/measure, e.g. an underlying tax assessment, is non-appealable and final.[9]

A Dispute Resolution Complaint shall contain the following information:[10]

- name, address, tax identification number and other information necessary to identify the Affected Person and any other person concerned;[11]
- the Member States concerned by the Dispute Resolution Complaint;[12]
- the tax period concerned;[13]
- detailed information and copies of supporting documents regarding the facts and circumstances of the case, including details of the structure of the transaction and the relationships between the Affected Person and the other parties involved in the transactions, as well as the facts recognized in good faith in a mutually binding agreement between the Affected Person and the German Federal Central Office of Taxation or another Competent Authority of a Member State concerned.[14] In this regard, the TDRM Law uses the term 'mutually binding agreement' ('*verbindliche Vereinbarung*') as used by Directive 2017/1852 although this term is not defined yet in German tax law. The explanatory notes to the TDRM Law, however, clarify that the term mutually binding agreement shall cover the binding ruling ('*verbindliche Auskunft*') pursuant to section 89 of the German General Fiscal Code ('*Abgabenordnung*')

8. Section 4 para. 3 TDRM Law.
9. Section 4 para. 3 sentence 3 TDRM Law.
10. Listed in section 5 TDRM Law.
11. Section 5 No. 1 TDRM Law.
12. Section 5 No. 2 TDRM Law. This requirement is not known by the Directive 2017/1852.
13. Section 5 No. 3 TDRM Law.
14. Section 5 No. 4 lit a TDRM Law.

as well as the factual agreement (*'tatsächliche Verständigung'*) pursuant to sections 204 et seq. of the German General Fiscal Code (*'Abgabenordnung'*);[15]

- detailed information and copies of supporting documents regarding the nature and the date of the action/measure giving rise to the Question in Dispute, including, where applicable, details of the income received in the other Member State and the inclusion of such income in the taxable income in the other Member State, as well as details of the tax charged or that will be charged in relation to such income in the other Member State and the related amounts in the currencies of the Member States concerned;[16]
- reference to the applicable provisions of domestic tax law, Conventions and Agreements; in case more than one Agreement or Convention is applicable, it shall be specified which Agreement or Convention is being interpreted in relation to the relevant Question in Dispute;[17]
- an explanation of why there is a Question in Dispute;[18]
- details of any remedy initiated by the Affected Person in relation to the Question in Dispute and any court decisions concerning the Question in Dispute including copies of all documents;[19]
- a declaration of the Affected Person committing itself to answer quickly and completely any appropriate request for further information by the Federal Central Office of Taxation or a Competent Authority of another Member State concerned and provide any respective documents;[20]
- to the extent available, copies of: (i) any tax assessment, (ii) any tax audit report or other equivalent documents leading to the Question in Dispute and (iii) other documents issued by the German tax authorities regarding the Question in Dispute;[21]
- to the extent available, information on any complaint submitted by the Affected Person under another MAP or arbitration procedure regarding the same Question in Dispute and the same tax period including copies of all documents;[22]
- a declaration of the Affected Person committing itself to comply with section 4 paragraph 4 TDRM Law, meaning not to file any proceedings under the MAP or dispute resolution procedure under an Agreement or Convention with regard to the Question in Dispute;[23] and
- any further information the Affected Persons considers necessary regarding the Question in Dispute.[24]

15. *See* explanatory notes to the TDRM Law (*Bundestagdrucksache* No. 19/12112, p. 32).
16. Section 5 No. 4 lit b and c TDRM Law.
17. Section 5 No. 5 TDRM Law.
18. Section 5 No. 6 TDRM Law.
19. Section 5 No. 7 TDRM Law.
20. Section 5 No. 8 TDRM Law.
21. Section 5 No. 9 TDRM Law.
22. Section 5 No. 10 TDRM Law.
23. Section 5 No. 11 TDRM Law. This requirement is not known by the Directive 2017/1852.
24. Section 5 No. 12 TDRM Law.

Within two months after the Dispute Resolution Complaint has been filed, the German Federal Central Office of Taxation informs the Affected Person on the one hand and the Competent Authority(s) of the other Member State(s) concerned on the other hand about the filed Dispute Resolution Complaint. The German Federal Central Office of Taxation further informs the Competent Authority(s) of the other Member States concerned in which language the Dispute Resolution Complaint was filed and in which languages it intends to communicate during the relevant proceedings.

D. THE RESOLUTION OF THE QUESTION IN DISPUTE UNDER THE MAP

D.1. Decision of the Competent Authority with Reference to the Complaint

In preparation for its decision to either accept or reject the Dispute Resolution Complaint, the Federal Central Office of Taxation may request further information from the Affected Person.[25] Such further information has to be requested within three months after the German Federal Central Office of Taxation has received the Dispute Resolution Complaint; the Affected Person in turn has to submit its answer within three months after receiving the request.

In principle, the German Federal Central Office of Taxation decides within six months after receiving the Dispute Resolution Complaint to accept or reject the Dispute Resolution Complaint.[26] In case additional information has been requested, the six-month period starts the day after the Federal Central Tax Office has received the respective answer from the Affected Person. In case the Affected Person has filed an appeal under the domestic law of one of the Member States concerned, the six-month period starts the day after: (i) the decision in such appeal procedure becomes legally binding, (ii) the appeal procedure has been finally settled by other means or (iii) the appeal procedure has been suspended.[27] If the German Federal Central Office of Taxation did not make a decision within the six-month period, the Dispute Resolution Complaint is deemed accepted.[28]

The German Federal Central Office of Taxation may decide to reject the Dispute Resolution Complaint if:

- the filing of the Dispute Resolution Complaints does not meet the formal requirements;[29]
- further information required after the filing of the Dispute Resolution Complaint has not been submitted in time (three-month period);
- there is no Question in Dispute of the Affected Person; or

25. Section 7 TDRM Law.
26. Section 8 para. 1 sentence 1 TDRM Law.
27. Section 8 para. 1 sentence 3 TDRM Law.
28. Section 8 para. 4 TDRM Law.
29. Pursuant to section 5 TDRM Law.

- the Dispute Resolution Complaint has not been filed within the three-year period after the receipt of first notification of the action/measure having resulted, or that will result, in the Question in Dispute.

D.2. MAP

If a Dispute Resolution Complaint has been filed, the TDRM Law foresees a MAP, as follows.

As the default rule, a MAP is initiated if the Competent Authorities of all the Member States concerned accept the Dispute Resolution Complaint.[30] However, a MAP is also initiated if: (i) an Advisory Commission in case of an initial spilt decision has decided to accept the Dispute Resolution Complaint and (ii) at least one Competent Authority initiates the MAP.[31] If in the latter case no Competent Authority initiates a MAP within sixty days after the Advisory Commission notified the German Federal Central Office of Taxation about its decision, the Advisory Commission shall provide an opinion to resolve the Question in Dispute (for details see below in section E).[32] In case the decision of the Advisory Commission overrules a rejection of the Dispute Resolution Complaint of the German Federal Central Office of Taxation, the TDRM Law requires the Federal Central Tax Office to initiate a MAP.[33]

If a MAP is initiated, the German Federal Central Office of Taxation shall seek to resolve the Question in Dispute together with the Competent Authority(s) of the other Member State(s) concerned within two years.[34] Such two-year period starts when the last notification of the acceptance of the Dispute Resolution Complaint by a Competent Authority of a Member State concerned is received by the Affected Person. Such two-year period will be extended by one further year if so suggested by a Competent Authority to the other Competent Authority(s) by means of a written justification.[35] During the MAP, the German Federal Central Office of Taxation has again the possibility to request further information.[36] Such request shall not extend the two-year period or three-year period (as applicable).

In case the Competent Authorities of the Member States concerned reach an agreement on how to resolve the Question in Dispute, such agreement will become binding for the competent local tax authorities and enforceable for the Affected Person once the Affected Person has waived any right to (further) challenge (under domestic law) the underlying action/measure that gave rise to the dispute vis-à-vis the German Federal Central Office of Taxation.[37] In case such agreement cannot be reached by the

30. Section 13 para. 1 TDRM Law.
31. Section 10 para. 5 sentence 1 TDRM Law.
32. Section 17 para. 2 TDRM Law.
33. Section 10 para. 5 sentence 2 TDRM Law. In case the Advisory Commission overrules a rejection of a Competent Authority of another Member State it is within the discretion of the German Federal Central Office of Taxation to initiate a MAP.
34. Section 13 para. 1 and 2 TDRM Law.
35. Section 13 para. 4 TDRM Law.
36. Section 14 TDRM Law.
37. Section 15 para. 1 und 2 TRDM Law.

Competent Authorities within the two-year period or three-year period (as applicable), the German Federal Central Office of Taxation informs the Affected Person without undue delay about the reasons for the failure to reach an agreement.[38] In such case, the Affected Person may request a decision by the Advisory Commission (see section E. below).

D.3. Appeal of the Taxpayer Against the Decision Rejecting the Complaint

In case the German Central Federal Office of Taxation rejects the Dispute Resolution Complaint the Affected Person may challenge the rejection by means of an appeal (*'Einspruch'*) pursuant to sections 347 et seq. of the German General Fiscal Code (*'Abgabenordnung'*).[39] Such appeal is, in principle, only available in case all Competent Authorities of the Member States concerned reject the Dispute Resolution Complaint (as foreseen by Article 5 para 3 of Directive 2017/1852).[40] Section 9 paragraph 1 TDRM Law ensures that the appeal may not be rejected as being time-barred where a decision of the Competent Authority(s) of the other Member State(s) concerned has not been issued before the end of the one-month appeal period available in Germany against the decision of the German Federal Central Office of Taxation.[41]

In case of a split decision of the Competent Authorities, i.e. at least one Competent Authority accepts the Dispute Resolution Complaint and at least one other Competent Authority rejects it, the Affected Person may request the formation of the Advisory Commission to decide about the acceptance or rejection of the Dispute Resolution Complaint.[42] If the Advisory Commission decides to accept the Dispute Resolution Complaint, this decision shall prevail over any rejecting decisions of a Competent Authority.

E. DISPUTE RESOLUTION PROCEDURE

E.1. Request of Appointment of the Advisory Commission

The Advisory Commission is in charge to resolve the Question in Dispute in two cases:

- The Affected Person requests the formation of an Advisory Commission within fifty days after being informed by the German Federal Central Office of

38. Section 16 para. 1 TDRM Law.
39. Explanatory notes to the TDRM Law (*Bundestagdrucksache* No. 19/12112, p. 33).
40. In fact, the TDRM Law does not explicitly mention the possibility of an appeal against the rejection. However, according to the explanatory notes to the TDRM Law (*Bundestagdrucksache* No. 19/12112, p. 33), an appeal shall be allowed based on the respective 'general rules of the German General Fiscal Code (*Abgabenordnung*)'.
41. In such cases, the *restutio in integrum* (*Wiedereinsetzung in den vorherigen Stand*) according to section 110 German General Fiscal Code (*Abgabenordnung*) is available.
42. *See* for details section 10 TDRM Law.

Taxation that the Competent Authorities have not reached an agreement during the MAP.[43]
- The Advisory Commission which has been set up to decide about the acceptance or rejection of a Dispute Resolution Complaint (because of a split decision of the Competent Authorities) decides to accept the Dispute Resolution Complaint and no Competent Authority initiates a MAP within the sixty-day period (see above D.22.).[44]

The German Federal Central Office of Taxation may reject the request of an Affected Person to set up an Advisory Commission in the first case where: (i) the Affected Person has violated German tax laws; (ii) such violation has been sanctioned by means of imprisonment, financial penalty (‘*Geldstrafe*’) or financial fine (‘*Geldbuße*’); and (iii) such violation is connected with the Question in Dispute.[45] In case a respective criminal/fine proceeding is pending, the German Federal Central Office of Taxation may suspend the dispute resolution (as of the time of the acceptance of the Dispute Resolution Complaint) until the termination of such criminal/fine proceeding.[46] Furthermore, the German Federal Central Office of Taxation may deny the formation of an Advisory Commission in exceptional cases where the Question in Dispute does not involve Double Taxation.[47]

E.2. Appointment of the Advisory Commission

In the event that the MAP has ended without an agreement, the German Federal Central Office of Taxation participates in the formation of an Advisory Commission, which has to be set up within 120 days after receiving the request of the Affected Person. In the event that an Advisory Commission has already been set up to decide on the acceptance or rejection of the Dispute Resolution Complaint, such Advisory Board will remain in existence to resolve the Question in Dispute in case no MAP will be initiated by a Member State; the 120-day period applied for the initial formation of the Advisory Board already.

The Advisory Commission is composed of

- a chair;
- one representative of each Competent Authority of the Member States concerned; and
- one independent person of standing appointed by each Competent Authority of the Member States concerned.[48]

43. Section 17 para. 1 TDRM Law.
44. Section 17 para. 2 TDRM Law.
45. Section 20 para. 1 sentence 1 TDRM Law.
46. Section 20 para. 1 sentence 2 TDRM Law.
47. Section 20 para. 2 TDRM Law.
48. Section 21 TDRM Law.

The Competent Authorities may agree to double the number of representatives and/or independent persons of standing for each Competent Authority.

The EU Commission provides a list of all independent persons of standing nominated by the Member States. The German Ministry of Finance (*'Bundesfinanzministerium'*) appoints at least three individuals being eligible for an Advisory Commission.[49] In principle, the German Federal Central Office of Taxation and the Competent Authority(s) of the other Member State(s) concerned agree on the rules to appoint the independent persons of standing. Based on the same rules, the Competent Authorities shall appoint a substitute for each independent person of standing. In case the Competent Authorities are unable to find an agreement, the independent persons of standing and their substitutes shall be chosen by lot.[50]

The representatives of the Competent Authorities and the independent persons of standing shall elect a chair from the list of independent persons of standing provided by the EU Commission. Until otherwise agreed, the chair shall be a judge.[51]

The by-laws (*'Geschäftsordnung'*) of the Advisory Commission shall be agreed upon by the German Federal Central Office of Taxation and the Competent Authority(s) of the other Member State(s) concerned.[52] Such by-laws shall include *inter alia*:

- a description and the characteristics of the Question in Dispute;
- a description of the legal and factual question to be resolved;
- the time frame of the dispute resolution procedure;
- the composition of the Advisory Commission; and
- the rules governing the participation of the Affected Person and third parties (e.g., exchange of memorandums, information and evidence).[53]

Within the 120-day period for the formation of the Advisory Board, the German Federal Central Office of Taxation shall notify the Affected Person the by-laws of the Advisory Commission, the date by which the Advisory Commission shall have taken its decision on the Question in Dispute as well as any applicable provisions under domestic law.[54]

E.3. Alternative Dispute Resolution Commission

The German Federal Central Office of Taxation and the Competent Authority(s) of the other Member State(s) concerned may agree to set up an alternative dispute resolution commission that may deliver an opinion on the Question in Dispute instead of the Advisory Commission. Such alternative dispute resolution commission may also be set up in the form of a committee that is of permanent nature.[55] Such alternative dispute

49. Section 26 para. 1 TDRM Law.
50. Section 24 para. 1 sentence 2 TDRM Law.
51. Section 24 para. 5 TDRM Law.
52. Section 27 para. 1 TDRM Law.
53. Section 27 para. 3 TDRM Law.
54. Section 27 para. 2 TDRM Law.
55. Section 29 TDRM Law.

resolution commission may apply alternative dispute resolution processes and techniques.[56] In principle, the main rules of procedure for the Advisory Commission shall apply accordingly.[57]

F. COMMON PROCEDURAL PROVISION

The procedural provisions described in the following for the Advisory Commission are, as a rule, also applicable for an Alternative Dispute Resolution Commission.

F.1. Procedural Language

The procedural language of the TDRM procedure is German (section 3 TDRM Law). Earlier drafts of the TDRM Law included English as a second procedural language;[58] however, this option has been removed in an early stage of the legislative procedure.

F.2. Information, Evidence and Hearings

The Affected Person may provide the Advisory Commission with any information, evidence or documents that may be relevant for the decision (to the extent the German Federal Central Office of Taxation and the Competent Authority(s) of the other Member State(s) concerned agree to them).[59] In addition, upon request of the Advisory Commission, the Affected Person as well as the German Federal Central Office of Taxation shall provide the Advisory Commission with any information, evidence or documents necessary for the decision.[60] The TDRM Law makes it clear that such obligation to disclose information, evidence and documents is given despite any applicable fiscal secrecy ('*Steuergeheimnis*') pursuant to section 30 German General Fiscal Code ('*Abgabenordnung*').[61] However, the German Federal Central Office of Taxation may refuse a request in case: (i) it is unable to obtain the requested information under applicable domestic law; (ii) such information concerns trade secrets, business secrets, industrial secrets or professional secrets;[62] or (iii) the disclosure of such information would be contrary to the public policy (*öffentliche Ordnung*).[63]

56. Section 30 para. 3 TDRM Law.
57. That is, *inter alia* sections 17, 19, 23 and 27 TDRM Law.
58. Section 3 of the published draft bill of the German Federal Ministry of Finance (*Referentenentwurf des Bundesfinanzministeriums*).
59. Section 23 para. 1 TDRM Law.
60. Section 23 para. 2 TDRM Law.
61. Section 23 para. 2 sentence 2 TDRM Law. According to section 23 para. 5 TDRM Law members of the Advisory Commission who are not qualified as officials (*Amtsträger*) within the meaning of section 30 para. 1 German General Fiscal Code (*Abgabenordnung*) in connection with section 7 German General Fiscal Code (*Abgabenordnung*) are also obliged to preserve the fiscal secrecy.
62. Section 32 TDRM Law states generally that any domestic rules protecting trade secrets, business secrets, industrial secrets or professional secrets shall apply and remain unaffected by the TDRM Law.
63. Section 23 para. 3 TDRM Law.

The Affected Person may, upon the consent of the German Federal Central Office of Taxation and the other Competent Authority(s) of the other Member State(s) concerned, request to appear or to be represented before the Advisory Commission. Upon request of the Advisory Commission, the Affected Person shall appear or be represented before the Advisory Commission.[64]

F.3. The Opinion of the Advisory Commission

The Advisory Commission has to take a decision within six months after being established.[65] The Advisory Commission may resolve to extend such six-month period for additionally three months in case it considers this to be appropriate to deliver an opinion on the Question in Dispute.[66]

The Advisory Commission shall take a decision based on the provisions of the applicable Agreement or Convention as well as on any applicable domestic law.[67] Such decision shall be adopted by the simple majority of the members of the Advisory Commission; where a majority cannot be reached, the vote of the chair shall decide.[68] The chair communicates the decision to the German Federal Central Office of Taxation and the Competent Authority(s) of the other Member State(s) concerned.[69]

F.4. Final Decision of Competent Authorities

The German Federal Central Office of Taxation shall agree with the Competent Authority(s) of the other Member States concerned on how to resolve the Question in Dispute within six months after the notification of the opinion of the Advisory Commission.[70] Such final decision may deviate from the opinion of the Advisory Commission. If, however, an agreement cannot be reached within the six-month period, the opinion of the Advisory Commission shall be binding.[71] In case the German Federal Central Office of Taxation has not notified the Affected Person of the final decision within thirty days after the end of the six-month period, the Affected Person may file an appeal according to section 347 paragraph 1 sentence 2 German General Fiscal Code ('*Abgabenordnung*') to obtain the final decision.[72] The final decision shall be binding for Germany; however, it shall not be considered a precedent for other Dispute Resolution Complaints.[73]

64. Section 23 para. 4 TDRM Law.
65. Section 17 para. 3 TDRM Law.
66. Section 17 para. 3 TDRM Law.
67. Section 17 para. 4 TDRM Law.
68. Section 17 para. 5 TDRM Law.
69. Section 17 para. 6 TDRM Law.
70. Section 18 para. 1 TDRM Law.
71. Section 18 para. 2 TDRM Law.
72. Section 18 para. 3 sentence 2 TDRM Law.
73. *See* for details section 18 paras 4 and 5 TDRM Law.

F.5. Costs

In principle, the Member States concerned shall share equally the costs and fees for the independent persons of standing.[74] However, in case the Dispute Resolution Complaint will be withdrawn by the Affected Person or in case the Advisory Commission decided that a rejection of a Dispute Resolution Complaint was correct, such costs and fees for the independent persons of standing shall be borne by the Affected Person.[75] In no case Germany reimburses any costs that are incurred by the Affected Person.[76]

74. Section 31 para. 1 TDRM Law.
75. Section 31 para. 3 TDRM Law.
76. Section 31 para. 2 TDRM Law.

CHAPTER 6
Ireland

Joseph Duffy

A. IMPLEMENTING MEASURES ADOPTED BY IRELAND IN RESPECT OF DIRECTIVE 2017/1852

On 5 July 2019, the EU (Tax Dispute Resolution Mechanisms) Regulations 2019 (S.I. No. 306/2019) (hereinafter the 'Regulations') was published in the Official Gazette of the Government of Ireland, to implement Directive 2017/1852. The Regulations entered into force on 1 July 2019 and apply to complaints submitted on or after that date in relation to disputes on income or capital for tax years starting on or after 1 January 2018.

B. GENERAL PROVISIONS

B.1. Subject Matter and Scope

The Regulations lay down the rules governing the procedures for settling tax disputes between Ireland and the other Member States arising from the interpretation and application of the Tax Treaties and the Arbitration Convention.

The scope of the Regulations does not differ from that set out in Directive 2017/1852 itself. Specifically, the Regulations do not introduce new criteria to determine the allocation of taxing power between States or determine where a treaty or convention can be implemented.

The regime applies to complaints submitted on or after 1 July 2019 in relation to a Question in Dispute which involves income or capital earned in a tax year commencing on or after 1 January 2018. It may also be applied to a complaint submitted before 1 July 2019, or a complaint involving income or capital earned in a tax year commencing before 1 January 2018 in circumstances where the Revenue Commissioners of Ireland (hereinafter the 'Revenue Commissioners') agree such with the Competent Authorities of the relevant Member States.

B.2. Definitions

Regulation 3 of the Regulations provides the following definitions:[1]

- 'Court' means the High Court of Ireland;
- 'Minister' means the Irish Minister for Finance;
- 'Revenue Commissioners' means the Revenue Commissioners of Ireland.

The Revenue Commissioners have been designed as the Competent Authority for Ireland for the purpose of the Regulations. The Revenue Commissioners will comply with the obligations imposed by Directive 2017/1852 on a Competent Authority of a Member State.

Terms not defined by the Regulations, unless the context requires another interpretation, have the meaning attributed to them by the Tax Treaties applicable on the date of receipt of the first notification of the act that has or may have given rise to the Question in Dispute.

In the absence of a definition provided by the relevant Tax Treaty, an undefined term shall have the meaning given to it, at that specific time, by the domestic law of the Member State concerned for the purposes of the taxes to which Tax Treaty applies, taking into account that any meaning given by the applicable tax laws of that Member State takes precedence over the meaning given to that term by other non-tax-related laws of that Member State.

C. COMPLAINT TO START A MAP

C.1. Filing a Complaint to Start a MAP

It is hoped that Directive 2017/1852 and the Regulations will help combat the delays in resolving double taxation disputes within EU by streamlining processes to resolve tax disputes. The Regulations, through Directive 2017/1852, aim to improve the MAP under the Tax Treaties and to enable EU resident taxpayers to access arbitration in cases where the MAP is failing. An illustration of the need for Directive 2017/1852 can be seen in the statistics relating to Irish MAPs. In 2018 there were sixteen MAP cases initiated during the year with twenty-two MAP cases left pending at the end of the year in relation to disputes under the Arbitration Convention.[2]

1. The definitions reported in this paragraph are used also for the purposes of this chapter.
2. The EU Joint Transfer Pricing Forum: Overview of numbers submitted for Statistics on Pending Mutual Agreement Procedures under the Arbitration Convention at the end of 2018. Published in July 2019.

The key component of Directive 2017/1852 and, by extension, the Regulations is that it provides for an EU-wide MAP which taxpayers can avail of in a situation where a dispute arises between Member States under a Tax Treaty. The taxpayer is obliged to notify Member States involved of their desire to access the MAP, although in cases where the taxpayer is an individual or an SME, the taxpayer is only required to notify the Revenue Commissioners under the Regulations. Crucially, taxpayers have three years to initiate a complaint and request a MAP.[3]

Directive 2017/1852 and Regulations place an obligation on Member States to resolve or not resolve the Question in Dispute[4] by mutual agreement within two years (with the possibility of an extension of one year)[5] at the request of the taxpayer, which is an improvement on the more malleable deadlines under the existing MAP framework. Complaints may be rejected by the concerned Member States if the dispute does not relate to double taxation or if there is no actual dispute involved.[6]

A MAP request will only be accepted when the relevant Competent Authorities have all information '*considered necessary to undertake the substantive consideration of the case*'.[7] This requirement may prove onerous for many taxpayers and could delay the commencement of any MAP under the Regulations given the Revenue Commissioners' discretionary ability to request additional information that is not prescribed under the Regulations. Where a complaint is accepted and an agreement is reached between the Member States, the Revenue Commissioners will inform the taxpayer who is free to accept or reject the agreement. If a request for MAP is denied by the Revenue Commissioners, the taxpayer can appeal such refusal to the Irish Tax Appeal Commissioners.[8] The right to avail of a MAP under the Regulations is in addition to any rights a taxpayer has under an applicable Tax Treaty. However, importantly, once a MAP under the Regulations is initiated, any other MAP commenced under a Tax Treaty must be ceased.

The two forms of arbitration provided for under Directive 2017/1852 (discussed in detail below) are the Advisory Commission[9] and the Alternative Disputes Resolution Commission.[10] The taxpayer can request arbitration on a matter if the dispute has not been resolved within two years or a mutual agreement has been reached but the taxpayer has rejected the decision. Directive 2017/1852 provides limited details on how the Alternative Disputes Resolution Commission will be comprised, and in this light, it appears the Revenue Commissioners and relevant Competent Authorities will be afforded flexibility in curating the Alternative Disputes Resolutions Commission. Under the Alternative Disputes Resolution Commission, it is possible to opt for

3. Pursuant to Regulation 21 of the Regulations.
4. In this chapter, 'Question in Dispute' means the matter giving rise to a dispute between Ireland and a relevant Member State arising from the interpretation and application of a double taxation arrangement made between Ireland and another Member State.
5. Pursuant to Regulation 9(1)(b) of the Regulations.
6. Pursuant to Regulation 8(5)(c) of the Regulations.
7. Pursuant to Regulation 8(4)(a) of the Regulations.
8. Pursuant to Regulation 10(1) of the Regulations.
9. Pursuant to Regulation 11 of the Regulations.
10. Pursuant to Regulation 15 of the Regulations.

alternative methods of arbitration including final best offer (also known as 'baseball arbitration').

The Revenue Commissioners and the relevant Competent Authorities have six months from the date of the decision of the Advisory Commission or the Alternative Disputes Resolution Commission to decide whether to accept the decision.[11] The Revenue Commissioners and the relevant Competent Authorities have the option to deviate from the decision given; however, if they fail to agree on how to resolve the dispute in question, then the decision of the Advisory Commission or the Alternative Disputes Resolution Commission is binding.

Details of a decision of the Advisory Commission or the Alternative Disputes Resolution Commission must be in writing. The decision will be published if the taxpayer consents to publication. If the Affected Person does not consent to publication, an abstract of the final decision will be published containing certain information including a description of the issue, the subject matter and the final outcome.

Directive 2017/1852 and Regulations should prove to be effective in assisting with double taxation disputes in Ireland and the EU, principally due to the broader scope which underpins the provisions. Directive 2017/1852 is much broader than many existing bilateral MAPs, for example, the Arbitration Convention, which is limited to complaints involving transfer pricing and permanent establishment issues. Directive 2017/1852 covers all double taxation issues and is, therefore, much broader than the Arbitration Convention. A strength of the directive is that it requires a decision to be reached within a shorter time frame and also that it now provides a structured appeals process.

The taxpayer should also gain a much greater level of influence in the arbitration process from Directive 2017/1852 as well as seeing a streamlining of the process across Member States; for example, the taxpayer does not have to accept the decision of the Revenue Commissioners and has the option to go to arbitration before the Advisory Commission or the Alternative Disputes Resolution Commission. The taxpayer also has the right under Directive 2017/1852 to request to appear before the Advisory Commission or the Alternative Disputes Resolution Commission. The taxpayer's enhanced role in the process as well as the improved timelines and the recourse available to taxpayers for non-implementation, in particular, should be critical in supporting Directive 2017/1852 in achieving its aim of enabling more effective dispute resolution in double taxation issues between Ireland and other Member States.

Pursuant to Regulation 8 of the Regulations, the Affected Person can submit a request for the opening of a MAP concerning a disputed matter to the Revenue Commissioners and to the Competent Authority of the other Member State. The request must be submitted within three years from the date of receipt of the first notification of the action resulting in, or which will result in, the Question in Dispute, regardless of whether the Affected Person has recourse to any other remedies that may be available

11. Pursuant to Regulation 19(1) of the Regulations.

under the law of Ireland or any relevant Member State.[12] This request must accompany specified information as set out in the schedule contained within the Regulations.[13]

For this purpose, the schedule requires a reference to the applicable national rules of the Member State which issued the act or other equivalent document.

The Regulations clarify that the filing of a complaint to start a MAP would not require the prior establishment of domestic litigation procedures.

Importantly, it is specified that the MAP would not be precluded by measures of domestic law which would render the tax assessment final.[14] However, the Regulations do not pinpoint the domestic measures (e.g., tax settlement procedure, self-correction of the tax return, acquiescence to the tax assessment notice) or provide further elements to indicate which measures would not prevent the start of a MAP.

In this regard, it is also necessary to provide specific measures to clarify how the Revenue Commissioners should proceed on the taxes already settled and/or paid according to the domestic measures that differ from the amounts due after a MAP has been concluded between the involved Competent Authorities.

When the Affected Person files an appeal on the Question in Dispute before the Courts, the proceedings can be suspended. In this case, the term will start from the date of suspension of the domestic tax proceeding: (i) concerning the Revenue Commissioner's decision on whether to accept or reject the complaint to start a MAP (i.e., six months from the receipt of the complaint)[15] and (ii) the term of two years from the date of the last notification of a decision to accept the complaint (which is extendible to three years) within which the Competent Authorities shall endeavour to resolve the Question in Dispute by mutual agreement.[16]

The application to start a MAP must be submitted simultaneously to the Revenue Commissioners and the concerned Competent Authority of the other Member State, containing the same information as necessarily required under the Regulations.

Any Affected Person shall submit his/her application in the official language of Ireland which is English or Irish.[17]

The Revenue Commissioners shall acknowledge receipt of the application within two months of the date of receipt of the application by notice in writing and shall, within the same period, inform the Competent Authorities of the other Member States involved in the complaint. In addition, the Revenue Commissioners will notify the relevant Competent Authorities of the language they intend to use in further communications throughout the proceedings.[18]

The application shall be accepted provided that the following information is provided:

12. Pursuant to Regulation 8(2)(iii) of the Regulations.
13. Pursuant to information to be contained in a complaint as per the Schedule of the Regulations.
14. Pursuant to Regulation 20(1) of the Regulations.
15. Pursuant to Regulation 8(5) of the Regulations.
16. Pursuant to Regulation 9(1)(b) of the Regulations.
17. Pursuant to Regulation 8(2)(ii) of the Regulations.
18. Pursuant to Regulation 8(3) of the Regulations.

- the name, address, tax identification number of each Affected Person and any other information necessary for the identification of each Affected Person and of any other person concerned;
- the tax year or tax years concerned;
- details of the following, including a copy of any supporting documents:
  - (i) the relevant facts and circumstances of the case, including:
    - (a) details of the structure of the transaction and the relationship between the Affected Person and the other parties to the relevant transactions, and
    - (b) any facts determined in good faith in a mutually binding agreement between the Affected Person and the Commissioners or the tax administration of a relevant Member State, where applicable.
  - (ii) the nature and date of the actions giving rise to the Question in Dispute, including, where applicable:
    - (a) details of the same income received in the other Member State and the inclusion of such income in the taxable income in the other Member State;
    - (b) details of the tax charged or that will be charged in relation to the income referred to in subclause (a) in the other Member State; and
    - (c) the related amounts in the currencies of the Member States concerned.
  - (iii) reference to the applicable national rules and to the arrangement, the interpretation or application of which is the subject of the Question in Dispute and, where more than one such arrangement is applicable, specification by the Affected Person of which arrangement is being interpreted in relation to the Question in Dispute, as that arrangement shall be the applicable arrangement for the purposes of these Regulations and the Directive; and
  - (iv) the following, together with copies of any supporting documents:
    - (a) an explanation of why the Affected Person considers that there is a Question in Dispute;
    - (b) the details of any appeals and litigation initiated by the Affected Person regarding the relevant transactions and of any court decisions concerning the Question in Dispute;
    - (c) a commitment by the Affected Person to provide timely and complete responses to all appropriate requests from, and to provide any documentation requested by, the Revenue Commissioners;
    - (d) a copy of any final tax assessment decision in the form of a final tax assessment notice, tax audit report or other equivalent document leading to the Question in Dispute and a copy of any other documents issued by the Revenue Commissioners and the tax authorities of the relevant Member States with regard to the Question in Dispute, where relevant; and
    - (e) any specific additional information requested by the Revenue Commissioners, or the Competent Authority of a relevant Member State,

that is considered necessary for them to undertake the substantive consideration of the particular case.

Should the Affected Persons decide to withdraw their complaint aimed at opening MAP, they must give notice in writing to the Revenue Commissioners and, at the same time, to the Competent Authority of the concerned Member State. Where such a notice is received by the Revenue Commissioners they shall, without delay, inform the Competent Authority of each relevant Member State of the termination proceedings.[19]

The Regulations provide for where an Affected Person submits a complaint, and is a natural person resident for tax purposes in Ireland or is an undertaking which, in accordance with Directive 2013/34/EU of the European Parliament and of the Council of 26 June 2013, is not a large business undertaking,[20] which is also resident for tax purposes in Ireland, the Affected Person need only notify the Revenue Commissioners.

Within two months of receiving the above notifications, the Revenue Commissioners should give notice in writing to that effect, at the same time, to the Competent Authority of each relevant Member State concerned.

According to Regulation 8 of the Regulations, if the Affected Person submits an application to start a MAP regarding a Question in Dispute under both the legislation and, alternatively, a Tax Treaty or the Arbitration Convention, the Regulations clarify that only the provisions of the Regulations shall apply.

In the first instance, from a literal interpretation, it seems that the provisions of the Regulations take precedence over the rules contained in the Tax Treaty to which Ireland entered into. This of course derogates from the widely acknowledged principle that the prevalence of the rules of international law that should prevail over national ones. However, considering that the rules laid down in the Regulations are procedural in scope and not substantive, it may be argued that the hierarchy of laws would not in fact be altered.

The Regulations also clarify that, in the event of a withdrawal or termination of the MAP, the same Affected Person may subsequently submit an application to start a MAP under the Tax Treaty or Arbitration Convention, in accordance with the terms and conditions laid down therein.

Regulation 8 of the Regulations lays down the rules concerning the preliminary phase of the MAP. Specifically, the Revenue Commissioners may, no later than three months from the date of receipt of the complaint, by notice in writing to the Affected Person, request the Affected Person to provide such additional information, specified in the notice, as the Revenue Commissioners consider it necessary to carry out the substantive consideration of the case.

Where the Revenue Commissioners request such information, the Affected Person shall, not later than three months from the date of receipt of the notice, provide the additional information to the Revenue Commissioners and, at the same time,

19. Pursuant to Regulation 8(7)(a) of the Regulations.
20. According to Article 3(4) of Directive 2013/34/EU, large undertakings are those undertakings which on their balance sheet dates exceed at least two of the three following criteria: (i) balance sheet total: EUR 20,000,000; (ii) net turnover: EUR 40,000,000; (iii) average number of employees during the financial year: 250.

provide a copy of the same information to the Competent Authority of each relevant Member State.[21]

Even if the Regulations do not provide further specifications, in all cases of additional requests, in order to reduce the uncertainty that may arise from a procedural standpoint, it would be appropriate to expressly provide in the Regulations a suspension of the above-mentioned terms within which the dispute must be resolved for the period starting from the date of request to the date of reply by the Affected Person.

In cases where Affected Persons filed the complaint only to the Revenue Commissioners (as they are natural persons and not a large business as further described in the Regulations),[22] the Affected Person will only have to answer the Revenue Commissioners, who will immediately forward a copy of the complaint to the Competent Authority of the other concerned Member State. Such additional information shall be deemed to have been received from all the Member States on the date of receipt.

Within six months from the date of receipt of the complaint to start a MAP or, within six months from the date of receipt of the additional information as provided by the Affected Person after a request was made by the Revenue Commissioners, the Revenue Commissioners may decide to settle unilaterally the Question in Dispute without involving the Competent Authority of each relevant Member State. If the Revenue Commissioners decide to resolve the dispute on a unilateral basis, they shall, without delay, give notice in writing to the Affected Person and the Competent Authority of each relevant Member State of the decision. After this point, the proceedings initiated under Directive 2017/1852 shall be terminated.[23]

It should be noted that the Regulations do not clarify the conditions under which the Revenue Commissioners may decide to settle the matter unilaterally or unfavourably against the Affected Person. In this respect, it would be appropriate, from an Irish domestic law perspective, to introduce mechanisms to seek jurisdictional protection against the unilateral initiative of the Revenue Commissioners (e.g., appeal to the Court as is the case for the decision to reject the application pursuant to Regulation 8 of the Regulations).

Where an Affected Person submits a complaint under Regulation 8 of the Regulations, any proceedings pending under the MAP or a dispute resolution procedure under a double taxation agreement or the Arbitration Convention shall come to an end with effect from the date of the first receipt of the complaint by the Revenue Commissioners or a Competent Authority of a relevant Member State.

21. Pursuant to Regulation 8(4)(a) of the Regulations.
22. Pursuant to Regulation 21 of the Regulations.
23. Pursuant to Regulation 8(6) of the Regulations.

D. THE RESOLUTION OF THE QUESTION IN DISPUTE UNDER THE MAP

D.1. Decision of the Competent Authority with Reference to the Complaint

The Revenue Commissioners shall make a decision to accept or reject the complaint to start a MAP no later than six months from the date of receipt by them of the complaint or not later than six months from the date of receipt of the additional information required in accordance with the Regulations or where the Question in Dispute is the subject of proceedings in Ireland or any relevant Member State, with respect to any remedy that may be available under the law of Ireland or the relevant Member State, not later than six months from the date on which a final judgment, order or decree of a court is delivered in those proceedings or those proceedings are suspended, discontinued or otherwise disposed of, which is the latest.[24]

The Revenue Commissioners shall give notice in writing to the Affected Person and the Competent Authority of each relevant Member State, without delay, of their decision on whether or not to accept or reject the complaint.

The complaint shall be rejected in the following cases:

- the Affected Person has failed to provide all or any of the information referred to in Regulation 8(2)(b) of the Regulations or where the additional information requested by the Revenue Commissioners has not been transmitted within the three months;
- in the opinion of the Revenue Commissioners there is no Question in Dispute; or
- the application was not submitted within the period of three years from the date of receipt of the first notification of the act.

When the Revenue Commissioners decide to reject a complaint, they must set out the general reasons for their decision in their written notice to the Affected Person and the relevant Competent Authority.

If the Revenue Commissioners fail to make a decision on a complaint before the above deadlines, the complaint shall be deemed to be accepted by the Revenue Commissioners and will be deemed to have given notice to the Affected Person of a decision to accept the complaint.

D.2. MAP

If the complaint is accepted, the Revenue Commissioners and the Competent Authorities of the other concerned Member State shall endeavour (i.e., they are not bound)[25] to resolve the Question in Dispute no later than two years from the date of the last

24. Pursuant to Regulation 8(5) of the Regulations.
25. Pursuant to Regulation 9(1) of the Regulations.

notification to accept the complaint, whether that decision is made by the Revenue Commissioners or a Competent Authority of a relevant Member State.

The two-year period can be extended by up to one year where there is a written justification for such an extension and this has been submitted by the Revenue Commissioners or the Competent Authority of another concerned Member State(s), to the Competent Authorities of the other concerned Member State(s).

When an agreement has been reached between the Revenue Commissioners and the Competent Authority of the other concerned Member State, the Revenue Commissioners shall notify the Affected Person of the decision taken within thirty days of the date of conclusion of the MAP.[26]

If the Revenue Commissioners and the Competent Authorities of the other concerned Member State(s) do not reach an agreement within the two-year deadline (or three years in a case where there has been an extension), the Revenue Commissioners shall inform the Affected Person of the general reasons for not reaching such an agreement.[27]

Where the Question in Dispute is the subject of proceedings by the Affected Person in Ireland or in a relevant Member State, in relation to any remedy that is available under Irish law or the relevant Member State, outside of what is provided for under the Regulations, the period of two years shall commence on the date on which the final judgment, order or decree is delivered in those proceedings or on the date on which those proceedings are suspended, discontinued or disposed of in some other manner.[28]

D.3. Appeal of the Taxpayer Against the Decision Rejecting the Complaint

In the event that both the Revenue Commissioners and the Competent Authorities of the other concerned Member State reject the complaint to start a MAP, the Affected Person may appeal the decision to the Appeal Commissioners in accordance with the provisions of the domestic law in force.

In such cases where the Affected Person is appealing before the Court, the Affected Person cannot submit a request to set up the Advisory Commission (*see* next section E.1) if:

- decision on the appeal has not yet been made;
- the Appeal Commissioners have decided to uphold the decision of the Revenue Commissioners to reject the complaint and that decision has been appealed and a decision on that further appeal has not yet been made; or
- the Appeal Commissioners have decided to uphold the decision of the Revenue Commissioners to reject the complaint and, within the time for bringing an appeal against the decision of the Revenue Commissioners, no such appeal has been brought or, if such an appeal has been brought, the Court has delivered

26. Pursuant to Regulation 19(4) of the Regulations.
27. Pursuant to Regulation 9(4) of the Regulations.
28. Pursuant to Regulation 9(5) of the Regulations.

its final judgment, decree or order in relation to the appeal upholding the decision of the Revenue Commissioners to reject the complaint, or the appeal has been otherwise discontinued or disposed of;

- in a case where the Affected Person has not made an appeal referred to in Regulation 10(1), paragraph (1)(a) of the Regulations shall only apply where the Affected Person has renounced any right of appeal under Regulation 10(1) of the Regulations and a declaration to that effect has been made by the Affected Person in writing to the Revenue Commissioners.

The Affected Person can also file an appeal before the Court if the complaint to start a MAP has been rejected by the Revenue Commissioners, but not by all the Competent Authorities of the other concerned Member State.[29]

E. DISPUTE RESOLUTION PROCEDURE

E.1. Request of Appointment of the Advisory Commission

Regulation 11 of the Regulations provides the procedural rules to start a dispute resolution procedure which could resolve the Question in Dispute where the Competent Authorities have not reached an agreement under the MAP. The Affected Party can submit a request to the Revenue Commissioners and the Competent Authority of the other concerned Member States to set up an Advisory Commission to overcome the failure to reach a mutual agreement during the first phase of the MAP.

In short, where a dispute has not been resolved within two years, the taxpayer can request an Advisory Commission to arbitrate on a matter. Similarly, recourse may also be had to an Advisory Commission where a mutual agreement has been reached between Member States, however, not accepted by the taxpayer.

The Affected Persons referred to in Regulation 21 of the Regulations (e.g., not large business undertakings) can submit a request to set up an Advisory Commission, only to the Revenue Commissioners, which, within two months from the date of receipt of the request, shall simultaneously notify the Competent Authorities of the other concerned Member State(s). On the date of such notification, the request shall be deemed to have been submitted by the Affected Persons to the Competent Authorities of all the concerned Member States.

The Advisory Commission shall be established in the following cases:

- where the complaint has been rejected by the Revenue Commissioners or by a Competent Authority in a relevant Member State, but not by all of the Competent Authorities concerned or where the Revenue Commissioners and the Competent Authority of each relevant Member State have accepted the complaint but have failed to reach a mutual agreement on how to resolve the

29. Pursuant to Regulation 11(2) of the Regulations.

question within the specified time under Regulation 9. In this circumstance, the Affected Person can file a request to set up an Advisory Commission only if:

(i) under the domestic law of the Member State in which the decision of rejection of the complaint was issued, no appeal against that decision may be filed;
(ii) there is no pending litigation;
(iii) the Affected Person has formally renounced, in a written declaration, his right to appeal against the decision of rejection of the complaint;

- where the complaint to start a MAP has been rejected by all the Competent Authorities of the concerned Member States and a judgment has been issued to the in favour of the Affected Person, following an appeal filed by that person before the Competent Court of a concerned Member State against the decision of the Competent Authority of that Member State;
- where the Competent Authorities of the concerned Member States have accepted the complaint to start a MAP but have not been able to reach an agreement on how to resolve the Question in Dispute through the MAP within two years or three years in the case of an extension.

The request to appoint the Advisory Commission must be made in writing within fifty days of receipt of the communication, of either of the following:

- the decision of rejection of a complaint; or
- that the Revenue Commissioners and the Competent Authorities of the other concerned Member States have not reached an agreement.[30]

The Revenue Commissioners can reject the complaint to start a MAP in cases where penalties have been imposed under domestic law for criminal offences such as tax fraud, wilful default or gross negligence.[31]

E.2. Appointment of the Advisory Commission

Pursuant to Article 6 of the Directive 2017/1852, the Advisory Commission shall be appointed within 120 days from the receipt of a request filed by the Affected Person. Once established, its chairman shall promptly inform the Affected Person.

The Advisory Commission shall be composed of:

- a chairman;
- one representative of each Competent Authority concerned. Where agreed by the Revenue Commissioners and the Competent Authorities, the number of such representatives may be increased to two;
- one independent person appointed by each Competent Authority concerned from a specific list of independent persons of standing (*see* section E.5. below).

30. Pursuant to Regulation 11(3) of the Regulations.
31. Pursuant to Regulation 20(4)(a) of the Regulations.

Where the Revenue Commissioners and the Competent Authorities agree, the number of such persons appointed may be increased to two.

The rules for the appointment of independent persons of standing shall be agreed between the Revenue Commissioners and the Competent Authorities of the concerned Member States. For each of the independent persons of standing appointed, a substitute shall be appointed, in accordance with the rules for the appointment of independent persons of standing, for cases where independent persons of standing are prevented from performing their duties. If the rules for the appointment of independent persons of standing have not been agreed, they shall be appointed by drawing lots.

Except where the independent persons of standing have been appointed by the Competent Court or national appointing body of the other concerned Member State(s),[32] the Revenue Commissioners may object to the appointment of an independent person of standing for any reason agreed in advance with the concerned Competent Authorities or for one of the following reasons:

- that person belongs to one of the tax administrations concerned or performs functions on behalf of one of those administrations or has been in that situation at any time during the preceding three years;
- at any time during the last five years preceding the date of his appointment, that person has or has had a material interest in, or is, or has been, employed by or an adviser to, an Affected Person;
- that person does not offer adequate objectivity for the settlement of the Question in Dispute;
- that person is employed by an undertaking which provides tax advice, or otherwise provides tax advice on a professional basis, or has been in that situation at any time during a period of at least three years before his appointment.

The Revenue Commissioners can require that a person of standing appointed to the Advisory Commission or his substitute to disclose any interest, relationship or other matter which might affect the independence or impartiality of that person or which might reasonably give rise to a suspicion of bias in the procedure. An independent person who is a member of the Advisory Commission must not, for a period of twelve months from the date of delivery of the decision of the Advisory Commission, be in a situation which would have led the Revenue Commissioners or a Competent Authority to object to his appointment if he had been in that situation at the time of his appointment to the Advisory Commission.

32. Pursuant to Regulation 12 of the Regulations.

E.3. Appointment of the Advisory Commission Made by a Competent Court

Regulation 12 of the Regulations provides for the rules relating to the appointment of the Advisory Commission by a Competent Court where the Competent Authorities of the Member States involved failed to timely set up the said Commission.

Where the Advisory Commission was not set up within 120 days from the request,[33] the Affected Party can apply to the Court to request the establishment of the said Commission.

If the Revenue Commissioners have not appointed at least one independent person and one substitute to an Advisory Commission, the Affected Person can appeal to the Court for the appointment of the independent person and his/her substitute from the list.[34]

Where the Revenue Commissioners and the Competent Authorities of all the other Member State(s) involved have failed to do so, the Affected Person may apply to the Court and to Competent Court of the other Member State(s) to appoint the two independent persons of standing from the list.

An application to the Court for appointments as above must be made not later than thirty days from the end of the period of 120 days from the date of receipt of the request by the Affected Person.

A decision by the Court on an application made under Article 12 of Directive 2017/1852 shall be final, unless by leave of the Court of Appeal an appeal from the decision shall lie to the Court of Appeal on a specified question of law.

E.4. List of the Independent Persons of Standing

The Minister for Finance shall nominate for inclusion on the list of persons of standing three persons who in the opinion of the Minister are competent and independent and can act with impartiality and integrity. These people are referred to in the Regulations as 'nominated persons'. Article 12 of Directive 2017/1852 clarifies that the list of independent persons of standing shall consist of all independent persons appointed by the Member States.

The Minister shall give notice in writing to the EU Commission of the names of each nominated persons and shall provide up-to-date information regarding the academic and professional qualifications of such persons, their skills, their experience and the existence of any conflict of interest. The Minister shall also specify in his notice which of the nominated persons, if any, may be appointed as chair and shall give notice to the EU Commission, without delay, of any changes to the list.

Where the Minister has reasonable cause to object to an independent person of standing remaining on the list because, in their opinion, the person lacks independence, the Minister shall inform the EU Commission and provide such evidence as they consider appropriate to support their objection.

33. Pursuant to Regulation 12 of the Regulations.
34. Pursuant to Regulation 12(2) of the Regulations.

No later than six months from receipt of a notification of objection and supporting evidence from the EU Commission, the Minister shall:

- take such steps as the Minister considers necessary to investigate the objection;
- consider the supporting evidence; and
- decide whether to retain on, or remove from, the list the nominated person concerned.

The Minister shall, without delay, give notice in writing to the EU Commission of the decision as to whether to retain or remove from the list the nominated person concerned. The Minister may also remove from the list for stated reasons a nominated person if, in the Minister's opinion, the person ceases to be independent.

The Minister shall fill any vacancy that arises on the list by nominating a person in accordance with Regulation 14, paragraph 1 of the Regulations (as set out here at E.3) and shall inform the EU Commission in writing of any changes to the list of nominated persons.

E.5. Alternative Dispute Resolution Commission

Regulation 15 of the Regulations provides that the Competent Authorities of each Member State can agree, instead of the Advisory Commission, to establish an Alternative Dispute Resolution Commission which shall have the purpose of delivering an opinion on how to resolve a Question in Dispute.

The Competent Authorities of the Member States can also agree to establish an Alternative Dispute Resolution Commission that is of a permanent nature (i.e., a standing commission).

The Revenue Commissioners may, subject to the rules of the functioning for the Alternative Dispute Resolution Commission referred to in Article 16 of the Regulations, agree on the composition of the Alternative Dispute Resolution Commission with the Competent Authority of each Member State and may appoint members to it.

The Revenue Commissioners may, for any reason outlined in Regulation 13(4), decide not to appoint, or may object to the appointment of, a person to the Alternative Dispute Resolution Commission. Regulation 13(5) and (6) shall apply to a person appointed to the Alternative Dispute Resolution Commission the same as those provisions that apply to an independent person of standing appointed to an Advisory Commission.

Instead of a dispute resolution based on the independent opinion process as provided for by the Advisory Commission, the Alternative Dispute Resolution Commission can apply different dispute resolution procedures or techniques to resolve the Question in Dispute. To this end, the Competent Authorities of the concerned Member States can agree on any other type of dispute resolution procedure to be applied by the Alternative Dispute Resolution Commission.

F. COMMON PROCEDURAL PROVISION

F.1. Procedural Rules of the Advisory Commission or Alternative Dispute Resolution Commission

Pursuant to Regulation 16 of the Regulations, the Revenue Commissioners and the Competent Authorities of the concerned Member States shall agree on the functioning rules of the Advisory Commission or the Alternative Dispute Resolution Commission and will sign the agreed rules. In particular, the Revenue Commissioners and the Competent Authorities shall agree on the functioning rules in respect of Article 11 of Directive 2017/1852 in relation to dispute resolution by the Advisory Commission.

Within 120 days from the receipt of the request submitted by the Affected Person to establish the Advisory Commission appointment, the Revenue Commissioners shall give notice in writing to the Affected Person of the following:

- the functioning rules of the Advisory Commission or the Alternative Dispute Resolution Commission;
- the deadline by which the opinion on the resolution of the Question in Dispute shall be delivered;
- references to the applicable provisions of any enactment and to any applicable arrangements.

If the independent persons of standing and the chairman of the Advisory Commission or the Alternative Dispute Resolution Commission have not reached an agreement with regard to the functioning rules or have not notified them to the Affected Person, the Affected Person can refer the matter to the Court in order to obtain the implementation of the functioning rules.

F.2. Costs of the MAP

Pursuant to Regulation 17 of the Regulations, unless the Revenue Commissioners and the Competent Authorities of the concerned Member States have agreed otherwise, the following costs shall be shared equally between the Member States:

- expenditure incurred by independent persons of standing, which must be equivalent to the average of the amount usually reimbursed to high-ranking civil servants of the concerned Member States; and
- the fees of the independent persons, where applicable, which are to be limited to EUR 1,000 per person per day for every day on which the Advisory Commission or Alternative Dispute Resolution Commission meets.[35]

In any case, where the Affected Person has submitted:

- a written notice of withdrawal of the MAP application; or

35. Pursuant to Article 12 of Directive 2017/1852.

- a request for setting up the Advisory Commission following a rejection to start a MAP on the grounds of Article 5(1) of Directive 2017/1852, (ii) the Advisory Commission decided that the Competent Authorities have rightly rejected the request, and (iii) with the agreement of the Competent Authorities of the concerned Member States,

all the costs of the MAP shall be borne by the Affected Person.

Lastly, it is specified that the costs incurred by the Affected Person shall not be borne by the Revenue Commissioners.[36]

F.3. The Opinion of the Advisory Commission or the Alternative Dispute Resolution Commission

Regulation 18 of the Regulations set forth the rules concerning the resolution of the controversy presented to the Advisory Commission or the Alternative Dispute Resolution Commission.

Where the Revenue Commissioners agree with the Competent Authority of each relevant Member State, the Affected Person may provide the Advisory Commission or the Alternative Dispute Resolution Commission with any relevant information, evidence or documents for the purpose of:

- the delivery by the Advisory Commission of a decision of admissibility of the complaint in question submitted under Regulation 11; or
- the delivery of an opinion by the Advisory Commission or the Alternative Dispute Resolution Commission under Article 14 of Directive 2017/1852 on how to resolve the Question in Dispute.

Affected Persons and Competent Authorities shall provide the relevant information, evidence or documents at the request of the Advisory Commission or the Alternative Dispute Resolution Commission. However, the Revenue Commissioners may refuse to provide information to the particular Commission when:

- obtaining the information requires carrying out administrative measures that are at variance with Irish law;
- the information cannot be obtained under Irish law;
- the information concerns trade secrets, business secrets, industrial secrets, professional secrets or trade processes;
- the disclosure of the information is contrary to public policy.

At the request of the Advisory Commission or the Alternative Dispute Resolution Commission, Affected Persons shall appear or be represented before the aforesaid Commission. The Affected Persons can also, at their request and with the agreement of the Revenue Commissioners, appear or be represented before the Commission.

36. Pursuant to Regulation 17(3) of the Regulations.

Any information of any kind accessed by the Advisory Commission or the Alternative Dispute Resolution Commission in their capacity as member of such commission shall be treated as confidential and should not be disclosed other than in the course of discharging their relevant functions as a member of their respective commission.[37]

Persons who contravene their confidentiality obligations or who make a false declaration for this purpose is deemed to commit an offence. A person convicted of an offence under this section is liable:

- on summary conviction, to a class a fine, or
- on conviction on indictment, to a fine not exceeding EUR 10,000.

Such summary proceedings may be brought by the Revenue Commissioners.

Where an offence under subparagraph (a) of Regulation 18 of the Regulations by a body corporate has been committed with the knowledge of, or attributable to the wilful neglect of, a director, manager, secretary or other officer of the body corporate, or a person who was purporting to act in such capacity, that person, as well as the body corporate, commits an offence and shall be liable to be punished as if he or she were guilty of the offence in question.

Where the affairs of a body corporate are managed by its members, the acts and defaults of a member in relation to their management will apply as if the member were a director or manager of the body corporate.[38]

F.4. Final Decision of the Competent Authorities

The Revenue Commissioners will agree with the Competent Authorities of each relevant Member State on how to resolve the Question in Dispute within six months of the date on which an opinion of the Advisory Commission or Alternative Dispute Resolution Commission was notified to them. The Revenue Commissioners may also, with the Competent Authority of each Member State, make a decision which deviates from the opinion of the Advisory Commission or Alternative Dispute Resolution Commission. However, if they cannot agree on how to resolve the Question in Dispute within the specified period, the Revenue Commissioners shall be bound by that opinion.

The Revenue Commissioners shall inform the Affected Person of the decision adopted within the dispute resolution procedure regarding the Question in Dispute within thirty days of the date on which that decision was taken. This decision will be either the agreement between the Competent Authorities or, where no agreement is reached, the opinion of the Advisory Commission or Alternative Dispute Resolution Commission and is referred to in the Regulations as the 'final decision'.[39] If an Affected

37. Pursuant to Regulation 18(6) of the Regulations.
38. Pursuant to Regulation 18(8) of the Regulations.
39. Pursuant to Regulation 19(4) of the Regulations.

Person does not receive notice of the final decision before the end of the specified period, that person may apply to the Court to obtain the final decision.

The final decision will be binding on the Revenue Commissioners; however, it will not constitute a precedent.[40]

Subject to the Affected Persons accepting the final decision and renouncing any right they may have under Irish law to seek any remedy available to them within sixty days of the notice of the final decision being given to them, the final decision will be implemented within the relevant time period. The relevant time period will depend on the specific nature of the claim.

Where the claim by the Affected Person involves a repayment of tax, the Revenue Commissioners will make a repayment of tax within sixty days from the date on which the claim to the repayment of tax would become a valid claim. The claim is deemed valid if it were a repayment of tax under section 865(1) of the Taxes Consolidation Acts 1997 (TCA). This section of the TCA sets out what is required for a claim for a repayment of tax to be valid. Where the claim involves an amendment of an assessment to tax, the Revenue Commissioners will amend the assessment within sixty days of the Affected Person providing the Revenue Commissioners will all information that is required for the purpose of making the amendment.[41]

The Revenue Commissioners will not implement a final decision where the Court, or the judicial body of a relevant Member State, decides that there was a lack of independence in respect of a member of either the Advisory Commission or Alternative Dispute Resolution Commission. In determining whether there has been a lack of independence, the Revenue Commissioners will assess the criteria outlined in Regulation 13 of the Regulations which deals with appointing members to the Advisory Commission. In respect of a judicial body of a relevant Member State, they will assess the criteria outlined in Article 8 of Directive 2017/1852.

If the Revenue Commissioners fail to implement the final decision within the relevant specified period, as set out above, the Affected Person can make an application to the Court for an order to require the Revenue Commissioners to implement the final decision in accordance with its terms.[42]

F.5. Enforcement of Decisions Taken under the MAP or Dispute Resolution Procedures

Regulation 19 of the Regulations set out the rules applicable to enforce the decisions adopted by the Competent Authorities under the MAP or a dispute resolution procedure.

Where a decision has been taken under the MAP or dispute resolution procedures, which results in a change of the taxable income or the taxes due, the Revenue Commissioners shall make a repayment of tax for a chargeable period or chargeable periods not later than sixty days from the date on which the claim to the repayment of

40. Pursuant to Regulation 19(6)(a) of the Regulations.
41. Pursuant to Regulation 19(6)(d) of the Regulations.
42. Pursuant to Regulation 19(6)(d) of the Regulations.

tax is made. Alternatively, if the decision does not involve a claim by the Affected Person for a repayment of tax but requires the Revenue Commissioners to amend an assessment to tax for a chargeable period or chargeable periods, the Revenue Commissioners shall amend the assessment for a chargeable period or chargeable periods not later than sixty days from the date in which the Affected Person has provided the Revenue Commissioners with all information reasonably required for the purposes of amending the assessment for the chargeable period.

Where the Revenue Commissioners fail to implement the final decision within the prescribed sixty-day periods, the Affected Person can apply to the Court for an order requiring the Revenue Commissioners to implement the final decision in accordance with its terms.

The Revenue Commissioners will not be obliged to implement the final decision where the Court in assessing criteria outlined in Regulation 13 of the Regulations, or a judicial body of a relevant Member State in its application of Article 8 of Directive 2017/1852, decides that there was a lack of independence in respect of any member of the Advisory Commission or Alternative Dispute Resolution Commission.

Where there is a dispute pending at domestic level, for the purposes of implementing the decision, the Affected Person must provide evidence, within sixty days of the date on which the decision was notified, that the withdrawal of the proceeding and/or any other form of appeal has been filed to the Court. To this end, the Regulations do not provide that, in the event of withdrawal of the judicial proceedings, the costs of the proceedings should be compensated between the parties.

F.6. Publicity

The Revenue Commissioners may agree with the Competent Authority of each relevant Member State to publish the final decision in its entirety, subject to the prior written consent of the Affected Person.[43]

If there is no agreement between the Revenue Commissioners and the Competent Authority involved, or if the Affected Person does not consent, the Revenue Commissioners will publish an abstract of the final decision containing the following information:

- a description of the issue;
- the subject matter;
- the date;
- the tax periods involved;
- the legal basis;
- the industry of reference;
- a short description of the final outcome; and
- the arbitration process applied.

43. Pursuant to Regulation 22 of the Regulations.

Before the publication, the Revenue Commissioners shall provide the Affected Person with a copy of the information referred under the list above. Within sixty days of receipt of the information, the Affected Person may request the Revenue Commissioners not to disclose information relating to any trade, business, industrial or professional secret or trade process, or that is contrary to public policy.

The Revenue Commissioners shall promptly notify the EU Commission of the information to be published under Regulation 22 of the Regulations.

F.7. Miscellaneous

According to Regulation 18 of the Regulations, the information required by the Revenue Commissioners in the context of the MAP shall be subject to and governed by the provisions of domestic law in force on the protection of personal data, trade, business, industrial, professional secrets or trade process.

The circumstance that the Question in Dispute is under review in the context of a MAP or a dispute resolution procedure shall not prevent the initiation or continuation of judicial proceedings, including criminal or administrative penalties under the domestic law.

In the event that judicial or administrative proceedings have been started under domestic law which may give rise to the application of penalties and are being conducted simultaneously with a MAP or a dispute resolution procedure, the Revenue Commissioners may suspend the proceedings from the date of acceptance of the complaint under Regulation 8(5)(b) of the Regulations until the date when the final judgment, order or decree of a court is delivered in those proceedings.

If for any reason a Question in Dispute no longer arises, the MAP or the dispute resolution procedure shall be terminated with immediate effect. The Revenue Commissioners shall inform the Affected Persons without delay, stating the general reasons that terminated the procedures.[44]

44. Pursuant to Regulation 8(8)(a) of the Regulations.

CHAPTER 7
Italy

Raul-Angelo Papotti

A. IMPLEMENTING MEASURES ADOPTED BY ITALY WITH RESPECT TO DIRECTIVE 2017/1852

The implementing measures of Directive 2017/1852 have been delegated by the Italian Parliament to the Government through Law No. 117/2019 (so-called *legge di delegazione europea*), published in Italian Official Gazette No. 245 of 18 October 2019 (hereinafter 'Law No. 117'), introducing principles and guidelines for the implementation of Directive 2017/1852. Law No. 117 entered into force on 2 November 2019.

More in detail, Article 8 of Law No. 117 provides that the Italian Government should take into account the following principles and criteria in order to fully implement in the national tax system Directive 2017/1852:

- introducing the provisions necessary to coordinate the judicial proceedings, under Legislative Decree No. 546 of 31 December 1992 (hereinafter 'Decree 546/1992'), with the domestic measures implementing Directive 2017/1852;
- coordinating and linking the provisions that will be included in the legislative decree to implement Directive 2017/1852 with the international tax obligations, including the Arbitration Convention as ratified by Law No. 99 of 22 March 1993;
- amending, in addition to the above, the other domestic law provisions for the purposes of implementing Directive 2017/1852, also taking into account international tax obligations;
- to set up the principles and the interactions with the domestic judicial proceedings to ensure an effective and consistent implementation of Directive

2017/1852, with particular reference to the options referred to in Article 16 of the same Directive.[1]

From a procedural perspective, Law No. 117 has provided that the legislative decree implementing Directive 2017/1852 shall be adopted on a proposal from the Minister for European Affairs and the Minister for Economic Affairs and Finance, in agreement with the Ministers for Justice and Foreign Affairs and for International Cooperation.

In light of the foregoing, Legislative Decree No. 49 dated 10 June 2020 (hereinafter in this chapter the 'Decree') was approved, setting forth the domestic implementing measures of Directive 2017/1852.

B. GENERAL PROVISIONS

B.1. Subject Matter and Scope

The Decree lays down the rules governing the procedures for settling disputes among the Competent Authorities of Italy and the other Member State(s) involved arising from the interpretation and application of the bilateral agreements and Tax Treaties entered into by Italy and of the Arbitration Convention.

In this respect, the scope of the Decree does not differ from the one provided by Directive 2017/1852. Indeed, the Decree does not introduce new criteria to determine

1. In detail, Article 16(4) of Directive 2017/1852 provides that, where a decision on a question in dispute has been rendered by the relevant court or other judicial body of a Member State, and the domestic law of that Member State does not allow it to derogate from the decision, that Member State may provide, alternatively, that:

   - before an agreement has been reached by the Competent Authorities of the Member States concerned under the MAP under Article 4 on that question in dispute, the Competent Authority of such Member State is to notify the other Competent Authorities of the Member States concerned of the decision of the relevant court or other judicial body and that that procedure is to be terminated as from the date of such notification;
   - before the Affected Person has made a request under Article 6(1), the provisions of Article 6(1) do not apply if the question in dispute had remained unresolved during the whole of the MAP under Article 4, in which case the Competent Authority of that Member State is to inform the other Competent Authorities of the Member States concerned of the effect of the decision of the relevant court or other judicial body;
   - the dispute resolution process under Article 6 is to be terminated if the decision of the relevant court or other judicial body was rendered at any time after an Affected Person has made a request under Article 6(1) but before the Advisory Commission or the Alternative Dispute Resolution Commission has delivered its opinion to the Competent Authorities of the Member States concerned in accordance with Article 14, in which case the Competent Authority of the relevant Member State concerned is to inform the other Competent Authorities of the Member States concerned and the Advisory Commission or the Alternative Dispute Resolution Commission of the effect of the decision of the relevant court or other judicial body.

   Moreover, Article 16 gives the option to the Member States to deny the access to the dispute resolution dispute in cases 'where penalties were imposed in that Member State in relation to the adjusted income or capital for tax fraud, wilful default and gross negligence'.

the allocation of taxing power between States, nor where a Tax Treaty or convention can be invoked.

Therefore, issues deriving from the interpretation of the Tax Treaties which relate to, for instance, the assessment of hidden permanent establishments, the qualification of the tax residence and the beneficial ownership status in connection to dividends, interest and royalty payments should be covered by the new procedures laid down by the Decree.

However, considering that Directive 2017/1852 provides rules 'to resolve disputes between Member States when those disputes arise from the interpretation and application of agreements and conventions that provide for the elimination of double taxation of income and, where applicable, capital', issues relating to the application of the Interest-Royalty Directive (Council Directive 2003/49/EC of 3 June 2003) and the Parent-Subsidiary Directive (Council Directive 2011/96/EU of 30 November 2011) should not be covered by the procedures governed by the Decree.

B.2. Definitions

Article 2 of the Decree provides the following definitions.[2]

- 'Competent Authority' means the authority designated by the Member State concerned;
- 'Competent Court' means the court or other body designated by the concerned Member State;
- 'Double Taxation' means the imposition by two or more Member States of taxes covered by an agreement or convention in respect of the same taxable income or capital when it gives rise to either: (i) an additional tax charge; (ii) an increase in tax liabilities; or (iii) the cancellation or reduction of losses that could be used to offset taxable profits. As clarified by the explanatory notes to the Decree, the Double Taxation refers to the case where the income is taxed several times both on the same person (i.e., legal double taxation) or on different persons (i.e., economic double taxation);
- 'Affected Person' means any person that is a resident of Italy or of a Member State for tax purposes, and whose taxation is directly affected by a question in dispute;
- 'Dispute resolution procedure with independent opinion' means a procedure ending with an opinion adopted by the Advisory Commission or the Alternative Dispute Resolution Commission based on an analysis of the facts and legal circumstances applicable to the dispute;
- 'Dispute resolution procedure with final offer' means a procedure ending with an opinion adopted by the Alternative Dispute Resolution Commission based on one of the proposals made by each Competent Authority involved in the dispute.

2. The definitions reported in this paragraph are used also for the purposes of this chapter.

The definition of 'Affected Person' provided by the Decree also includes individuals, as also expressly listed by Article 2(1)(d) of Directive 2017/1852. Therefore, should the requirements of the Decree be satisfied, individuals can apply to start a MAP under the Decree to tackle double taxation issues arising from the interpretation and application of the bilateral agreements and Tax Treaties entered into by Italy (e.g., dual resident cases).

In addition, individuals filing a complaint about the opening of a MAP under the Decree benefit from a simplification of the fulfilments necessary to start the MAP (*see* section C.1. below).

The Italian revenue agency ('*Agenzia delle Entrate*', hereinafter 'IRA') has been designed as the Competent Authority for Italy.

The Provincial and Regional Tax Courts (hereinafter 'Tax Courts') are the Italian Competent Court for the purposes of the Decree. According to Article 4 of Decree 546/1992, the Provincial Tax Courts are competent in relation to disputes brought against tax authorities located in their own district. If the dispute is brought against local ramifications of the IRA, with jurisdiction over all or part of the national territory, the Provincial Tax Court competent is the one in whose district it is located the office responsible for the dispute at stake. The Regional Tax Courts shall be responsible for appeals against the decisions issued by the Provincial Tax Courts, which are based in their district.

Finally, terms not defined by the Decree, unless the context requires another interpretation, have the meaning attributed to them by the relevant Tax Treaty applicable on the date of receipt of the first notification of the act that has or may have given rise to the question in dispute. In the absence of a definition provided by the relevant Tax Treaty, an undefined term shall have the meaning given to it, at that specific time, by the domestic law of the Member State concerned for the purposes of the taxes to which the Tax Treaty applies, taking into account that any meaning given by the applicable tax laws of that Member State takes precedence over the meaning given to that term by other non-tax-related laws of that Member State.

C. COMPLAINT TO START A MAP

In dealing with a controversy which may cause double taxation, one of the most important points of attention to be taken into account in defining the possible strategy is that a MAP does not replace the legal remedies put forward by the domestic tax framework.

Indeed, according to Article 25(1), first sentence, of the OECD Model Tax Convention, a MAP request can be submitted by a taxpayer '*irrespective of the remedies provided by the domestic law of those States*'. In this respect, as also noted by the IRA in Circular No. 21 of 5 June 2012[3] (hereinafter the 'Circular 21/2012'), most of the Tax Treaties entered into by Italy contain, in their accompanying Protocol, an interpretative

3. Guidelines and procedures in relation to MAPs started on the basis of a Tax Treaty and/or the Arbitration Convention are included in Circular Letter No. 21/E of 5 June 2012, which was issued by the IRA. This document sets out in detail how MAP functions within Italian tax framework

provision regarding the MAP article whereby the expression *'irrespective of the remedies provided by the domestic law'* should be interpreted as the MAP is not alternative to the domestic judicial proceedings which shall be, in any case, started by the taxpayer.[4] Also, under Article 6 of the Arbitration Convention, a taxpayer can file a request to the Competent Authority *'irrespective of the remedies provided by the domestic law of the Contracting States concerned'*.

Therefore, where a MAP is initiated, in general, the taxpayer is also required to file an appeal before the competent Tax Court to avoid that, pending the MAP, the tax claims challenged by the IRA through the issue of a notice of assessment[5] become final (i.e., no longer subject to possible amendments or withdrawal).

In a first scenario, should the Competent Authorities reach an agreement eliminating the double taxation in the context of a MAP started under a Tax Treaty and/or the Arbitration Convention before that a judgment is rendered by the competent Tax Court, a prerequisite for the execution of the MAP grounded on a Tax Treaty and/or on the Arbitration Convention is the acceptance of its outcome by the taxpayer and the simultaneous withdrawal of the domestic judicial proceedings.[6] This being said, the taxpayer can in any case reject the results of the MAP and continue the judicial proceedings.

However, the 'parallel' continuation of, on the one hand, the MAP and, on the other hand, the domestic judicial proceedings might cause that the judgment issued by the competent Tax Court could conflict with the agreement entered into the Competent Authorities in the context of the MAP.

In MAPs based on a Tax Treaty and/or the Arbitration Convention (and not covered by the Decree), where the judgment of first degree has been delivered before an agreement is reached under the MAP, the Italian competent authority will not have the chance to deviate from that judgment in the context of the MAP with the consequence that the double taxation may not be eliminated. This conclusion holds true unless, as noted by Circular 21/2012, the foreign Competent Authority decides to enter into a mutual agreement consistent with the domestic judicial decision rendered by the competent Italian Tax Court.

---

until the Decree and the various stages of that procedure, whereby a distinction is made between MAPs under Tax Treaties and under the Arbitration Convention.

4. According to the OECD, as to Tax Treaties entered into by Italy, the provision generally incorporated the relevant Protocol which reads: *'[...] the expression 'irrespective of the remedies provided by the domestic law' means that mutual agreement procedure is not alternative with the national contentious proceedings which shall be, in any case, preventively initiated, when the claim is related with an assessment of the taxes not in accordance with this Convention"*. For further details *see OECD (2017), Making Dispute Resolution More Effective – MAP Peer Review Report, Italy (Stage 1): Inclusive Framework on BEPS: Action 14, OECD/G20 Base Erosion and Profit Shifting Project, OECD Publishing, Paris. http://dx.doi.org/10.1787/9789264285835-en.* Pursuant to the Tax Treaty entered into by Italy and Germany and the relative Protocol, the expression *'irrespective of the remedies provided by the domestic law (...) means that invoking a mutual agreement procedure cannot replace the domestic remedies'*.
5. In Italian language *'avviso di accertamento'*. From a procedural standpoint, pursuant to Article 21 of Decree 546/1992, the appeal of the taxpayer against the notice of assessment issued by the IRA should be notified within sixty days from the notification of the notice of assessment.
6. *See* para. 4.2.5 of Circular 21/2012.

Moreover, the judgment rendered by a competent Tax Court would rule out the possibility to enter into the arbitration phase of the Arbitration Convention.

In order to avoid that a judgment may anticipate a possible agreement of the Competent Authorities in the context of a MAP grounded on a Tax Treaty and/or the Arbitration Convention, Article 39(1-*ter*) of Decree 546/1992 provides that the proceedings can be suspended where a MAP under a Tax Treaty or the Arbitration Convention has been started. The suspension request should be filed by both the taxpayer and the IRA to the competent Tax Court. By doing so, the domestic proceedings would be suspended so that the risk of having a judgment rendered before the conclusion of a MAP would be entirely mitigated.

On a separate profile, it should be noted that the filing of a MAP request pursuant to the applicable Tax Treaty and/or the Arbitration Convention would not suspend per se the collection of the taxes under the notice of assessment issued by the IRA. Indeed, as a general principle, a provisional payment equal to one-third of the taxes (plus related interest) claimed by the IRA with the notice of assessment is required in case of filing of the appeal to the competent Provincial Tax Court.

With reference to MAPs based on a Tax Treaty, there are no specific procedures aimed at suspending the tax collection. However, the taxpayer could get access to the remedies ordinarily available, such as the administrative suspension or the suspension granted by a Tax Court provided for, respectively, by Article 39(1) of Presidential Decree No. 602 of 20 September 1973 and Article 47 of Decree 546/1992.[7]

In relation to pending MAPs grounded on the Arbitration Convention, the IRA may authorize the suspension of the tax collection[8] where the request of starting a MAP has been accepted. According to Circular 21/2012, in case the taxpayer filed an appeal on the same issues covered by the MAP, the suspension is granted if the taxpayer withdraws from the domestic judicial proceedings.[9]

In evaluating the best strategy to resolve international double taxation, it is also necessary to evaluate the procedural ramifications related to the interplays between MAPs and the domestic tax settlement procedures[10] under Italian law. Indeed, before the implementation of Directive 2017/1852, the tax settlement procedures in general precluded the possibility for the taxpayer to resolve international double taxation through a MAP under a Tax Treaty and/or the Arbitration Convention.

In relation to MAPs started on the basis of a Tax Treaty, in case the taxpayer does not challenge the notice of assessment issued by the IRA in which the tax claims that give rise to the double taxation are reported, the taxes assessed will become final with the consequence that, in the context of a MAP, it would not be possible for the Italian

7. *See* para. 4.2.7 of Circular 21/2012.
8. *See* Article 3(2) of Law No. 99 of 1993 implementing the Arbitration Convention.
9. *See* para. 5.7 of Circular 21/2012.
10. The Italian tax framework provides for several settlement procedures depending on the stage in which the dispute is (e.g., pre-litigation versus litigation). In particular, the so-called *accertamento con adesione* is the typical settlement procedure available in a pre-litigation context, while the '*mediazione tributaria*' and the '*conciliazione giudiziale*' relate to a subsequent phase in which the taxpayer has already filed the appeal against the notice of assessment before the competent Tax Court.

competent authority to deviate from the tax claims raised with the notice of assessment.

As clarified by Circular 21/2012,[11] the same consequences of not timely challenging the notice of tax assessment will arise where the taxpayer settled the dispute with the IRA under the pre-litigation tax settlement procedure (the so-called *accertamento con adesione* procedure) pursuant to Legislative Decree No. 218 of 19 June 1997 or through either the tax mediation (the so-called *mediazione tributaria*) or the judiciary settlement (the so-called *conciliazione giudiziale*), provided for, respectively, by Article 17-*bis* and Articles 48 and 48-*bis* of Decree 546/1992. From the standpoint of the Italian competent authority, the MAP could be started but it cannot deviate from the results agreed pursuant to the said settlement procedures. In this respect, Circular 21/2012 clarified that the Competent Authority of the other State may however explore the possibility of a unilateral corresponding (downward) adjustment in order to eliminate or mitigate double taxation.

With reference to MAPs started pursuant to the Arbitration Convention, according to Circular 21/2012, the settlement of tax disputes through the domestic settlement procedures would exclude, in the context of a MAP, the possibility for the Italian competent authority to change the taxes settled, as already noted above in relation to MAPs grounded on a Tax Treaty. To this end, the access to a MAP under the Arbitration Convention would be denied in order to avoid a potential conflict between the outcomes of the settlement and the arbitration procedure under the Arbitration Convention.

Since the taxes settled have become final – with the consequence that any renegotiation within a MAP based on the Arbitration Convention is precluded – Circular 21/2012 provides that the only viable route for the Competent Authority of the other State is to explore the possibility to perform a unilateral corresponding downward adjustment in order to eliminate or mitigate the double taxation. This possibility, however, can be granted provided that the taxpayer has submitted a MAP request on the basis of a Tax Treaty.

On a separate profile, Circular 21/2012 specifies also that Articles 6 and 7 of the Arbitration Convention provide that the MAP is alternative to the domestic judicial appeal; where the Competent Authorities do not reach an agreement, the arbitration phase will begin. To this end, differently from tax settlements, not appealing against the notice of assessment before the competent Tax Court does not prevent the taxpayer from starting a MAP under the Arbitration Convention. Where a taxpayer does not challenge the notice of assessment and files a request to start a MAP, it proves the taxpayer's willingness to resolve the double taxation through a MAP which envisages the arbitration phase.

Following the clarifications laid down by Circular 21/2012 of the IRA, despite the wording is not clear, in all cases in which the taxpayer has not challenged the notice of assessment by paying in full the taxes assessed, reduced penalties[12] and interest

11. *See* para. 7 of Circular 21/2012.
12. According to Article 15(1) of Legislative Decree No. 218 of 19 June 1997, penalties are reduced up to one-third of the minimum penalties applicable by law where the taxpayer pays the

claimed by the IRA (the so-called *acquiescenza*), the mere acceptance of the claims that give rise to the double taxation should not prevent the taxpayer from initiating a MAP under the Arbitration Convention being the behaviour of the taxpayer consistent with the circumstances that the arbitration phase is alternative to the domestic judicial proceedings.

To this end, it should be taken into account that, where the taxpayer has filed an appeal against the notice of assessment, the arbitration phase could be activated only where the taxpayer has allowed the time provided for the appeal to expire or has withdrawn any such appeal before a decision has been delivered.

Conversely, in case of 'pure' tax settlement procedures (e.g., '*accertamento con adesione*', '*mediazione*' and '*conciliazione giudiziale*'), Circular 21/2012 clearly prevents the chance to the Italian competent authority to review and changes the terms of the settlement in the context of a MAP.

Even if the new procedures laid down by Directive 2017/1852, as implemented by the Decree, are innovative and overcome certain juridical limitations of the procedures started until now on the basis of Tax Treaty and/or the Arbitration Convention, as it will be pointed out in the following sections, a careful analysis of the interplay between the domestic remedies and the procedures governed by the Decree should be done in order to evaluate how best to resolve and tackle an issue that may lead to double taxation.

C.1. Filing of a Complaint to Start a MAP

Pursuant to Article 3 of the Decree, any Affected Person is entitled to submit a request for the opening of a MAP concerning a disputed matter to the IRA and to the Competent Authority of the other Member State. The request must be submitted within three years from the date of receipt of the first notification of the act (or other equivalent document) containing the measure that has or may have led to the question in dispute.[13]

For this purpose, it is specified that the Affected Person should refer to the domestic law of the Member State which issued the act or other equivalent document.

Article 3(2) of the Decree clarifies that the filing of a complaint to start a MAP would not require the prior initiation of domestic litigation procedures. In addition, it is specified that the MAP would not be precluded per se by the tax settlement procedures laid down by the domestic tax framework[14] which would render the notice of tax assessment final. As anticipated, this is a groundbreaking aspect as it overcomes,

assessed taxes, reduced penalties and interest within the deadline to file the appeal to the competent Tax Court (i.e., sixty days from the notification of the notice of assessment).

13. It is expressly clarified that in the case of submission of a MAP request following a formal notification issued by a tax audit report ('*processo verbale di constatazione*'), the period of three years starts to run from the notification of the relevant notice of assessment ('*avviso di accertamento*').
14. Such as the '*acquiescenza*', '*accertamento con adesione*' and '*mediazione tributaria*' as mentioned by the explanatory notes to the Decree.

at least partially, the previous position assumed by the IRA with Circular 21/2012 in relation to domestic tax settlement procedures.

However, according to the explanatory notes to the Decree, the voluntary correction of the tax return by the Affected Person (so-called *ravvedimento operoso*) would prevent the start of a MAP governed by the Decree.

Conversely, the complaint to start a MAP cannot be filed where a judgment on the merit of the question in dispute has already been rendered (even if still appealable by the Affected Person) or a Tax Court has issued a decision following a judicial settlement (so-called *conciliazione giudiziale*) within the meaning of Articles 48 and 48-*bis* of Decree 546/1992.[15]

In any case, the filing of a complaint to start a MAP under the Decree would not preclude the Affected Person from availing himself of the domestic tax procedures to settle and/or resolve the question in dispute, including the chance to file an appeal before the Tax Court against the notice of tax assessment which gave rise to the question in dispute.

Should the Affected Persons file an appeal on the question in dispute before the competent tax court, the proceedings can be suspended pursuant to Article 39(1-*ter*)(b) of Decree 546/1992 and, in this event, according to Article 15(2) of Presidential Decree No. 602 of 29 September 1973, the collection of the taxes claimed assessed is suspended.[16] Moreover, the terms concerning: (i) the IRA decision on whether to accept or reject the complaint to start a MAP (i.e., six months from the receipt of the complaint) and (ii) the term of two years (extensible to three years), within which the Competent Authorities shall endeavour to resolve the question in dispute,[17] will start from the date of suspension of the domestic tax proceedings.

The complaint to start a MAP must be submitted simultaneously to the IRA and to the concerned Competent Authority of the other Member State(s) and must contain the same information and the indication of all the Member States involved.

Any Affected Person shall submit his/her complaint in one of the official languages of the concerned Member States, in accordance with domestic law, or in a language different from one of the official languages, if accepted by the concerned Member State.

In this respect, the Decree clarifies that the request filed to the IRA shall be written in Italian or accompanied by a sworn translation into Italian.

The documentation enclosed to the complaint shall be accompanied by a translation in Italian or, alternatively, in English. In any case, the IRA could require a sworn translation of the supporting documentation into Italian if it is appropriate.

Within two months from the date of receipt of the complaint, the IRA shall:

15. According to Articles 48 and 48-*bis* of Decree 546/1992, the parties can reach a settlement during the course of the tax proceedings.
16. Generally, a provisional payment equal to one-third of the taxes (plus related interest) claimed by the IRA with the notice of assessment is required in case of filing of the appeal to the competent Tax Court of First Instance, except where the competent tax court has granted the suspension of the tax collection upon request of the taxpayer.
17. *See also* Article 16(3) of Directive 2017/1852.

- notify the Affected Person, acknowledging the receipt of the complaint; and
- inform the Competent Authorities of the other Member State(s) involved of the receipt of the complaint as well as about the language (or languages) it intends to use in its communications.

The complaint shall only be admitted if the Affected Person provides the following information:

- the name, address, tax identification number and other information necessary for the identification of the Affected Person(s) that filed the complaint and any other Affected Person(s);
- the tax periods concerned;
- detailed information on:
  - (i) the facts and circumstances of the case, including details of the structure of the transaction and the relations between the Affected Person and the other parties involved in the transactions, as well as the facts recognized in good faith in an agreement, including those pursuant to Article 31-*ter* of Presidential Decree No. 600 of 29 September 1973, mutually binding between the Affected Persons and the IRA or the Competent Authorities of the other concerned Member State(s);
  - (ii) the kind and date of the document or other equivalent document which led or could lead to the question in dispute, including, where applicable, details of the income realized in Italy or in the other Member State and the inclusion of such income in the taxable income in Italy or in the other Member State;
  - (iii) taxes levied or due on that income pursuant to the domestic law or in the other Member State;
  - (iv) the relevant amounts converted in the currencies of the concerned Member States;
- a copy of any supporting document relating to the information referred to in points (i) to (iv) above;
- the applicable domestic and Tax Treaty provisions. Where more than one Tax Treaty is applicable, the persons which filed the complaint shall specify which Tax Treaty is to be interpreted in relation to the question in dispute. In that case, the Tax Treaty shall apply for the purposes of the Decree;
- the following additional information together with a copy of any supporting documents:
  - (i) an explanation of the reasons according to which the Affected Persons consider that there is a question in dispute;
  - (ii) details of any appeals filed by the Affected Persons in relation to the question in dispute and any judgments or decisions of the courts in relation to that question in dispute;
  - (iii) a declaration of commitment from the Affected Persons to answer fully and promptly to all relevant requests of the IRA or other Competent

Authority and to provide the necessary documentation at the request of the IRA or other Competent Authorities;

(iv) a copy of the notice of tax assessment, tax audit report or other equivalent document that give rise to the question in dispute and a copy of any other document issued by the IRA or the Competent Authority of the other Member State(s), where applicable.

The complaint shall also contain information on any other complaint about the opening of a MAP or other dispute resolution procedure submitted under a Tax Treaty and/or an Arbitration Convention, as well as an express undertaking by the Affected Persons not to pursue the 'parallel' ongoing procedure initiated on the same question in dispute resolution mechanism following the opening of the MAP under the Decree (i.e., the Affected Persons should terminate the existing MAP started pursuant to the Arbitration Convention or a Tax Treaty).

In order to simplify the access to the MAP and reduce its costs, the complaint to start a MAP (or the notification of its withdrawal, *see* section C.2. below) could be submitted only to the IRA if the Affected Person is a natural person resident for tax purposes in Italy or an undertaking which, in accordance with Directive 2013/34/EU of the European Parliament and of the Council of 26 June 2013, is not a large business undertaking[18] and does not belong to the category of a large group,[19] which is also resident for tax purposes in Italy.

Within two months of the date of receipt of the above notification (also in case of withdrawal), the IRA should simultaneously notify the Competent Authorities of the other concerned Member State(s). On the date of such notification, such communications shall be deemed to have been submitted by the Affected Persons to the Competent Authorities of all the Member States concerned.

C.2. Withdrawal of a Complaint to Start a MAP

Should the Affected Persons decide to withdraw their complaint about the opening of a MAP, they must at the same time notify in writing to the IRA and all the Competent Authorities of the concerned Member State(s). Such notification shall terminate, with immediate effect, all procedures under the Decree. Upon receipt of such notification, the IRA shall promptly inform the Competent Authorities of the other Member State(s) of the end of the procedures.

18. According to Article 3(4) of Directive 2013/34/EU, large undertakings are those undertakings which on their balance sheet dates exceed at least two of the three following criteria: (i) balance sheet total: EUR 20,000,000; (ii) net turnover: EUR 40,000,000; (iii) average number of employees during the financial year: 250.
19. Pursuant to Article 3(7) of Directive 2013/34/EU, large groups shall be groups consisting of parent and subsidiary undertakings to be included in a consolidation and which, on a consolidated basis, exceed the limits of at least two of the three following criteria on the balance sheet date of the parent undertaking: (i) balance sheet total: EUR 20,000,000; (ii) net turnover: EUR 40,000,000; (iii) average number of employees during the financial year: 250.

C.3. Complaint Filed According to Tax Treaties or the Arbitration Convention

According to Article 4 of the Decree, if the Affected Person submits an application to start a MAP with respect to a question in dispute pursuant to the Decree, a Tax Treaty or the Arbitration Convention, only the provisions of the Decree shall apply. Indeed, the submission of a complaint to start a MAP shall terminate any other ongoing proceedings on the same question in a dispute started pursuant to a Tax Treaty or the Arbitration Convention.[20]

In the first instance, the plain wording of the applicable provisions would suggest that the Decree takes precedence over the rules contained in the applicable Tax Treaty or in the Arbitration Convention – thereby derogating from the acknowledged principle of prevalence of international law. However, considering that the rules laid down in the Decree are procedural in scope and not substantive, it may be argued that the hierarchy of laws would not be altered.

Also, the Decree clarifies that, in the event of withdrawal or termination of the MAP, the same Affected Person may subsequently submit an application to start a MAP under the Tax Treaty or the Arbitration Convention, in accordance with the.terms and conditions laid down therein.

Furthermore, it should be noted that the Decree does not provide for an effective coordination between the implementing rules of Directive 2017/1852 and the provisions in place with reference to the procedure referred to in Article 31-*quater*(1)(c) of Presidential Decree No. 600 of 29 September 1973 (hereinafter 'Procedure 31-*quater*').

In brief, Procedure 31-*quater* provides that the applicant may be granted the right to benefit from a corresponding adjustment, through the filing of a specific written request, in respect of a final primary adjustment at arm's length performed by a State having a Tax Treaty in force with Italy allowing an adequate exchange of information.

This being said, pursuant to Point 6.1, first sentence, of Implementing Act No. 108954 of the IRA Director dated 30 May 2018, which detailed explanatory notes of Procedure 31-*quater*, the application directly activates the underlying procedure for the resolution of international disputes under which Procedure 31-*quarter* is grounded (i.e., a Tax Treaty or the Arbitration Convention).

In this respect, considering the scope of the Decree, it would be necessary to provide that Procedure 31-*quater* can be based also on the implementing provisions of Directive 2017/1852 with the consequent effects in legal and procedural terms. In fact, if Procedure 31-*quater* ends with the non-recognition of a downward adjustment, the elimination of double taxation could be still possible and, in any case, obtained in the context of the 'underlying' MAP whose activation has been simultaneously requested through Procedure 31-*quater*. As a result, there is a need for coordination between the provisions of the Decree and those provided for in Procedure 31-*quarter*; this could be obtained by explicitly stating the possibility of referring to the procedure laid down by the Decree when applying for Procedure 31-*quater*.

20. *See also* Article 5(4) of Directive 2017/1852.

D. THE RESOLUTION OF THE QUESTION IN DISPUTE UNDER THE MAP

D.1. Decision of the Competent Authority with Reference to the Complaint

Article 5 of the Decree lays down the rules concerning the preliminary phase of the MAP. In detail, the IRA could request specific additional information within three months from the date of receipt of the complaint, where the requested information is necessary for the purposes of the case.

The persons receiving the request shall reply within three months from the date of its receipt. A copy of the reply shall be sent by the persons providing the information simultaneously to the Competent Authorities of the other concerned Member State(s).

In case the Affected Person filed the complaint only to the IRA under Article 3(12) of the Decree (e.g., natural person, not large business undertakings), the Affected Person will answer only to the IRA, which at the same time shall forward a copy of the answer to the Competent Authorities of the other concerned Member State(s). Such additional information shall be considered as received by all the Member States on the date of receipt.

Within six months from the date of receipt of the complaint to start a MAP or, if later, within six months from the date of receipt of the additional information as provided by the Affected Persons after a request made by the IRA, the IRA may decide to settle unilaterally the question in dispute, notifying promptly this decision to the Affected Persons and the Competent Authorities of the other Member State(s). In such a case, the MAP laid down by the Decree shall not be started.

It should be noted that the Decree does not clarify the conditions under which the IRA may decide to settle the matter unilaterally. In this respect, it would be appropriate, from an Italian domestic law perspective, to introduce mechanisms to seek jurisdictional protection against the unilateral initiative of the IRA (e.g., appeal to the Tax Court as provided for the decision to reject the application pursuant to Article 8 of the Decree, *see* section D.3. below).

With respect to the decision of the Competent Authority with reference to the complaint, the IRA shall take a decision on whether to accept or reject the complaint to start a MAP within six months from the date of receipt[21] or within six months from the date of receipt of the additional information required pursuant to Article 5 of the Decree, giving timely notice to the Affected Person and to the Competent Authorities of the involved other Member State(s), pursuant to Article 6(1) of the Decree.

The complaint shall be rejected in the following cases:

- the complaint does not contain the information required under Article 3 (*see* section C.1. above), or the additional information requested by the IRA has not been transmitted within the three months;
- there is not a questionable issue subject to unilateral or bilateral resolution;

21. Where the Affected Person filed an appeal concerning the question in dispute before a Tax Court, the deadline shall start to run from the date of such suspension granted by the Tax Court.

- the application was not submitted within the period of three years from the date of receipt of the first notification of the act (or other equivalent document) containing the measure that has or could have led to the question in dispute;
- a final judgment (‘*sentenza passata in giudicato*’) on the substance of the question in dispute has been rendered by a Tax Court or a judgment following a judicial settlement (the so-called *conciliazione*) has been issued within the meaning of Articles 48 and 48-*bis* of Decree 546/1992.

When informing the Affected Person, the IRA shall state the reasons which led to the rejection of the complaint.

If the IRA does not take a decision on the complaint within the applicable deadline reported above, the application shall be deemed to have been granted (so-called *silenzio assenso*).

The IRA shall at the same time forward a copy of the reply to the Competent Authorities of the other involved Member State(s).

With respect to the possibility that the IRA may reject the complaint as there is not a questionable issue subject to unilateral or bilateral resolution, particular attention should be addressed to self-adjustments executed by the taxpayer.

According to the OECD, the request of starting a MAP under a Tax Treaty could be filed where the taxpayer has performed also self-adjustments to amend its tax returns previously filed. Indeed, the Commentary on Article 25 of the OECD Model provides that the access to a MAP should be granted also in the case of ‘*bona fide taxpayer-initiated adjustments which are authorised under the domestic laws of some countries and which permit a taxpayer, under appropriate circumstances, to amend a previously filed tax return in order to report a price in a controlled transaction, or an attribution of profit to a permanent establishment, that is, in the taxpayer's opinion, in accordance with the arm's length principle*’.

For instance, according to applicable tax laws in certain jurisdictions (e.g., Italy, Germany), if the taxpayer, after submitting the relevant tax return, becomes aware – before the expiry of the statute of limitations – that a tax return is incorrect or incomplete and has led or may lead unpaid taxes, the taxpayer is obliged (or may have the interest[22]) to amend that tax return. Moreover, if the taxpayer is aware, during a tax audit, that the tax returns previously submitted for years which are not subject to that tax audit are incorrect or incomplete, the taxpayer must (or may have the interest to) correct the relevant tax returns. Also, in certain cases, the applicable tax laws may require that, with regard to tax returns that will be submitted after the completion of the tax audit, the taxpayer could be required to reflect the results of the tax audit in

22. Indeed, the taxpayer may benefit from a special penalty regime in amending voluntarily its incorrect tax returns. This is the case of the self-correction of a tax return (‘*ravvedimento operoso*’) pursuant to Articles 13 and 13-*bis* of Legislative Decree No. 472 of 18 December 1997.

such returns, if the findings raised by the competent tax authority have effects also with respect to these years still subject to audit.[23]

In all the above-mentioned cases, the taxpayer may be obliged (or have the interest) to amend the tax returns already filed so that a self-adjustment increasing the taxable income would be performed on a voluntary basis.

With respect to the starting point of the three-year period within which the taxpayer should file the request to start a MAP pursuant to Article 25(1) of the OECD Model Tax Convention,[24] the Commentary provides that, in self-assessment cases, the notification effecting that assessment or the date on which the taxpayer files the self-assessed return would be the starting point for the three-year period to run.[25]

23. For example, after a tax audit carried out by the Competent Authority with reference to fiscal years 2014-2017, the taxpayer should (or may have the interest to) adjust its tax return for fiscal year 2018 in accordance with the principles set out in the notice of assessment issued in 2019 for fiscal years 2014-2017.
24. In this respect, from a practical point of view, in order to ensure an effective functioning of MAP, the taxpayers should have the necessary time to present a MAP request. To this end, according to Article 25 (1), second sentence, of the OECD Model Convention, '*the case must be presented within three years from the first notification of the action resulting in taxation not in accordance with the provisions of the Convention*'. However, not all the Tax Treaties entered into by Italy allow taxpayers to present a MAP request within a period of at least three years from the first notification of the action resulting in taxation not in accordance with the provisions of the relevant Tax Treaty. Such Tax Treaties are not in line with the OECD Model Convention. The lack of the said minimum period creates uncertainty for taxpayers and Competent Authorities on the availability of the MAP. For example, certain Tax Treaties entered into by Italy provide a period to file a MAP request less than three years (generally two years) from the first notification of the action resulting in taxation not in accordance with the provisions of the relevant Tax Treaty. As to such Tax Treaties, it should be noted that it is not entirely clear the starting date of the period for filing a MAP request. According to the tax practitioners addressing the matter, the said period should start from the formal notification of the notice of assessment by the tax authorities triggering a taxation not in accordance with the applicable Tax Treaty. The IRA clarifies that when taxation not in accordance with a Tax Treaty arises from the application of a domestic tax or withholding tax, the term for a valid submission of a MAP request runs either from: (i) the date of notification by the tax authority of the refund denial submitted with respect to the application of a refund of a withholding tax or (ii) from the ninetieth day following the submission of the refund's request without a decision by the tax authority. On the contrary, in the case where taxation not in accordance with the provisions of a Tax Treaty is triggered by adjustments carried out by the tax authorities, the initial term of the period within which the taxpayer may submit a MAP request runs from the date of notification of the notice of assessment. The said Tax Treaties entail the risk that the access to MAP could be denied to a taxpayer because the latter did not submit the MAP request within the shorter deadline set forth by the relevant Tax Treaty. However, in such a scenario, the taxpayer could submit a MAP request under the Arbitration Convention.

    Certain other Tax Treaties entered into by Italy do not include a time limit for the submission of a MAP request. In such a case, in practice, the Italian competent authorities take into account such request when it has been filed in compliance with the domestic statute of limitation. Such Tax Treaties entail the risk that the access to MAP could be denied to a taxpayer since the period under the domestic statute of limitation is less than three years as from the first notification of the action resulting in taxation not in accordance with the provisions of the relevant Tax Treaty.
25. In addition, the Commentary clarifies that, where a taxpayer pays additional tax in connection with the filing of an amended return reflecting a bona fide taxpayer-initiated adjustment, the starting point of the three-year time limit would generally be the notice of assessment resulting from the amended return.

In this respect, Point 4 of the Code of Conduct for the effective implementation of the Arbitration Convention[26] clarifies that the date of the first notification of the tax assessment notice (or equivalent measure) which results or is likely to result in double taxation is considered as the starting point for the three-year-period deadline for submitting the request to start a MAP according to Article 6(1) of the Arbitration Convention. It is worth stressing in this respect that Italy made a reservation to Point 4 of the Code of Conduct stating that the application of the Arbitration Convention should be limited to those cases where there is a transfer pricing adjustment.

In certain recent experiences, due to such reservation made by Italy, the Italian competent authority has refused to enter into an agreement under a MAP having as object transfer price adjustments which gave rise to double taxation not originated from an adjustment made by the foreign tax authorities but from self-adjustments performed by the taxpayer. Indeed, according to the Italian competent authority, a self-adjustment performed by a taxable person does not constitute a transfer pricing adjustment within the meaning of Point 4 of the Code of Conduct of the Arbitration Convention and, therefore, it cannot constitute an 'action' undertaken by a State within the meaning of Article 6 of the Arbitration Convention.

Also after the implementation of Directive 2017/1852 in the Italian tax framework, in the absence of specific new provisions regulating the treatment of self-adjustments in the context of MAPs and dispute resolution procedures, one may argue that the above restrictive position of the IRA with respect to self-adjustments may be upheld,[27] considering also that the explanatory notes to the Decree have expressly excluded from the scope of the new resolution procedures the cases in which the Affected Person has availed himself of the voluntary correction of the tax return (so-called *ravvedimento operoso*).

D.2. MAP

If the complaint is accepted, the IRA and the Competent Authorities of the other concerned Member State(s) shall endeavour (i.e., are not bound) to settle the question

26. As adopted and revised in 2009 by the European Council.
27. In light of the position taken by the Italian Competent Authority, in order to avoid a possible rejection of the application to open a MAP on the basis of the reservation made by Italy in relation to Point 4 of the Code of Conduct, one possible practical solution may consist in filing a refund of the higher taxes paid in connection to the amended tax returns filed voluntarily by the taxpayer. Such tax refund application should be addressed by the taxpayer to the tax authority of the State in which the self-adjustments have been performed.

    As presumably the Competent Authority will reject the tax refund application filed by the taxpayer, the request to start a MAP could be based on the rejection of the tax refund issued by the competent tax authority (i.e., an 'action' undertaken by a State within the meaning of Article 6 of the Arbitration Convention) and not only on (mere) self-adjustments performed by the taxpayer.

in dispute by a MAP within two years from the date of the last notification of the decision accepting the complaint by one of the Member States.[28]

The two-year period could be extended by up to one year where a reasoned written request of the IRA or the Competent Authority of another concerned Member State(s) is submitted to the Competent Authorities of the other concerned Member State(s).

Considering that the Italian domestic framework does not allow to derogate from a final decision provided by a Tax Court, where the question in dispute has been the subject of a final judgment ('*sentenza passata in giudicato*') of a Tax Court or a judgment following a judicial settlement within the meaning of Articles 48 and 48-*bis* of Decree 546/1992 has been rendered before an agreement is reached, the IRA shall notify such judgment to the Competent Authorities of the other concerned Member State(s) and the MAP shall terminate from the date of such notification.

As already noted by Circular 21/2012 issued by the IRA before the implementation of Directive 2017/1852, Italy is one of those jurisdictions where administrative authorities cannot deviate from the decision of a judicial body. However, differently from the previous position taken by the IRA through Circular 21/2012 according to which a judgment rendered by a Tax Court would preclude the IRA to deviate from that judgment in the context of the MAP, the Decree now provides that only a final judgment ('*sentenza passata in giudicato*') would prevent the conclusion of an agreement in the context of a MAP started under the Decree.

In execution of an agreement reached by the Competent Authorities under a MAP pursuant to Article 7 of the Decree, the IRA shall notify the Affected Person of the decision taken within thirty days of the date of conclusion of the MAP. If the IRA and the Competent Authorities of the other concerned Member State(s) did not reach an agreement within the two-year deadline (or three year in case of extension), the IRA shall inform the Affected Person of the general reasons for not reaching such an agreement.

In the event that a question in dispute deriving from an assessment performed by the Italian tax authorities was previously subject to a domestic settlement procedure, the IRA should recalculate the increase or decrease in taxes due following the introduction of the MAP. The purpose of this provision is not to bind the IRA to the tax settlements entered into by the taxpayer with the IRA.

D.3. Appeal of the Taxpayer Against the Decision Rejecting the Complaint

In the event that both the IRA and the Competent Authorities of the other concerned Member State(s) have rejected the complaint to start a MAP, the Affected Person can file an appeal before the Tax Court in accordance with the provisions of the domestic law in force.

28. Where the Affected Person filed an appeal on the question in dispute before the Tax Courts, the deadline shall start to run from the date of such suspension granted by the Tax Court, also in case of extension of up to one year of the ordinary deadline.

In case of appeal against the rejection of the complaint, the Affected Person who appealed, as the case may be, before the Tax Court or to the Competent Court of the other Member State(s) cannot submit a request to set up the Advisory Commission (*see* section E.1. below) if:

- the appeal against the rejection of the complaint is still pending in accordance with the domestic law of the Member State concerned;
- the decision of rejection of the complaint can be further appealed in accordance with the domestic law of the Member State concerned;
- the decision to reject was confirmed, as the case may be, by the Tax Court or by the Competent Court of the other concerned Member State and that decision cannot be appealed anymore according to the applicable law.

Even if the Decree does not provide further clarifications, it also seems necessary to coordinate any litigation pending before the Competent Courts of different jurisdictions in the event of rejection by all the Competent Authorities, e.g. by requiring the submission of the appeal to only one of the possible Competent Courts (including the competent Italian Tax Courts). A solution could be that which qualifies as competent the national court that is first appealed by the Affected Person.

E. DISPUTE RESOLUTION PROCEDURE

A point of attention that until now has concerned practitioners in dealing with international controversies under the Arbitration Convention is represented by the need to withdraw the domestic tax proceedings to get access to the arbitration phase under the Arbitration Convention.

Even if the access to the MAPs is *'irrespective of the remedies provided by the domestic law of the Contracting States concerned'*, Circular 21/2012 has observed that, since Italy is one of the jurisdictions that does not allow the Competent Authority to derogate from a judgment, the arbitration phase is prevented where a judgment is provided by a domestic Tax Court.[29] As a result, on the basis of Article 7(3) of the Arbitration Convention, the arbitration phase can be activated only where the taxpayer has allowed the time provided for the appeal to expire or has withdrawn any such appeal before a decision has been delivered.

Moreover, according to the IRA, should the request for opening a MAP be submitted before the withdrawal of the judicial proceedings, the term of two years to set up an advisory commission pursuant to Article 7(1) of the Arbitration Convention and get access to the arbitration phase starts from the date in which the taxpayer has withdrawn from the judicial proceedings.

In this respect, it should be pointed out that the withdrawal of the judicial proceedings to get access to the arbitration phase under the Arbitration Convention may expose de facto the taxpayer to the uncertainty on how the dispute may end. For example, it could happen that, after the taxpayer has withdrawn from the judicial

29. *See* para. 5.6 of Circular 21/2012.

proceedings, the Competent Authorities, having acquired the advisory commission's opinion, decide to conclude an agreement that the taxpayer may consider unsatisfactory and wrongful from a technical standpoint (possibly in light of the opinion put forward by the advisory commission). The withdrawal of the judicial proceedings would leave the taxpayer with no other options with the consequence that the only viable route would be to accept the agreement entered into by the Competent Authorities. Therefore, from a strategic standpoint, the access to the arbitration phase of the MAP should be carefully evaluated.

This being said, as noted also by Circular 21/2012, in the event that the taxpayer has submitted a MAP opening request and filed in parallel an appeal before the Tax Court on the same issues covered by the MAP, the judicial proceedings do not prevent per se the MAP from starting. Indeed, the existence of the judicial proceedings would only disallow the access to the arbitration phase but not to the MAP under the Arbitration Convention. This being said, it would be of utmost importance to file also a request to suspend the judicial proceedings in order to avoid that a judgment is rendered by the competent Tax Court which would: (i) rule out the possibility for the Italian competent authority to enter in the context of a MAP into an agreement which deviates from the judgment and (ii) exclude in any case the chance to get access to the arbitration phase.

Also, as previously noted by Circular 21/2012, the Italian competent authority would not be able to enter into an agreement under a MAP procedure started under a Tax Treaty and/or the Arbitration Conventions where a judgment intervened before the Competent Authorities reached an agreement pending the MAP[30] (*see* section C. above). In addition, the decision of a judicial authority would prevent the arbitration under the Arbitration Convention. Indeed, as anticipated above, the arbitration phase may be activated only and insofar as the associated enterprise has allowed the time provided for the appeal to expire or has withdrawn any such appeal before a decision has been delivered. Moreover, should the request for opening the procedure be submitted before withdrawing from the judgment, the term of two years – pursuant to what is established in Article 7(1), second period, and 7(3) – runs from the date in which the taxpayer has withdrawn from the first grade of appeal. In the event that the taxpayer simultaneously submits a MAP opening request and carries on the appeal against the assessment notice (regarding elements thereof pertaining to the adjustments leading to double taxation), the existence of a litigation proceeding does not prevent the MAP from beginning and/or the Competent Authorities from exchanging views regarding the case or information on the pending judicial proceeding. However, in the event a judicial decision even if not final occurred before the decision of the Competent Authorities, the latter will not be removed unless the foreign Competent Authority accepts a mutual agreement with the Italian competent authority consistent to the domestic judicial decision.

As better detailed in the following sections, the Decree now provides that the IRA should reject the request to set up an Advisory Commission to resolve the question in

30. *See* paras 4.5.2 and 5.6 of Circular 21/2012.

dispute only where a Tax Court has rendered a final judgment ('*sentenza passata in giudicato*'). Therefore, a judgment not yet final should not preclude the start of a dispute resolution procedure after that the Competent Authorities have not reached an agreement within two years under a MAP started under the Decree.

E.1. Request of Appointment of the Advisory Commission

Article 9 of the Decree provides the procedural rules relating to the dispute resolution procedure in all cases in which the Competent Authorities have not reached an agreement under the MAP started pursuant to Article 3 (*see* section C.1.). Indeed, the Affected Person can submit a request to the IRA and the Competent Authority of the other concerned Member States to set up an Advisory Commission and, *inter alia*, get access to the arbitration phase in order to overcome the failure by the Competent Authorities to reach an agreement during the MAP phase.

The Affected Persons referred to in Article 3(12) of the Decree (e.g., not large business undertakings) can submit a request to set up an Advisory Commission, only to the IRA, which, within two months from the date of receipt of the request, shall simultaneously notify the Competent Authorities of the other concerned Member State(s). On the date of such notification, the said request shall be deemed to have been submitted by the Affected Persons referred to in Article 3(12) to the Competent Authorities of all the concerned Member States.

The Advisory Commission shall be established in the following cases:

- where the complaint to start a MAP has been rejected by at least one, but not all, of the Competent Authorities of the other concerned Member State(s). In this circumstance, the Affected Person can file a request to set up an Advisory Commission only if:
  (i) under the domestic law of the Member State in which the decision of rejection of the complaint was issued, no appeal against that decision may be filed;
  (ii) there is no pending litigation;
  (iii) the Affected Person has formally waived, in a written declaration, his right to appeal against the decision of rejection of the complaint:
- where the complaint to start a MAP has been rejected by all the Competent Authorities of the concerned Member States and a judgment has been issued in favour of the Affected Person, following an appeal filed by that person[31] before the Competent Court of one of a concerned Member State against the rejection decision of the Competent Authority of that Member State;
- where the Competent Authorities of the concerned Member States have accepted the complaint to start a MAP but have not been able to reach an agreement on how to resolve the question in dispute through the MAP within two years or three years in case of extension.[32]

31. Article 8(1) of the Decree.
32. Article 7(1) and 7(2) of the Decree.

The request to appoint the Advisory Commission must be made in writing within fifty days from the receipt of the notification (alternatively):

- of the decision by the IRA of rejection of the complaint;[33]
- of the communication on the Competent Authorities' failure of reaching an agreement under the MAP;[34] or
- of the favourable decision of the Competent Court following an appeal filed by that person before the Competent Court of one of a concerned Member State against the rejection of the complaint of the Competent Authority of that Member State.

Where the Competent Authorities of the concerned Member States have accepted the complaint to start a MAP but have not been able to reach an agreement on how to resolve the question in dispute through the MAP within two years (or three years in case of extension) and the question in dispute has been the subject of a final judgment ('*sentenza passata in giudicato*') issued by a Tax Court or a judgment following a judicial settlement has been rendered within the meaning of Articles 48 and 48-*bis* of Decree 546/1992, the IRA shall inform the Competent Authorities of the other concerned Member States of the preclusive effects of the domestic decision on the possibility to set up an Advisory Commission to resolve the question in dispute.[35]

Moreover, the IRA can reject the complaint to set up an Advisory Commission in cases where penalties have been imposed under domestic law for one of the criminal offences referred to in Title II of Legislative Decree No. 74 of 10 March 2000 which has risen from the question in dispute.[36] In particular, the following criminal offences would prevent the MAP:

- fraudulent declaration through the use of invoices or other documents for non-existent transactions;
- fraudulent declaration by other artifices;
- unfaithful tax return;
- omitted tax return;
- issuance of invoices or other documents for non-existent operations;
- omitted payment of withholding taxes due or certified;
- omitted VAT payments;
- offset of undue or non-existent tax credits;
- fraudulent tax evasion.

It should be noted that the exclusion from a MAP procedure should operate only in the case where criminal penalties have been effectively imposed and not also in the case of mere initiation of criminal investigation (this is particularly important in case – for instance – of audits on hidden permanent establishments in Italy of foreign companies or groups that normally trigger per se criminal exposure).

33. Article 6(1) of the Decree.
34. Article 7(5) of the Decree.
35. *See also* Article 16(4)(b) of Directive 2017/1852.
36. *See also* Article 16(6) of Directive 2017/1852.

The IRA can also refuse to start a MAP where the question in dispute does not lead to Double Taxation.[37] In such a case, it shall promptly inform the Affected Person and the Competent Authorities of the other involved Member States.

E.2. Appointment of the Advisory Commission

Pursuant to Article 10 of the Decree, the Advisory Commission shall be appointed within 120 days from the receipt of the request filed by the Affected Person. Once established, its chairman shall promptly inform the Affected Person.

The Advisory Commission shall be composed of:

- a chairman;
- one representative of each of the involved Competent Authority. Where agreed by the Competent Authorities, the number of such representatives may be increased to two for each of the Competent Authority;
- one independent person appointed by each Competent Authority of the concerned Member States from a specific list of independent persons of standing (*see* section E.4. below). Where agreed by the Competent Authorities, the number of such persons appointed may be increased to two for each Competent Authority.

The rules for the appointment of independent persons of standing shall be agreed between the Competent Authorities of the concerned Member States. For each of the independent persons of standing appointed, a replacement shall be chosen, in accordance with the rules for the appointment of independent persons of standing, for cases where independent persons of standing are prevented from performing their duties. If the rules for the appointment of independent persons of standing have not been agreed, they shall be appointed by drawing lots.

Except where the independent persons of standing have been appointed by the Competent Court or national appointing body of the other concerned Member State(s),[38] the IRA may reject the appointment of an independent person for any reason agreed in advance with the concerned Competent Authorities or for one of the following reasons:

- that person belongs to one of the tax administrations concerned or performs functions on behalf of one of those administrations or has been in that situation at any time during the preceding three years;
- at any time during the last five years preceding the date of his appointment, that person has or has had a significant holding or voting right or is or has been employed or advised by an Affected Person;
- that person does not offer adequate objectivity for the resolution of the dispute;

37. *See also* Article 16(7) of Directive 2017/1852.
38. According to Article 11(2) of the Decree.

- that person is employed by an undertaking which provides tax advice, or otherwise provides tax advice on a professional basis, or has been in that situation at any time during a period of at least three years before his appointment.

The IRA can require that a person appointed under or his substitute to disclose any interest, relationship or other matter which might affect the independence or impartiality of that person or which might reasonably give rise to a suspicion of bias in the procedure. An independent person who is a member of the Advisory Commission must not, for a period of twelve months from the date of delivery of the decision of the Advisory Commission, be in a situation which would have led a Competent Authority to object to his appointment if he had been in that situation at the time of his appointment to the Advisory Commission.

The representatives of the Competent Authorities and the independent persons appointed shall appoint a chairman from the list of persons of standing provided by the Decree (*see* section E.4. below). Unless otherwise agreed by the representatives of each Competent Authority and the independent persons of standing, the chairman shall be a judge.

E.3. Appointment of the Advisory Commission Made by a Competent Court

Article 11 of the Decree provides for the rules relating to the appointment of the Advisory Commission by a Competent Court where the Competent Authorities of the Member States involved failed to timely set up the said Commission.

Indeed, in case the Advisory Commission was not set up within 120 days from the request,[39] the Affected Party can file an appeal to the President of the Regional Tax Court of Lazio to request the establishment of the said Commission.

If the IRA has not appointed at least one independent person and one replacement, the Affected Person can appeal to the Regional Tax Court of Lazio for the appointment of the independent person and his/her replacement from the list referred to in Article 12 (*see* section E.4. below).

Where the IRA and the Competent Authorities of all the other Member States involved have failed to appoint two independent persons included in the list referred to in Article 12, the Affected Person may appeal to the Regional Tax Court of Lazio and to Competent Court of the other Member State(s) to appoint two independent persons included in the list referred to in Article 12. These independent persons shall appoint the President by drawing lots from the list of independent persons in accordance with Article 10(4) of the Decree.

The Affected Persons shall submit their request for the appointment of independent persons of standing and their replacement to each of their respective States of residence if more than one Affected Person is involved in the procedure, or to the

39. Pursuant to Article 10(1) of the Decree.

Member State(s) whose Competent Authorities have failed to appoint at least one independent person and one replacement if only one Affected Person is involved.

All the above-mentioned requests related to the appointment of independent persons of the Advisory Commission shall be submitted only after the expiry of the 120-day period referred to in Article 10(1) of the Decree and within thirty days of the expiry of that period.

The Regional Tax Court of Lazio shall take a decision on the appointment of the independent persons and their replacements and notify the applicant thereof. The decision of Regional Tax Court of Lazio could be appealed under Article 28 of Decree 546/1992. The Regional Tax Court of Lazio shall inform the IRA, which shall promptly inform the Competent Authority of the other concerned Member State(s).

The procedure for the appointment of independent persons of standing and their substitutes is governed by the rules set out in Title VIII of Section IV of the Italian Code of Civil Procedure (i.e., arbitration functioning rules).

E.4. List of the Independent Persons of Standing

Article 12 of the Decree clarifies that the list of independent persons of standing shall consist of all independent persons appointed by the Member States.

For the purposes of the above-mentioned list, the Italian Ministry of the Economy and Finance shall appoint at least three persons who are competent and independent and able to operate with impartiality and integrity, considering the academic and professional qualifications of such persons, their skills, their experience and the existence of any conflict of interest. To this end, ordinary judges in service may also be appointed as independent persons, provided that they have been or have been for at least five years judicial officers of legitimacy, with proven experience in the tax field. Ordinary judges are indicated to the Minister of Economy and Finance by the Superior Council of the Judiciary (‘*Consiglio Superiore della Magistratura*’).

A further decree of the Minister for the Economy and Finance will establish the criteria and procedures for the composition of the list of independent persons appointed by Italy, as well as their removal from that list.

E.5. Alternative Dispute Resolution Commission

In accordance with Directive 2017/1852, Article 13 provides that the Competent Authorities of the concerned Member States can agree, instead of the Advisory Commission, to establish an Alternative Dispute Resolution Commission which shall have the purpose to give an opinion on how to resolve the question in dispute.

The Competent Authorities of the Member States can also agree to establish an Alternative Dispute Resolution Commission of a permanent nature (i.e., a standing Commission).

Without prejudice of the rules related to the independence of its members laid down by the Decree,[40] which are applicable also for the purposes of the Alternative Dispute Resolution Commission, this latter may differ in terms of composition and form from the Advisory Commission.

Instead of a dispute resolution based on an independent opinion as provided for by the Advisory Commission, the Alternative Dispute Resolution Commission can apply different dispute resolution procedures or techniques to resolve the question in dispute in a binding manner. To this end, the Competent Authorities of the concerned Member States can agree on any other type of dispute resolution procedure to be applied by the Alternative Dispute Resolution Commission, including the so-called final offer arbitration process.[41]

The Competent Authorities of the concerned Member States shall decide on the functioning rules (*see* section F.1.), including also how to allocate the procedure costs[42] and provide information related to the question in dispute to the Alternative Dispute Resolution Commission.[43]

F. COMMON PROCEDURAL PROVISIONS

F.1. Rules of Functioning for the Advisory Commission or Alternative Dispute Resolution Commission

Pursuant to Article 14 of the Decree, the Competent Authorities of the concerned Member States shall define the functioning rules of the Advisory Commission or the Alternative Dispute Resolution Commission. In particular, the functioning rules shall include:

- the description and characteristics of the question in dispute;
- the terms of reference on which the Competent Authorities of the Member States agree as regards the legal and factual questions to be resolved;
- the form of the dispute resolution body (i.e., the Advisory Commission or the Alternative Dispute Resolution Commission), as well as the type of procedure for alternative dispute resolution (e.g., the final offer arbitration process), where the procedure differs from the one related to the 'independent opinion' that would be provided by an Advisory Commission;
- the timeline of the MAP;
- the composition of the Advisory Commission or the Alternative Dispute Resolution Commission (including the number and names of its members,

40. *See* paras 5 and 6 of Article 10 of the Decree.
41. According to the 'final offer' arbitration process, both parties (i.e., the Competent Authorities) shall submit their final offer to the Alternative Dispute Resolution Commission, which may choose any offer upon its discretion. In this respect, the Alternative Dispute Resolution Commission must select the position of one of the Competent Authority and cannot take a compromise position.
42. Article 15 of the Decree (*see* section F.2.).
43. Paras 10 and 11 of Article 16 of the Decree (*see* section F.3.).

indication of their competence and qualifications and disclosure of their conflicts of interest);
- the rules governing the participation of the Affected Person and third parties in the procedure, the exchange of briefs, information and evidence, costs, the type of dispute resolution procedure to be used and other relevant procedural or organizational matters;
- the logistical aspects of the procedure carried out by the Advisory Commission and the manner according to which it will disclose its position.

Where an Advisory Commission is set up to give an opinion when the complaint has been rejected,[44] only the following aspects shall be defined by the Competent Authorities:

- the description and characteristics of the question in dispute;
- the timeline of the MAP;
- the composition of the Advisory Commission or the Alternative Dispute Resolution Commission (including the number and names of its members, indication of their competence and qualifications and disclosure of their conflicts of interest);
- the rules governing the participation of the Affected Person and third parties in the procedure, the exchange of briefs, information and evidence, costs, the type of dispute resolution procedure to be used and other relevant procedural or organizational matters.

Within 120 days from the receipt of the request submitted by the Affected Person to establish the Advisory Commission appointment, the IRA shall communicate to the Affected Person:

- the functioning rules of the Advisory Commission or Alternative Dispute Resolution Commission;
- the deadline by which the opinion on the resolution of the question in dispute shall be adopted;
- the references of the applicable domestic law provisions of the Member States and the applicable agreements or conventions.

Where the Competent Authorities have not notified the functioning rules to the Affected Persons, the independent persons of standing and the chairman shall complete the rules of functioning in accordance with the standard rules established by the EU Commission and shall transmit them to the Affected Persons within two weeks from the date on which the Advisory Commission or the Alternative Dispute Resolution Commission was set up. If the independent persons of standing and the chairman have not reached an agreement with regard to the functioning rules or have not notified them to the Affected Person, this latter can refer the matter to the President of the

44. *See* Article 9(3)(a) and (b) of the Decree.

Regional Tax Court of Lazio or to the Competent Court of one of the other concerned Member States in order to obtain the implementation of the functioning rules.

F.2. Costs of the MAP

Pursuant to Article 15 of the Decree, unless the concerned Member States of the Competent Authorities have agreed otherwise, the following costs shall be shared equally between the Member States:

- expenditure incurred by independent persons of standing, which must be equivalent to the average of the amount usually reimbursed to senior officials of the concerned Member States; and
- the fees of the independent persons, where applicable, which are to be limited to EUR 1,000 per person per day for every day on which the Advisory Commission or Alternative Dispute Resolution Commission meets.

However, the said costs shall be borne by the Affected Person if it has submitted:

- a written notice of withdrawal of the MAP application; or
- a request for setting up the Advisory Commission following a rejection of the complaint to start a MAP on the grounds of Article 6(2) of the Decree (*see* section D.1. above) and the Advisory Commission decides that the Competent Authorities have rightly rejected the request with prior agreement of the Competent Authorities of the concerned Member States.

Lastly, it is specified that the costs incurred by the Affected Person shall not be borne by the concerned Member States.

F.3. Resolution of the Controversy by the Advisory Commission

Article 16 of the Decree set forth the rules concerning the resolution of the controversy by the Advisory Commission.

Where the complaint filed by the Affected Person has been rejected by: (i) only one Competent Authority[45] or (ii) all the Competent Authorities but a Competent Court has ruled in favour of the Affected Person against the rejection of the complaint,[46] the Advisory Commission shall take a decision on acceptance of the request to start a MAP within six months from the set-up of that Commission and shall notify its decision to the Competent Authorities of the involved Member States within thirty days from the date on which a decision has been taken.

If the Commission confirms that the Affected Person has provided all the information required and that the question in dispute meets the conditions requested by Articles 3 and 5(2) of the Decree, the MAP shall be initiated at the request of one of

45. *See* Article 9(3)(a) of the Decree.
46. *See* Article 9(3)(b) of the Decree.

the concerned Competent Authorities. The Competent Authority shall notify the said request to the Advisory Commission, to the other Competent Authorities involved and to the Affected Person. In this case, the period within which the Competent Authorities are required to resolve the question in dispute (i.e., two years or three years in case of request for extension) starts from the notification date of the decision adopted by the Commission on the acceptance of the request to open the MAP.

If none of the Competent Authorities has requested to start the MAP within sixty days from the notification date of the Commission decision, this latter shall issue an opinion on how to resolve the question in dispute. The opinion shall be issued within six months from the date on which the Commission has been set up. For this purpose, the Commission shall be deemed to have been set up on the date on which the said sixty-day period has expired.

In cases where all the Competent Authorities rejected the complaint, but a Competent Court ruled in favour of the Affected Person, the Advisory Commission shall issue an opinion on how to resolve the question in dispute. As above, the opinion shall be issued within six months from the date on which the Commission has been set up and the Commission shall be deemed to have been set up on the date on which the said sixty-day period has expired.

Where the Competent Authorities have failed to reach an agreement during the MAP phase within two years from the date of the last notification of the decision accepting the complaint by one of the Member States (or three years in case of extension), the Advisory Commission issues an independent opinion within six months from the date on which the Advisory Commission has been set up.

Where the Advisory Commission considers that the delivery of an opinion on the question in dispute requires more than six months, that period can be extended by three months. In that case, it shall inform the Competent Authorities of the Member States involved and the Affected Persons of that extension.

The Advisory Commission shall ground their respective opinions on the provisions of the applicable Tax Treaty or the Arbitration Convention and on any applicable domestic law rules. The opinion is adopted by the Commission through a simple majority of its members. If no majority can be reached, the chairman vote shall determine the final opinion. The chairperson shall notify the Competent Authorities of the opinion rendered by the Commission.

In any case, the Advisory Commission shall deliver its opinions in writing.

If a final judgment ('*sentenza passata in giudicato*') by a Tax Court has been issued by a Tax Court with reference to the question in dispute after the filing by the Affected Person of the request to set up the Advisory Commission but before that the Advisory Commission has notified its opinion to the IRA, this latter shall inform the other Competent Authorities of the involved Member States and the Commission which rendered the opinion that, as a consequence of the domestic judgment, the dispute resolution procedure is terminated.[47]

47. *See also* Article 16(4)(c) of Directive 2017/1852.

The above applies also in case of judgment rendered by a Tax Court following a judicial settlement pursuant to Articles 48 and 48-*bis* of Decree 546/1992.

The Affected Persons can, with the agreement of the Competent Authorities, provide the Advisory Commission with any information, evidence or documents which could be relevant to the decision or opinion. Affected Persons and Competent Authorities shall provide the information, evidence or documents at the request of the Advisory Commission.

However, the Competent Authorities may refuse to provide information to that Commission when:

- obtaining the information requires carrying out administrative measures that are against domestic law;
- the information cannot be obtained under the domestic law of the Member State concerned;
- the information concerns trade secrets, business secrets, industrial secrets, professional secrets or trade processes;
- the disclosure of the information is contrary to public policy;

At the request of the Advisory Commission, Affected Persons shall appear or be represented before the aforesaid Commission. The Affected Persons can also, at their request and with the agreement of the Competent Authorities of the Member States, appear or be represented before the Advisory Commission.

Pursuant to Article 17, the independent persons of standing and any other members of the Advisory Commission or the Alternative Dispute Resolution Commission appointed by the Italian Competent Authority shall be subject to the obligations of professionals and professional secrecy provided by domestic laws, regulations or administrative provisions in relation to the information they receive as members of those Commissions. In the event of a breach of these obligations, the penalties provided for by domestic law shall apply.

Affected Persons and, where appropriate, their representatives shall undertake to treat in confidence the information and documents they receive during the dispute resolution procedures. To this end, they shall make a declaration to the Competent Authorities of the involved Member States if requested in the course of those procedures. In the event of a breach of confidentiality obligations, regarding the aforementioned persons, resident for tax purposes in the territory of the State, unless the act constitutes a crime, a fine of a sum from EUR 25,000 to EUR 125,000 shall apply according to the procedures and terms set forth in Law No. 689 of 24 November 1981.

F.4. Decision of the Competent Authorities Following the Dispute Resolution Procedure

Under Article 18, the IRA and the other Competent Authorities concerned shall agree on how to resolve the question in dispute within six months from the notification of the opinion of the Advisory Commission or the Alternative Dispute Resolution Commission.

The IRA and the other Competent Authorities concerned can adopt a decision that does not take into consideration the opinion of the Advisory Commission or the Alternative Dispute Resolution Commission. However, if they cannot agree on how to resolve the question in dispute, the concerned Competent Authorities shall be bound by that opinion.

In the event that the question in dispute arising from an audit carried out by the IRA has been already settled in accordance with the domestic law provisions in force before the issuance of a decision under the dispute resolution procedure, the IRA redetermines the amount of the taxes due. On this important matter, however, the Decree does not clarify how the IRA should proceed from a procedural standpoint, including the effect on penalties and interest paid under the domestic settlement (*see* section F.5. below).

In any case, the decision taken by the competent tax authorities will not constitute a precedent.

The IRA shall inform the Affected Person of the decision adopted within the dispute resolution procedure regarding the question in dispute within thirty days of the date on which that decision was taken. If the IRA has not communicated its decision on the question in dispute within thirty days, the Affected Person can file an appeal with the Tax Court in accordance with the procedure laid down in Article 70 of Decree 546/1992 (i.e., judgment to enforce) in order to obtain that the decision be properly communicated.

If, after the notification of the opinion of the Advisory Commission or the Alternative Dispute Resolution Commission, a final judgment ('*sentenza passata in giudicato*') given by a Tax Court or a decision which has been rendered by Tax Court following the judicial settlement pursuant to Articles 48 and 48-*bis* of Legislative Decree 546/1992 intervenes, the IRA shall inform the Competent Authorities of the other Member States concerned and the said Commissions of the effects of that decision terminating the dispute resolution procedure.

F.5. Enforcement of Decisions Taken under the MAP or Dispute Resolution Procedures

Article 19 sets forth the rules applicable to enforce the decisions adopted by the Competent Authorities under the MAP[48] (*see* section D.2. above) or a dispute resolution procedure[49] (*see* section F.4. above).

Through the implementation of a decision taken under a MAP or a dispute resolution procedure, which results in a change of the taxable income or of the taxes due, the IRA shall provide for the refund or cancellation of undue taxes or, conversely, execute the collection of the amounts due. To this end, it should be noted that the IRA should reimburse also interest paid by the Affected Person (if any) even if Article 19(1) does not expressly provide for it.

48. Article 7 of the Decree.
49. Article 18 of the Decree.

In this respect, by way of derogation from the ordinary statute of limitations,[50] for the purposes of implementing the decisions deriving from a MAP or a dispute resolution procedure, the ordinary statutes of limitations shall be doubled.

Considering the different phases of a MAP to which the arbitration phase may follow under a dispute resolution procedure, in practice the mere doubling of the terms may not be sufficient to ensure that Affected Persons are able to resolve the question in dispute.

In this respect, the following 'real life' example may be interesting: an Affected Person has received a notice of assessment for the year 2018 served in 2024.[51] In accordance with Article 3(1) of the Decree, that person applies for a MAP in 2027 with the consequent failure of the Competent Authorities to reach an agreement in 2030 (the IRA used the one-year extension of the former deadline of Article 7(2) of the Decree).

Following a request of the Affected Person to set up the Advisory Commission to settle the question in dispute, the opinion is given in 2031 and the final agreement between the Competent Authorities is also given in 2031. In this case, if the statute of limitations were doubled, the initial complaint in respect of the year 2018 would be definitively closed.

However, Article 15 of the Directive provides that: '(...) the final decision shall be implemented under the national law of the Member States concerned which as a result of the final decision shall amend their taxation, irrespective of any time limits prescribed by the national law'. Therefore, one could argue that a decision taken by the Competent Authorities in the context of a procedure governed by the Decree should be implemented even beyond the doubling of the ordinary statute of limitations.

Any higher taxes due as a result of the recalculation pursuant to the decision taken under a MAP[52] or a dispute resolution procedure[53] shall be subject to:

- penalties, except where the higher taxes due have already been settled in accordance with the provisions of domestic law (e.g., through the '*accertamento con adesione*' procedure), and
- interest from the date of the decision taken under a MAP or a dispute resolution procedure.

Conversely, only in the event that the original tax claim put forward by the IRA has been fully annulled, the refund of the penalties is allowed upon presentation of a special application by the Affected Person.

In the opinion of the author, both the application of penalties on any higher taxes due according to the MAP or a dispute resolution procedure and the limitation applicable to the refund of penalties only where the claim underlying the question in

50. According to Article 43 of Presidential Decree No. 600 of 29 September 1973, the deadline is represented by 31 December of the fifth year following the year in which the relevant income tax return has been filed. In case of omitted tax return, the term is represented by 31 December of the seventh year following the year in which the income tax return should have been filed.
51. Within 31 December of the fifth year (2024) following the year in which the relevant income tax return has been filed (2019 for the year 2018).
52. Article 7(6) of the Decree.
53. Article 18 of the Decree.

dispute is totally annulled do not seem to be fully in line with the goals of Directive 2017/1852, considering that penalties would be applicable in any case to any higher taxes following an agreement, except in case of a previous domestic settlement procedure.

Indeed, the application of penalties in case of higher taxes due, as recalculated under the agreement reached by the Competent Authorities, may somehow reduce the appeal of starting a MAP under the Decree.

Moreover, the refund of penalties not due under the agreement should always be possible and not only in case the claim underlying the question in dispute is totally cancelled. That said, the refund of the penalties should be executed by the IRA together with undue taxes and interest, without the need for the Affected Person to submit an appropriate application for claiming back the penalties previously paid.

In any case, the Decree clarifies that, where the Affected Person settled with the IRA the question in dispute in accordance with the domestic law provisions in force, the sums provisionally collected by the IRA shall be taken into account.

A decision deriving from a MAP or a dispute resolution procedure shall be implemented on condition that the Affected Person accepts that decision in writing within sixty days from the notification and at the same time renounces to other legal remedies (e.g., appeal before a Tax Court).

Where there is a dispute pending at domestic level, for the purposes of implementing the decision, the Affected Person must provide evidence, within sixty days from the date on which the decision of the Competent Authorities has been notified, that a withdrawal, even if partial, of the judicial proceedings and/or any other form of appeal has been filed to the Tax Court with respect to the issues covered by the MAP or the dispute resolution procedure. To this end, the Decree does not provide that, in the event of withdrawal from the judicial proceedings, the costs of the proceedings should be compensated between the parties (while the ordinary rule, indeed, puts expenses at the charge of the succumbent party).

The decisions adopted by the Competent Authorities in the context of a MAP or a dispute resolution procedure shall constitute legal title for the collection of the sums due by the Affected Person and for the payment of the amounts to be refunded.

Article 19(7) of the Decree provides that all the above shall apply also with reference to refund or collection of taxes which have become final according to domestic law provisions.

If the decision adopted by the Competent Authorities in the context of a MAP or a dispute resolution procedure is not implemented by the IRA, the Affected Person can appeal to the Tax Court, in accordance with the procedure laid down in Article 70 of Decree 546/1992, to request the enforcement of that decision by a so-called *commissario ad acta*.

The decision adopted by the Competent Authorities in the context of a dispute resolution procedure shall not be implemented where, following an appeal by the Affected Person, the Regional Tax Court of Lazio rules that the independent persons appointed for the purposes of the dispute resolution procedure at stake did not have the independence requirements laid down by Article 10 of the Decree (*see* section E.2. above) at the moment of the appointment or when the decision was rendered.

F.6. Publicity

The Competent Authorities can agree to publish and disclose in full the decisions taken in the context of a dispute resolution procedure pursuant to Article 18 of the Decree (*see* section F.4.), subject to the consent of each of the Affected Persons.

If the Competent Authorities involved or the Affected Persons did not give their consent to the full publication of a decision, the Competent Authorities shall publish a summary of the decision reporting:

- a description of the issue;
- the subject matter;
- the date;
- the tax periods involved;
- the legal basis;
- the industry of reference;
- a short description of the final outcome; and
- the arbitration process applied.

Before the publication, the IRA shall provide the Affected Person with the information listed above. Within sixty days of receipt of the information, the Affected Person may request the IRA not to disclose information relating to any trade, business, industrial or professional secret or trade process, or that is contrary to public policy.

The IRA shall promptly notify the EU Commission of the information to be published under Article 20 of the Decree.

F.7. Miscellaneous

According to Article 21 of the Decree, the information required by the IRA in the context of the MAP shall be subject to and governed by the provisions of domestic law in force on the protection of personal data, trade, business, industrial, professional secrets or trade process.

The circumstance that the question in dispute is under review in the context of a MAP or a dispute resolution procedure shall not prevent per se the establishment or continuance, according to domestic law, of judicial proceedings or administrative procedures which may give rise to the application of penalties relating to the same question in dispute.

In the event that judicial or administrative proceedings were started under domestic law and that gave rise to the application of penalties for one of the criminal violations referred to in Title II of Legislative Decree No. 74 of 10 March 2000[54] (e.g., unfaithful tax return) and such proceedings were conducted simultaneously with a MAP or a dispute resolution procedure, the IRA can suspend the said procedures from

54. *See also* section E.1.

the date of acceptance of the complaint to start a MAP until the date of the final outcome of the judicial or administrative proceedings.[55]

If for any reason a question in dispute becomes no longer at stake, the MAP or the dispute resolution procedure shall be terminated with immediate effect. The IRA shall inform the Affected Persons without delay, stating the general reasons that terminated the procedures.

F.8. Amendments to Other Domestic Law Provisions

The Decree provides that the decision rejecting the complaint to open a MAP submitted pursuant to, alternatively, Directive 2017/1852, a Tax Treaty or the Arbitration Convention can be appealed by the taxpayer before a Tax Court.[56]

Moreover, the Decree provides also that the domestic proceedings before a Tax Court shall be suspended:

- at the request of both the Affected Person and the IRA, if a complaint according to a Tax Treaty or the Arbitration Convention[57] has been filed;
- at the sole Affected Person's request, where a request for the opening of a MAP under Directive 2017/1852 has been filed.

The Decree provides also that, if a MAP request has been submitted pursuant to Directive 2017/1852, the suspension of the proceedings under Article 39(1-*ter*)(b) shall entail the suspension of the provisional collection of one-third of the taxes claimed by the IRA. In this case, the suspension of the collection shall be carried out by the competent local office of the IRA and shall operate until the conclusion of the procedures under Directive 2017/1852.

Finally, it is now provided that the downward corresponding adjustment of the taxable income, under Article 31-*quater*(1)(a) of Presidential Decree No. 600 of 29 September 1973, shall be performed by following the conclusion of the procedures, among others,[58] laid down by Directive 2017/1852.

F.9. Implementation Rules

Article 23 of the Decree states that the procedural rules (e.g., request for the refund of the penalties not due under Article 19(3) of the Decree) for implementing the Decree shall be established through one or more Acts of the IRA Director.

55. *See also* Article 16(6) of Directive 2017/1852.
56. *See* Article 19(1) of Decree 546/1992.
57. *See* Article 39(1-*ter*) of Decree 546/1992.
58. The provision includes MAP under the Tax Treaties and the Arbitration Convention.

G. SPECIAL PROVISIONS

G.1. Provision for the Budget of the State

For the implementation of Directive 2017/1852, an overall cost of EUR 893,750, starting from 2020, has been estimated.

However, it should be noted that the domestic tax framework during the last years has changed and now taxpayers are more interested in the instruments for the resolution of international tax controversy or for reducing operational tax risks (e.g., bilateral and unilateral advance pricing agreements).

In light of the increasing appeal of the resolution of international controversy through MAPs, the IRA should be provided with the necessary additional financial resources in terms of personnel to effectively tackle and deal with the increasing number of applications, also considering that, thanks to Directive 2017/1852, the complaints could significantly grow in the next few years.

H. FINAL AND TRANSITORY PROVISIONS

H.1. Entry into Force

The provisions of Decree entered into force on 25 June 2020 and shall apply to complaints to start a MAP submitted as from 1 July 2019 on questions in dispute relating to income or capital issues which refer to the tax period beginning on 1 January 2018.

In spite of the last period of Article 23 of Directive 2017/1852, Article 25 of the Decree does not provide the faculty for the IRA to agree with the other Competent Authorities involved in the context of a MAP or a dispute resolution procedure to apply Directive 2017/1852 with regard to any complaints that were submitted prior to 1 July 2019 or to earlier tax periods than those beginning on 1 January 2018.

CHAPTER 8

Luxembourg

Alain Goebel

A. IMPLEMENTING MEASURES ADOPTED BY LUXEMBOURG WITH RESPECT TO DIRECTIVE 2017/1852

Directive 2017/1852 has been transposed in Luxembourg by the law dated 20 December 2019[1] (hereinafter the 'Law of 20 December 2019'). The Law closely follows Directive 2017/1852 and only adjusts the text by referring to the Luxembourg domestic elements where required. It is noteworthy to mention that the MAP provided by the Tax Treaties is ruled by a Circular Letter L.G. - Conv. D.I. No. 60 of 28 August 2017. These rules are quite similar to the ones established by the Law of 20 December 2019 that applies only to disputes between Luxemburg and one or more other Member States, but fail to oblige the Contracting States to settle the dispute.

B. GENERAL PROVISION

B.1. Subject Matter and Scope

The Law of 20 December 2019 lays down rules to resolve disputes between Luxemburg and one or more other Member States when these disputes arise from the interpretation and application of agreements and conventions concluded between Luxembourg and the other Member State(s) that provide for the elimination of double taxation of income and, where applicable, capital (hereinafter the 'Agreements'). It also lays down the rights and obligations of the affected persons when such disputes arise.

1. *Loi du 20 décembre 2019 instaurant un mécanisme de règlement des différends fiscaux*, Mémorial A No. 890, available at http://www.scl.lu/eli/etat/leg/loi/2019/12/20/a890/jo.

It is noteworthy to mention that the concept of double taxation is quite wide and covers three different situations, namely: (i) the case of an additional tax charge, (ii) the case of an increase of the tax charge and (iii) the case of a reduction or cancellation of losses that could have been used to offset taxable profits.[2] Also, both situations of economic[3] and judicial[4] double taxation are included.[5]

During the adoption process of the Law of 20 December 2019, the parliamentary works highlighted that only disputes between Member States were within the scope of the Law of 20 December 2019, which in 2019 raised the question of how the United Kingdom should be treated, given its imminent exit from the EU.[6] Although no response could be given from a Luxembourg perspective only, it was suggested that the question should be solved by amending the relevant provisions under the double tax treaty concluded between Luxembourg and the United Kingdom.[7] This solution seems to make sense, given that Luxembourg would not be in a position to take a unilateral decision on the application of the Directive without the consensus of the other Member States. Ultimately, the question could be brought before the ECJ in due time.

C. COMPLAINT TO START A MAP

C.1. Filing of a Complaint to Start a MAP

The procedure starts with a complaint to be filed by the affected person on the question in dispute to the competent Luxemburg authority – which is the *Administration des contributions directes* (hereinafter the 'ACD') – and the competent tax authority of the other Member State(s) in dispute (hereinafter the 'Competent Authorities'), requesting the resolution thereof.[8]

The Law of 20 December 2019 provides that the complaint must be submitted within three years from the receipt of the first notification of the action resulting in, or that will result in, the question in dispute, regardless of whether the affected person has recourse to the remedies available under the domestic law or of the law of any other Member State(s) concerned.

The affected person must simultaneously submit the complaint with the same information to all tax authorities in dispute and indicating which other Member State(s) is/are concerned. The increase of the administrative burden on the taxpayer due to a simultaneous filing with all the tax authorities concerned has been justified by the fact that it avoids any asymmetry of information between the various authorities

2. *See* parliamentary works No. 7431, p. 15.
3. That is, two different taxpayers are subject to tax on the same income or capital, e.g. in case of a unilateral transfer pricing adjustment.
4. That is, the same taxpayer is subject to tax in two States on the same income, e.g. in case of a divergent application of a double tax treaties by the tax authorities of the relevant States or if no double tax treaty has been concluded between these States.
5. *See* parliamentary works No. 74312, p. 4.
6. *See* parliamentary works No. 74312, p. 3.
7. *See* parliamentary works No. 74319, p. 6.
8. Article 3 of the Law of 20 December 2019.

that handle the complaint.[9] However, this has been criticized given that after a single filing with the ACD, the latter could exchange the relevant information with the foreign tax authorities concerned.[10] Such a regime has further been adopted for individuals and smaller undertakings.[11]

The complaint must be drafted in one of Luxembourg's official languages, i.e. French, German or Luxemburgish (although in practice Luxembourgish is never used for written requests). In case the official language of the other concerned Member State(s) is none of the aforementioned, the complaint may be drafted in English.

The ACD has two months to acknowledge the reception of the complaint and to inform the other Competent Authorities of such acknowledgement and of the language they intend to use for the procedure.

In order for the complaint to be accepted, the affected person has to provide the ACD and the other Competent Authorities with the information listed in Directive 2017/1852. The Law of 20 December 2019 reiterates that list, and the affected person has, in this regard, to provide the following information:

- the name(s), address(es), tax identification number(s) and any other information necessary for identification of the affected person(s) who presented the complaint and of any other person concerned;
- the tax periods concerned;
- details of the relevant facts and circumstances of the case (including details of the structure of the transaction and of the relationship between the affected person and the other parties to the relevant transactions, as well as any facts determined in good faith in a mutually binding agreement between the affected person and the tax administration, where applicable) and more specifically, the nature and the date of the actions giving rise to the question in dispute (including, where applicable, details of same income received in the other Member State and of inclusion of such income in the taxable income in the other Member State, and details of the tax charged or that will be charged in relation to such income in the other Member State), as well as the related amounts in the currencies of the Member States concerned, with a copy of any supporting documents;
- reference to the applicable national rules and to the Agreements; where more than one Agreement is applicable, the affected person making the complaint must specify which Agreement is being interpreted in relation to the relevant question in dispute;
- the following information together with copies of any supporting documents:
  (i) an explanation of why the affected person considers that there is a question in dispute;

9. *See* parliamentary works No. 7431, p. 15.
10. *See* parliamentary works No. 74316, p. 2.
11. *See* section 8 hereinafter.

(ii) the details of any appeals and litigation initiated by the affected person regarding the relevant transactions and of any court decisions concerning the question in dispute;
(iii) a commitment by the affected person to respond as completely and quickly as possible to all appropriate requests made by the ACD and to provide any documentation at the request of the latter;
(iv) a copy of the final tax assessment decision in the form of a final tax assessment notice, tax audit report or other equivalent document leading to the question in dispute and a copy of any other documents issued by the tax authorities with regard to the question in dispute where relevant;
(v) information on any complaint submitted by the affected person under another MAP or under another dispute resolution from an Agreement and an express commitment by the affected person that they will put to an end any other ongoing proceedings under a MAP or a dispute resolution procedure from such Agreement; and

- any specific additional information requested by the ACD that is considered necessary to undertake the substantive consideration of the particular case.

The Law of 20 December 2019, as Directive 2017/1852, states that any such specific additional information may be requested by the ACD or the other Competent Authorities within three months from the receipt of the complaint, and must be provided within three months from the receipt of the request. Other requests for such information may occur during the MAP. Moreover, the Law states that the affected person can invoke applicable laws on trade, business, industrial, professional or trade processes secret.

C.2. Withdraw of a Complaint to Start a MAP

The affected person can withdraw the complaint by presenting a written notification to the ACD and to the other Competent Authorities. This notification will put to an end any dispute resolution procedure engaged with respect to the Law of 20 December 2019. Upon receipt, the ACD must inform the other Competent Authority on the termination of the procedure.

Moreover, the Law of 20 December 2019 states that if the dispute ceases to exist, the procedure engaged by the complaint would immediately come to an end.[12]

D. THE RESOLUTION OF THE QUESTION IN DISPUTE UNDER THE MAP

D.1. Decision of the Competent Authority Concerning the Complaint

The ACD has six months from the receipt of the complaint or from the receipt of specific additional information requested to take a decision upon the acceptance or rejection of

12. Article 3 (11) of the Law of 20 December 2019.

such complaint.[13] Alternatively, the ADC may decide to resolve the dispute unilaterally.

Within this six-month period, the ACD can decide to resolve the dispute on a unilateral basis, without involving the other Competent Authorities. If so, the ACD notifies the other Competent Authorities and the affected person of its decision. This notification puts the procedure to an end.

The ACD may accept or reject the complaint within the six-month period. If the ACD does not take a decision upon the acceptance or rejection of the complaint, the latter will be deemed to be accepted.[14]

If the complaint has been accepted by the ACD and the other Competent Authorities, the MAP will proceed. In case the ACD has accepted the decision, but the Competent Authority of at least one other Member State in dispute rejected the complaint, the Advisory Commission may be seized by the affected person.[15]

The ACD can reject the complaint if:[16]

- the complaint lacks specific additional information requested by the ACD;
- there is no question in dispute; or
- the complaint was not submitted within the three-year period from the receipt of the first notification of the measure that led to the dispute.

The rejection decision must be notified to the affected person within the six-month period previously mentioned.

The affected person possesses two remedies in case of a rejection decision. The first one is regulated by national rules and the second one by a specific provision of Directive 2017/1852 and the Law of 20 December 2019.

D.2. MAP

If the ACD as well as the other Competent Authorities accept the complaint, they must endeavour to resolve the dispute within a period of two years from the latest notification of acceptance of either Competent Authority.[17] The ACD may request to extend the two-year period by one year. If so, the ACD must request it to the other Competent Authorities by written request and with justification.

The outcome could then be that either the ACD or the other Competent Authorities have or have not reached an agreement.

13. Article 3 (5) of the Law of 20 December 2019.
14. Article 5 (2) of the Law of 20 December 2019.
15. Article 6 (1) a) of the Law of 20 December 2019.
16. Article 5 of the Law of 20 December 2019.
17. Article 4 of the Law of 20 December 2019.

D.3. Appeal of the Taxpayer Against the Decision Rejecting the Complaint

If the ACD and the other Competent Authorities reject the complaint, the affected person may introduce an appeal against the ACD's decision at the Luxembourg administrative tribunal.[18] The appeal must include the proof of the rejection decision of the ACD, as well as evidence of the rejection decision of the other Competent Authorities; otherwise the appeal is inadmissible. The decision of the administrative tribunal may be subject to appeal before the Luxembourg administrative court following the domestic procedure. If an appeal before the Luxembourg administrative jurisdictions has been introduced, their decision will be considered by the Advisory Commission when deciding on the admissibility of the complaint.

Second, if at least one of the ACD or the other Competent Authorities has accepted the complaint, the affected person may seize the Advisory Commission.[19] However, if the affected person introduced an appeal before the Luxembourg administrative tribunal, the Advisory Commission cannot be seized if the:

- rejection decision may still be appealed before the administrative court;
- procedure is still pending before the administrative tribunal or the administrative court; or
- rejection decision has been definitely confirmed by the administrative tribunal or the administrative court.

D.4. Termination of the Dispute Resolution Procedure

If an agreement has been reached, such agreement becomes a binding decision that needs to be notified to the affected person. This decision is enforceable by the affected person if the latter accepts the decision and renounces the right to any other remedy.

If proceedings regarding such other remedies have already commenced, the decision becomes binding and enforceable once the affected person has provided evidence to the ACD that actions have been taken to terminate those proceedings. Such evidence must be provided no later than sixty days from the date on which the decision has been notified to the affected person.

If no agreement has been reached within the two or three-year period, the ACD notifies the affected person thereof by indicating the general reasons for the failure to reach agreement. In this case, the affected person may seize the Advisory Commission.

18. Article 5 (3) of the Law of 20 December 2019.
19. Article 6 (1), a) of the Law of 20 December 2019.

E. DISPUTE RESOLUTION PROCEDURE

E.1. Request of Appointment of the Advisory Commission

In disputes under certain circumstances, the affected person may seize the Advisory Commission. However, the ACD, in accordance with the other Competent Authorities, may agree to set up an Alternative Dispute Resolution Commission and to overrule the affected persons' decision.[20]

Upon request of the affected person, the ACD and the other Competent Authorities must set up an Advisory Commission,[21] where:

- the complaint submitted by such affected person was rejected by at least one, but not all of the Competent Authorities concerned; or
- the Competent Authorities concerned had accepted the complaint that was submitted by the affected person but failed to reach an agreement on how to resolve the question in dispute by mutual agreement within the applicable time limit.

However, the affected person can only request the constitution of the Advisory Commission if:

- no appeal can be made;
- no appeal is pending; or
- the affected person has formally renounced the right for appeal.

The request must include a declaration to this effect.

The request must be made in writing, within fifty days from the receipt date of the notification of the rejection of the claim or the notification of the failure to reach agreement or the notification of the decision by the administrative tribunal or the administrative court, as the case may be. The Advisory Commission must be set up no later than 120 days from the date of the receipt of the request. Once the Advisory Commission is set up, its president informs the affected person.

E.2. Appointment of the Advisory Commission

The Advisory Commission is composed of:[22]

- one chair;
- one representative of each Competent Authority concerned. If the ACD and the other Competent Authority agree, the number of such representatives may be increased to two for each Competent Authority;

20. Article 10 (1) of the Law of 20 December 2019.
21. Article 6 of the Law of 20 December 2019.
22. Article 8 of the Law of 20 December 2019.

- one independent person of standing, who shall be appointed by the ACD, as well as the other Competent Authority from the list of 'independent persons of standing'.[23] If the Competent Authorities agree, the number of such persons appointed may be increased to two for each Competent Authority.

The Advisory Commission may be competent in two situations: either to verify whether a complaint is acceptable or to advise on the resolution of the dispute itself.

In the first case, a decision must be made within six months from the date of the set-up of the Advisory Commission. The Advisory Commission notifies its decision to the ACD and to the other Competent Authorities within thirty days from the adoption of the decision. If the Advisory Commission accepts the complaint, the MAP can be requested by the ACD or the other Competent Authorities. In case the ACD requests the engagement of the MAP, it must inform the Advisory Commission, the affected person, as well as the other Competent Authorities. If neither the ACD nor the other Competent Authority has requested the MAP within sixty days, the Advisory Commission shall provide an opinion on how to resolve the dispute. Similarly, when no agreement has been reached following the MAP, the Advisory Commission delivers an opinion on how to resolve the question.

E.3. List of Independent Persons of Standing

The rules of appointment of the 'independent persons of standing' are agreed between the ACD and the other Competent Authorities. Following the same rules as the appointment of the 'independent persons of standing', a substitute is nominated for each independent person in case the latter may not be able to fulfil their functions. When no appointment rules have been agreed upon, the appointment of such persons will be carried out by drawing lots from a list of 'independent persons of standing'. The ACD may object the appointment of any independent person of standing for any reason agreed upon between all Competent Authorities or any following reason:

- that person belongs to or is working on behalf of one of the tax administrations concerned or was in such a situation at any time during the previous two years;

23. The list of 'independent persons of standing' comprises at least three individuals who are competent and independent, and who can act with impartiality and integrity. The 'independent persons of standing' are appointed by the Minister of Finance. The names of the appointed independent persons are notified to the EU Commission, along with complete and up-to-date information regarding those persons' professional and academic background, their competence, their expertise and any conflicts of interest they may have. The notification may specify which of those persons may be appointed as chair. Any change in the list must be notified to the EU Commission without delay. If Luxembourg has reasonable cause to object to an independent person of standing for reasons of lack of independence, it must inform the EU Commission and provide appropriate evidence to support their concern. If an *independent person of standing* appointed by Luxembourg is subject to an objection from another Member State, the Minister of Finance, after receiving the notification of the objection, will, within six months take all necessary measures to investigate this complaint and will decide whether to retain or remove that person from the list. The Minister of Finance notifies the EU Commission without delay.

- that person has, or has had, a material holding in or voting right in or is or has been an employee of or adviser, at any time during the last five years prior to the date of his appointment, to any affected person concerned;
- that person does not offer a sufficient guarantee of objectivity for the settlement of the dispute or disputes to be decided;
- that person is an employee with an enterprise that provides tax advice or otherwise gives tax advice on a professional basis, or was in such a situation at any time during a period of at least three years prior to the date of his appointment.

However, the ACD cannot object to the appointment of an independent person of standing who was appointed by order of the president of the Luxembourg district court or, as the case may be, by the Court of Appeal,[24] or by any competent court or national appointing body of the other Member States in dispute. It has to be noted that the competence of the judicial courts (i.e., the Luxembourg district court or the Court of Appeal) as opposed to the administrative courts (administrative tribunal and administrative court) is justified by the fact that the appointment of an independent person of standing is not per se a tax question and hence not of the competence of the administrative courts.[25]

When appointed, the independent person of standing and their substitute must disclose any interest, relationship or any other matter that is likely to affect that person's independence or impartiality or might reasonably create an appearance of bias in the proceedings. Moreover, the independent person of standing must not be in such situation for 12 months after the decision of the Advisory Commission they were part of. The chair of the Advisory Commission is appointed by the representatives of the other Competent Authorities alongside with the appointed independent persons of standing. Except if agreed otherwise between the ACD and the Competent Authority of the other concerned Member States, the chair is a judge.

E.4. Alternative Dispute Resolution Commission

The ACD may agree with the other Competent Authorities to establish an Alternative Dispute Resolution Commission instead of an Advisory Commission.[26] They can also

24. If the Advisory Commission has not been set up within 120 days from the date of the receipt of the request, or if the ACD did not appoint an *independent person of standing* or a substitute, the Advisory Commission is set up, and the *independent person of standing* is appointed, by order of the president of the Luxembourg district court, upon request of the affected person, the ACD being present or duly called. The same appointment procedure will be held if none of the Competent Authorities appointed an *independent person of standing* and substitute. The affected person must submit the request to appoint the *independent persons of standing* and their substitute to the Competent Authority of the other concerned Member States that did not proceed to the appointment. The affected persons may submit their referral at the end of the 120-day period, and until 30 days after. The order of the Luxembourg district court to reject the set-up of the Commission or to accept or reject the referral for nomination of independent persons may be subject to an appeal in front of the Court of Appeal.
25. *See* parliamentary works No. 7431, p. 18.
26. Article 10 of the Law of 20 December 2019.

agree to set up this Commission in the form of a committee that is of a permanent nature.

Except for the rules regarding the independence and impartiality of the independent persons, the composition and form of the Alternative Dispute Resolution Commission can differ from those of the Advisory Commission. The main difference between the two commissions (hereinafter the 'Commissions'), apart from their constitution, is that the Alternative Dispute Resolution Commission may apply any dispute resolution processes or technique to solve the question in dispute in a binding manner, provided that such procedure is agreed upon between the ACD and the other Competent Authorities.

Unless provided otherwise by the ACD and the other Competent Authority, the rules of functioning, as well as the rules on information, evidence, and hearings, costs and proceedings of the Advisory Commission also apply to the Alternative Dispute Resolution Commission.

F. COMMON PROCEDURAL PROVISIONS

F.1. Procedural Rules of the Advisory Commission or Alternative Dispute Resolution

The ACD must provide the affected person within 120 days with the following information:[27]

- the rules of functioning for the Advisory Commission;
- the date by which the opinion on the resolution of the question in dispute shall be adopted;
- references to any applicable legal provisions in the national law of the Member States and to any applicable agreements or conventions.

The rules of functioning are signed between the ACD and the other Competent Authorities. The rules provide in particular:

(a) the description and the characteristics of the question in dispute;
(b) the terms of reference on which the ACD and the other Competent Authority agree as regards the legal and factual questions to be resolved;
(c) the form of the dispute resolution body, as well as the type of process for any Alternative Dispute Resolution, if the process differs from the independent opinion process applied by an Advisory Commission;
(d) the time frame for the dispute resolution procedure;
(e) the composition of the Advisory Commission (including the number and names of the members, details of their competence and qualifications, and disclosing any conflicts of interest of the members);

27. Article 11 of the Law of 20 December 2019.

(f) the rules governing the participation of the affected person(s) and third parties in the proceedings, exchanges of memoranda, information and evidence, the costs, the type of dispute resolution process to be used, and any other relevant procedural or organizational matters; and
(g) the logistical arrangements for the Advisory Commission's proceedings and delivery of its opinion.

In case the Advisory Commission is requested to decide on the acceptance of the complaint, only the information of the (a), (d), (e) and (f) is needed in the rules of functioning. In case the rules of functioning are incomplete or were not notified to the affected person, the standard Rules of Functioning from the Examination Procedure provided by Article 5 of Regulation (EU) No 182/2011 apply.

When the ACD has not notified the rules of functioning to the affected person, the independent persons of standing and the chair complete the rules of functioning with the standard Rules of Functioning mentioned above and notify the affected person within two weeks from the set-up of the Advisory Commission.

When the independent persons of standing and the chair failed to reach an agreement on the rules of functioning, or if these rules have not been notified to the affected person, the latter may seize the president of the Luxembourg district court to obtain the notification of the rules of functioning or an order of execution of the above-mentioned standard Rules of Functioning.

F.2. Costs of the MAP

Unless otherwise agreed between the ACD and the other Competent Authority, the following costs are shared equally among the Member States:[28]

(a) the expenses of the independent persons of standing, which are to be an amount equivalent to the average of the usual amount reimbursed to high-ranking civil servants of the Member States concerned; and
(b) the fees of the independent persons, where applicable, which are to be limited to EUR 1,000 per person per day for every day on which the Advisory Commission meets.

The costs that are incurred by the affected person will not be borne by Member State.

Moreover, the cost referred to in (a) and (b) above will be borne by the affected person, if the ACD and the other Competent Authorities agree as such, when:

- the affected person presented a notification of withdraw of the complaint; or
- the Advisory Commission decides that the complaint was rightfully rejected.

28. Article 12 of the Law of 20 December 2019.

F.3. Information, Evidence and Hearings

The affected persons may provide the Advisory Commission with any information, evidence or documents that may be relevant for the decision.[29] Both the affected person and the Competent Authorities must provide any information upon request of the Advisory Commission. However, the ACD may refuse to provide the Advisory Commission with the following information:

- obtaining the information requires carrying out administrative measures that are against Luxembourg domestic law;
- the information cannot be obtained under Luxembourg national law;
- the information concerns trade secrets, business secrets, industrial secrets, professional secrets or trade processes;
- the disclosure of the information is contrary to public policy.

The affected person may, upon request and with the consent of the ACD and the Advisory Commission, appear or be represented before the Advisory Commission.[30] The affected person must appear or be represented upon request of the Advisory Commission.

The independent persons of standing or any other members of the Advisory Commission are subject to professional secrecy rules as provided by Article 458 of Luxembourg Criminal Code and paragraphs 22 and 412 of the Luxembourg General Tax Law (*Abgabenordnung* (AO)) with regards to information received in their capacity as members in the Advisory Commissions.[31] The affected person and, as the case may be, its representative shall undertake to treat any information that they receive during the proceedings of Advisory Commission as secret. They both make a declaration to this effect to the ACD.

F.4. The Opinion of the Advisory Commission

The Advisory Commission delivers its opinion to the ACD no later than six months after the date on which it was set up.[32] When the Advisory Commission accepts a complaint and has to deliver an opinion on how to resolve the dispute because no Competent Authority requested a MAP within the allocated time, the Advisory Commission is deemed to be set up at the end of the delay of sixty days during which the Competent Authorities could have requested for a MAP.[33] The six months period may be extended by three months if the Advisory Commission considers that the question in dispute is such that it would need more than six months. In this case, the Advisory Commission in charge informs the ACD and the other Competent Authorities of the prorogation.

29. Article 13 (1) of the Law of 20 December 2019.
30. Article 13 (2) of the Law of 20 December 2019.
31. Article 13 (3) of the Law of 20 December 2019.
32. Article 14 of the Law of 20 December 2019.
33. Article 6 (2) last paragraph of the Law of 20 December 2019.

The opinion delivered by the Advisory Commission is based upon provisions of the applicable Agreements, as well as upon any national rules.

The Advisory Commissions adopt their opinions by a simple majority of its members. Where a majority cannot be reached, the vote of the chair will determine the final opinion. The chair communicates the opinion of the Advisory Commission in charge to the ACD and to the other Competent Authorities.

F.5. Final Decision of the Competent Authorities

The ACD and the other Competent Authority have six months from the notification of the opinion of the Commissions[34] to agree on how to resolve the question in dispute. The Competent Authorities may deviate from the Commission's opinion; however, if they cannot reach an agreement, they will be bound by the opinion.

The final decision: (i) must be notified to the affected person by the ACD, (ii) is binding for Luxembourg and (iii) does not constitute a precedent. For the decision to be implemented, the affected person has to renounce the right to any domestic remedy within sixty days from the notification of the decision.

If the final decision has not been notified within thirty days from the date in which the decision has been made, the affected person may seize the president of the administrative tribunal to appoint a special commissioner for the notification of the final decision instead of the ACD and at the ACD's expense.[35] The appointment of the special commissioner by the administrative tribunal is not subject to appeal. The special commissioner has a delay fixed by the president of the administrative tribunal and during which he/she must fulfil his/her mission. The special commissioner is chosen among high-ranking civil servants of the Ministry of Finance. As a result of the appointment of the special commissioner, the ACD is no longer in charge of the case. The special commissioner is entitled to a compensation fixed by the president of the administrative tribunal according to the nature and the complexity of the case.

When the final decision has not been implemented by the ACD within three months from the acceptance of the final decision by the affected person, and its renouncing to any national remedies, the affected person may seize the president of the administrative tribunal that will appoint a special commissioner for the implementation of the final decision instead of the ACD and at the ACD's expense.

F.6. Publicity

The Commissions deliver their opinions by writing. An anonymized abstract will be published for all final decisions. However, if the ACD and the other Competent Authority agree, and with the consent of each affected person concerned, the final decisions may be published in their entirety.

34. Article 15 of the Law of 20 December 2019.
35. Article 15 of the Law of 20 December 2019.

The published abstract will contain a description of the issue and the subject matter, the date, the tax periods involved, the legal basis, the industry sector, and a short description of the final outcome. It will also contain a description of the arbitration methodology used.

Before publishing the final decisions the ACD must notify the affected person who then has sixty days to ask the LTA not to publish information concerning trade, business, industrial, professional or trade process secrecy, or that is contrary to public policy. The ACD must also communicate to the EU Commission the information published.

F.7. Interaction with National Proceedings

The Law of 20 December 2019 provides for a series of precisions regarding the interaction with local laws and other proceedings.

Regarding the domestic statute of limitations rules, the Law of 20 December 2019 states that the affected person has always the possibility to use the tax dispute resolution mechanisms provided by the Law of 20 December 2019, even if the administrative measure that gave rise to a question in dispute has become final.[36] The MAP and the final decision are indeed considered as a new fact that entitles the ACD to issue a new tax assessment, even if the statute of limitations period has elapsed. Taxpayers should be aware that this provision may not necessarily be in their favour, since it applies irrespective of whether the final decision results in a lower or higher tax burden for the taxpayer. Also, the facts that gave rise to the dispute may simultaneously be subject to administrative or criminal procedures sanctioned by penalties. Accordingly, taxpayers should consider these risks when initiating the dispute resolution procedure.

Regarding previous domestic proceedings that have been commenced by the affected person before the ACD[37] or the administrative tribunal / court, the delay of three months for the ACD to decide on the admissibility of the complaint as well as the delay of two years for the ACD and the other Competent Authorities to reach an agreement are suspended and only commence from the date on which a judgment delivered in those proceedings has become final or on which those proceedings have otherwise been definitively concluded or where the proceedings have been suspended.

Once the decision of the administrative tribunal or court, as the case may be, is final, the ACD must notify the decision to the other Competent Authorities. This notification implies that:

- the MAP comes to an end at the day of the notification, unless an agreement has been reached before such notification;

36. Article 16 of the Law of 20 December 2019.
37. Under Luxembourg tax law, taxpayers must first file a complaint with the head of the ACD before being able to seize the administrative tribunal. In case the head of the ACD rejects the complaint, taxpayers may seize the administrative tribunal within three months. If no response of the head of the ACD is obtained within six months, taxpayers may seize the administrative tribunal without any time limit.

- the affected person can no longer request an Advisory Commission if the MAP failed to provide an agreement;
- the procedure of either Commission comes to an end if the decision was made after the request for the set-up of such Commissions, but before the Commission in charge could provide an opinion; in this case the ACD informs the other Competent Authorities and the Commission in charge of the effect of the decision.

The submission of the complaint will put to an end any other ongoing proceedings under a MAP or dispute resolution under an Agreement.

The ACD may deny access to the Advisory Commission in cases where penalties were imposed in Luxembourg in relation to the adjusted income or capital for tax fraud[38] wilful default[39] and gross negligence.[40] Where judicial or administrative proceedings were commenced that could potentially lead to such penalties, and these proceedings are being conducted simultaneously with any of the proceedings referred to in Law of 20 December 2019, ACD may suspend the proceedings under the Law of 20 December 2019 as from the date of acceptance of the complaint until the date of the final outcome of those proceedings.

The ACD may also refuse access to the Advisory Commission if it establishes that the dispute does not imply a double taxation issue.

G. SPECIAL PROVISIONS

G.1. Derogation

By way of derogation from the domestic rules on delays, the taxation of the taxpayer is adjusted according to the final decision notified and accepted.

G.2. Special Provisions for Individuals and Smaller Undertakings

The Law of 20 December 2019 foresees certain special provisions for individuals and smaller undertakings, i.e. not a large undertaking and does not form part of a large group:[41] these may submit the complaints, replies to a request for additional information, withdrawals and other requests to the ACD only.[42] The ACD must notify the other Competent Authorities at the same time and within two months from the receipt of such communications. The affected person is then deemed to have submitted the communication to all the Member States concerned as of the date of such notification.

38. As defined by para. 396 AO.
39. As defined by para. 166 AO.
40. As defined by para. 402 AO.
41. Both defined in Directive 2013/34/EU of the European Parliament and of the Council of 26 June 2013 on the annual financial statements, consolidated financial statements and related reports of certain types of undertakings, amending Directive 2006/43/EC of the European Parliament and of the Council and repealing Council Directives 78/660/EEC and 83/349/EEC.
42. Article 17 of the Law of 20 December 2019.

In case the ACD receives specific additional information, it must exchange such information with the other Competent Authorities. It shall be deemed that additional information has been received by all the Member States concerned as at the date of such receipt of information.

H. FINAL AND TRANSITORY PROVISIONS

H.1. Time Limits Applicable to the Appeals

The Law of 20 December 2019 entered in force on 27 December 2019 but applies to any complaint relating to questions of dispute relating to income or capital earned in a tax year commencing on or after 1 January 2018. The ACD and the other Competent Authorities may however agree on a case-by-case basis to apply the provisions of the Law of 20 December 2019 to a complaint submitted before the entry into force of the same law (i.e., Law of 20 December 2019) or relating to questions of dispute relating to income or capital earned in a tax year commencing before 1 January 2018.

H.2. Conclusions

The Law of 20 December 2019 constitutes a fair and accurate transposition of the entire Directive into Luxembourg law. It was largely welcomed as an additional option for taxpayers to solve tax disputed with other Member States, although the length of the procedure has been criticized. Whether or not the dispute resolution mechanisms provided by the Law of 20 December 2019 prove themselves as being efficient in the future seems indeed to be dependent on the reactivity and collaboration of the various tax authorities involved. At least the Law of 20 December 2019 has the merit that the dispute must be resolved at some point in time, which has not been the case previously.

CHAPTER 9

The Netherlands

Mark Van Casteren

A. IMPLEMENTING MEASURES ADOPTED BY THE NETHERLANDS WITH RESPECT TO DIRECTIVE 2017/1852

Directive 2017/1852 was implemented into Dutch law by the Law of 10 July 2019 on the adoption of a legal resolution mechanism to settle tax disputes between Member States[1] (hereinafter the 'Fiscal Arbitration Act').

B. GENERAL PROVISIONS

B.1. Subject Matter and Scope

Article 1 of Directive 2017/1852 describes the subject matter and scope of the Directive. The Fiscal Arbitration Act does not include a separate article on subject matter and scope. As it is clear (from the recitals and official explanation) that the Fiscal Arbitration Act forms the implementation of Directive 2017/1852 in Dutch law, it is also clear that the scope of the Fiscal Arbitration Act is in accordance with the scope of Directive 2017/1852: the Fiscal Arbitration Act provides for rules on a mechanism to resolve disputes between Member States which arise from the interpretation and application of Tax Treaties. It also lays down the rights and obligations of the affected persons when such disputes arise.

Directive 2017/1852 applies to any 'question in dispute'.[2]

1. '*Wet van 10 juli 2019, houdende Invoering van een wettelijk mechanisme ten behoeve van de beslechting van belastinggeschillen tussen lidstaten van de Europese Unie (Wet fiscale arbitrage).*'
2. *See* para. B.2. 'Definitions'.

B.2. Definitions

Article 1.1 of the Fiscal Arbitration Act provides for the following definitions:

- 'Other competent authority': the authority of another involved Member State or the authorities of other involved Member States which has or have been designated as such by the Member State concerned;
- 'Affected person': any person that is a tax resident of a Member State and whose taxation is directly affected by a question in dispute;
- 'Tax act': tax act as meant in Article 2, paragraph 1, part a, of the General Taxes Act;[3]
- 'Double taxation': the imposition of taxes covered by an agreement or convention for the elimination of double taxation, on the same taxable income or capital by two or more Member States, in case such results in an additional tax charge, an increase in tax liabilities, or the cancellation or reduction of losses that could be used to offset taxable profits;
- 'Question in dispute': means the issue which gave rise to the dispute between the Netherlands and the other Member State or other Member States, on the explanation or application of agreements and conventions for the elimination of double taxation on income or capital or on the explanation or application of the Arbitration Convention;
- 'Filing of a complaint': means using the entitlement that an affected person has under this act and Directive 2017/1852/EU to request the resolution of a dispute;
- 'Inspector': means the official appointed as such by ministerial regulation;
- 'Complaint': means a request of an affected person to resolve a dispute;
- 'Our Minister': means Our Minister of Finance;
- 'Directive 2013/34/EU': means Directive 2013/34/EU of the European Parliament and of the Council from 26 June 2013 on the annual financial statements, consolidated financial statements and related reports of certain types of undertakings, amending Directive 2006/43/EC of the European Parliament and of the Council and repealing Council Directives 78/660/EEC and 83/349/EEC;
- 'Preliminary relief judge of the District Court': means the preliminary relief judge as meant in the Code of Civil Procedure.

The Minister of Finance is designated the competent authority for the Netherlands. As such, the Minister of Finance is responsible for all contacts with and meeting all requirements under the Fiscal Arbitration Act and Directive 2017/1852 towards the EU Commission, the other competent authority and the arbitration commission.

Terms not defined in the Fiscal Arbitration Act, unless the context otherwise requires, have the meaning attributed to them by the relevant Tax Treaties applicable on the date of receipt of the first notification of the act that has or may have given rise

3. '*Algemene Wet inzake Rijksbelastingen*'.

to the question in dispute. Absent a definition in the relevant Tax Treaties, undefined terms shall have the meaning given to them at that specific time under the Dutch tax laws. The meaning given to these undefined terms under the Dutch tax laws has preference over the meaning given to these terms under any other laws.

The General Time Limits Act,[4] which provides for generally applicable rules on legal terms when these end on holidays or during weekends, does not apply to the Fiscal Arbitration Act. The specific time limits included in the Fiscal Arbitration Act must be implemented as prescribed by Directive 2017/1852. Directive 2017/1852 does not allow the Netherlands to apply any different time limits in the Fiscal Arbitration Act.

C. COMPLAINT TO START A MAP

C.1. Filing of a Complaint to Start a MAP

While filing a complaint under the Fiscal Arbitration Act, an affected person makes a clear choice: he chooses to use the legal possibility under the Fiscal Arbitration Act and Directive 2017/1852 to resolve a dispute instead of by applying any of the applicable provisions of the relevant Tax Treaty or the Arbitration Convention.

Pursuant to Article 2.1 of the Fiscal Arbitration Act, an affected person is entitled to file a complaint, together with all required data and information, simultaneously with the Minister of Finance (the Dutch competent authority) and the other competent authority. Article 2.7 Fiscal Arbitration Act provides for a simplified procedure for Dutch residents who do not qualify as a large undertaking or form part of a large group, as defined in Directive 2013/34/EU. In that case, the affected person needs to file the complaint with the Dutch competent authority only, instead of with both the Dutch competent authority and the other competent authority. The Dutch competent authority will in that case inform the other competent authority about the complaint and send the other competent authority all data and information, requests for withdrawal and other requests related to the complaint, within two months after the receipt thereof from the affected person. The affected person is deemed to have filed the complaint in such a case at the time that the Dutch competent authority will have informed the other competent authority about the filed complaint. This simplified procedure is implemented to avoid a substantial administrative burden for smaller businesses as a result of using the dispute resolution mechanism as provided for in the Fiscal Arbitration Act.

The complaint shall be submitted within three years from the receipt of the first notification of the action resulting in, or that will result in, the question in dispute, regardless of whether the affected person has recourse to any available remedies. The term of three years is not suspended as a result of filing objections or appeal against the decision on the basis of the tax act (such as a final tax assessment) that causes the question in dispute, or by applying any other domestic legal remedies. From a Dutch perspective, the complaint will in any case be filed in time if it will be filed within three

4. *'Algemene termijnenwet'*.

years from the date of the assessment or, if earlier, the date upon which the tax authorities informed the taxpayer about issuing the assessment (e.g., at the time they substantially motivated their position in a letter to the taxpayer). The Netherlands will try to explain the three-year rule as much as possible in the advantage of the affected person, as the Netherlands want to facilitate the use of the Fiscal Arbitration Act as much as possible.

The complaint, as well as all required data and information, must be stated in the Dutch or English language.

Within two months from the receipt of the complaint, the Dutch competent authority shall:

- acknowledge receipt of the complaint[5] to the affected person and the other competent authority; and
- inform the other competent authority about the preferred language or languages it intends to use for its communications during the relevant proceedings.[6]

The Fiscal Arbitration Act provides that the complaint is only admissible if the affected person making the complaint provides the competent authority and the other competent authority with the information listed in Article 2.2 Fiscal Arbitration Act. This list of required information is slightly more extensive than the list of information as provided for in Article 3, paragraph 3 of Directive 2017/1852. Article 2.2 includes the following nine elements:

(1) the name, address and tax identification number (or functional equivalent thereof) and all other information necessary for the identification of the affected person;
(2) the tax periods concerned and the affected Member States;
(3) details of the relevant facts and circumstances of the case, including the nature and date of the actions giving rise to the question in dispute as well as the relevant amounts, in the currencies of the Member States concerned, together with a copy of any supporting documents;
(4) reference to the applicable domestic legislation and the agreements and conventions as referred to above, including, if more agreements and conventions are applicable, reference to which specific agreement or convention needs to be explained for purposes of the question in dispute: this will then be referred to as the applicable agreement or the applicable convention;
(5) a written statement of the affected person and a copy of any supporting documents in relation to:
    (i) an explanation of why the affected person considers that there is a question in dispute;

5. Article 2.1 (4) Fiscal Arbitration Act.
6. Article 2.1 (5) Fiscal Arbitration Act.

(ii) the details of any appeals and litigation and any other domestic legal actions initiated by the affected person regarding the relevant transactions and any court decision concerning the question in dispute;

(iii) a commitment of the affected person to respond as completely and quickly as possible to all appropriate requests made by the Dutch competent authority and to provide any documentation at the request of the Dutch competent authority.

(6) as appropriate, a copy of the final decision on the tax assessment that gives rise to the question in dispute as included in: (a) the final tax assessment, (b) a tax audit report, or (c) another equivalent document;

(7) as appropriate, a copy of any document provided by the tax authorities with respect to the question in dispute;

(8) as appropriate, all available data and information on any complaints filed by the affected person under other mutual agreement proceedings or other dispute resolution proceedings, together with an explicit confirmation of the affected person that he agrees to stop these proceedings; and

(9) any specific additional information, requested by the Dutch competent authority and the other competent authority that is considered necessary to undertake the substantive consideration of the particular case.

Within three months from the receipt of the complaint, the Dutch competent authority may request any specific additional information that is considered necessary to undertake the substantive consideration of the particular case. Further requests for information may be made during the MAP if the competent authorities consider this necessary. An affected person that receives such request shall reply within three months of receiving the request. The affected person shall send a copy of his reply simultaneously to the Dutch competent authority and the other competent authority.[7]

The Dutch competent authority shall take a decision on the acceptance or rejection of the complaint within six months of the receipt thereof or within six months of the receipt of the specific additional information, whichever is later. The Dutch competent authority shall inform the affected person and the other competent authority of its decision without delay[8] (see also section D below).

Within the period of six months from the receipt of a complaint, or within six months of the receipt of the specific additional information, whichever is later, the Dutch competent authority may decide to resolve the question in dispute on a unilateral basis, without involving the other competent authority. In such case, the Dutch competent authority shall notify the affected person and the other competent authority without delay, following which the proceedings under Directive 2017/1852 shall be terminated.

7. Article 2.3 Fiscal Arbitration Act.
8. Article 2.5(1) Fiscal Arbitration Act.

C.2. Withdrawal of a Complaint to Start a MAP

An affected person can withdraw a complaint submitting a written notification of withdrawal to the Dutch competent authority and the other competent authority, simultaneously. Such notification shall terminate all proceedings under the Fiscal Arbitration Act. If the Dutch competent authority receives a notification of a withdrawal, the Dutch competent authority shall inform the other competent authority about the withdrawal without delay.[9] The affected person who withdraws a complaint can become liable for the costs of the advisory commission.[10]

If for any reason a question in dispute ceases to exist, all proceedings under the Fiscal Arbitration Act shall terminate with immediate effect. In such case, the Dutch competent authority shall inform the affected person about this, together with the general reasons, therefore, without delay.[11]

D. THE RESOLUTION OF THE QUESTION IN DISPUTE UNDER THE MAP

D.1. Decision of the Competent Authority Concerning the Complaint

In accordance with Article 2.5 of the Fiscal Arbitration Act, the Dutch competent authority will reject a complaint (within the six-month period) if there is no question in dispute or if the affected person has not (or not fully) complied with the formal requirements for filing the complaint (i.e., the affected person has not filed the complaint within the period of three years as required by Article 2.1 Fiscal Arbitration Act, the affected person has not submitted all required information in accordance with Articles 2.2 and 2.3 Fiscal Arbitration Act, or the complaint was not filed in either the Dutch or English language).

If the Dutch competent authority rejects the complaint, it will inform the affected person about its decision, including the general reasons for the rejection.

If the Dutch competent authority will not take a decision on the complaint within the required six-month period, the complaint shall be deemed to be accepted.[12]

Article 2.5(1) Fiscal Arbitration Act provides that no appeal is possible against the decision of the Dutch competent authority to accept or reject a complaint. Two important comments should be made in respect of this provision. First of all, it does not seem to be useful that an affected party should be entitled to appeal a decision from the competent authority that a complaint is accepted. If the affected person does not want to pursue the complaint anymore, it can always withdraw it in accordance with Article 2.5(5) Fiscal Arbitration Act.[13] Second, in line with Directive 2017/1852, appeal is

9. Article 2.5(5) Fiscal Arbitration Act.
10. *See* para. F.2. 'Costs of the Advisory Commission' below.
11. Article 2.5(6) Fiscal Arbitration Act.
12. Article 2.5(2) Fiscal Arbitration Act.
13. Although it may in that case become liable for certain costs; *see* para. F.2. 'Costs of the Advisory Commission' below.

possible against a decision by the Dutch competent authority to reject a complaint if the complaint will also have been rejected by the other competent authority.[14] So, Articles 2.5 and 2.6 Fiscal Arbitration Act in combination provide that the decision to reject a complaint by the Dutch competent authority is not open for appeal, unless the complaint is also rejected by the other competent authority. If the latter is the case, the affected person can appeal under the general domestic appeal procedure of the General Taxes Act.[15] In accordance with that domestic procedure, appeal should be filed with the court[16] within six weeks following the receipt of the rejection of the complaint by both the Dutch competent authority and the other competent authority.

If an affected person will appeal against the rejection of the complaint by the Dutch as well as the other competent authority, this will suspend the possibility for the affected person to request the formation of an advisory commission, pending the appeal.

As mentioned in section C of this chapter, an affected person makes a clear choice with filing a complaint under the Fiscal Arbitration Act: he chooses to use the legal possibility under the Fiscal Arbitration Act and Directive 2017/1852 to resolve a dispute instead of the applicable provisions of the relevant Tax Treaty or the Union arbitration convention. The affected person cannot take legal actions under Directive 2017/1852 and the relevant Tax Treaty or the Union arbitration convention simultaneously. Article 2.8 Fiscal Arbitration Act provides that the filing of a complaint with the Dutch competent authority and the other competent authority terminates all other procedures for mutual agreement or dispute resolution which may be pending under the application of an agreement or convention that is explained or applied in relation to the question in dispute. An affected person should therefore consider the consequences of filing a complaint carefully. The termination of all other procedures is obligatory and irreversible: a withdrawal of a complaint will not undo the termination of all other procedures.

D.2. MAP

If the complaint is accepted by both the Dutch competent authority and the other competent authority, they shall endeavour to resolve the question in dispute by mutual agreement within two years, starting from the last notification of a decision of one of the Member States on the acceptance of the complaint.[17] Upon a written and motivated request by the Dutch competent authority or the other competent authority to all other competent authorities of the relevant Member States, this two-year term can be extended by up to one year. As the Netherlands are in favour of a quick and efficient dispute resolution, it was indicated in the legislative procedures that the Netherlands aim not to use this extension possibility.

14. Article 2.6(1) Fiscal Arbitration Act.
15. '*Algemene wet inzake rijksbelastingen*'.
16. '*Fiscale bestuursrechter*'.
17. Article 3.1(2) Fiscal Arbitration Act.

As part of the MAP, the Dutch competent authority can request the affected person for additional data and information which may be relevant for resolving the question in dispute. The affected person will send this information, in Dutch or in English, to the Dutch competent authority and, simultaneously, copy the information to the other competent authority. It was clarified in the Dutch legislative proceedings that the affected person does not have the right to be heard, nor the right to receive the documents which are relevant to the case, in addition to the information and documents he provided himself. The affected person can request to be heard by the advisory commission.

The Dutch competent authority shall, without delay, notify the affected person when it has reached an agreement with the other competent authority on resolving the question in dispute. Together with this notification, the Dutch competent authority will send the affected person a settlement agreement,[18] which includes the binding and enforceable conditions of the agreement to resolve the question in dispute. The settlement agreement in any case includes an explicit confirmation by the affected person that he accepts the decision and waives his rights to any other Dutch legal remedy, where applicable.[19] Where proceedings regarding such other remedies have already commenced, the decision shall only become binding and enforceable once the affected person has provided evidence to the Dutch competent authority that action has been taken to terminate those proceedings. Such evidence shall be provided not later than sixty days from the date on which such decision was notified to the affected person. The settlement agreement that is sent to the affected person can still be amended or adjusted in consultation with the affected person. The affected person can also reject the proposed resolution of the question in dispute and decide not to sign the settlement agreement, but he does not have the right to appeal against the decision to resolve the question in dispute.

If the competent authorities concerned have not reached an agreement on how to resolve the question in dispute within the legal term, the Dutch competent authority shall inform the affected person thereof, indicating the general reasons for the failure to reach agreement.[20]

E. DISPUTE RESOLUTION PROCEDURE

E.1. Request of Appointment of the Advisory Commission

If:

- the complaint submitted by an affected person was rejected by at least one, but not all of the competent authorities of Member States concerned; or
- the competent authorities of the Member States concerned accepted the complaint that was submitted by the affected person but failed to reach an

18. As meant in Article 900, Book 7 of the Dutch Civil Code.
19. Article 3.4(2) Fiscal Arbitration Act.
20. Article 3.1(5) Fiscal Arbitration Act.

agreement on how to resolve the question in dispute by mutual agreement within the legal term,

the affected person can file a written request to the Dutch competent authority and the other competent authority to request that an advisory commission shall be set up by such competent authorities.[21]

For requesting the appointment of the advisory commission, a simplified procedure is available for Dutch residents who do not qualify as a large undertaking or form part of a large group, as defined in Directive 2013/34/EU. This is the same simplified procedure that is available while filing a complaint.[22] Following this simplified procedure, it is sufficient that the affected person will file the request to appoint an advisory commission with the Dutch competent authority only, instead of filing the request with the Dutch competent authority and the other competent authority. In the simplified procedure, the Dutch competent authority will inform the other competent authority about the request and send the other competent authority all data and information, requests for withdrawal and other requests related to the request, within two months after the receipt thereof from the affected person.

The affected person can only request to appoint an advisory commission provided he declares that it is not possible to file objections and appeal against the rejection of the filed complaint under the applicable national rules, and that no such objections or appeal is pending. Or, in case the applicable national rules include the possibility to appeal, the affected person must declare that he has formally waived his right of appeal against the rejection of the filed complaint. The Fiscal Arbitration Act provides that no appeal is possible against the rejection of a filed complaint in the Netherlands, unless the filed complaint is rejected by both the Dutch competent authority and the other competent authority. As a result, the above-mentioned condition will always be met, if the complaint is rejected by the Dutch competent authority only. Consequently, the condition is only relevant if the filed complaint is rejected by both the Dutch and the other competent authority. The reason for this additional condition to apply in that case is that if the affected person would at the same time, while making the request, successfully appeal the Dutch and other competent authority's decisions to reject the filed complaint, and, as a result, both the Dutch and the other competent authority would accept the complaint, they should enter the MAP first.

The affected person shall make the request to appoint an advisory commission in writing, not later than fifty days from the date upon which it is certain that the complaint has been rejected by at least one of the competent authorities and accepted by at least one other competent authority.

The advisory commission shall be set up not later than 120 days from the receipt of such request, and once set up, its chair shall inform the affected person thereof without delay. If the advisory commission is not set up within 120 days or the advisory commission that is set up does not meet the legal composition requirements, the

21. Article 4.1 Fiscal Arbitration Act.
22. Article 2.7 Fiscal Arbitration Act.

affected person can request the preliminary relief judge of the District Court to set up the advisory commission. If both the Dutch competent authority and the other competent authority did not appoint at least one independent person of standing,[23] the affected person can only request the relief judge of the District Court to appoint an independent person of standing for the Dutch competent authority. In order to start this process, the affected person must serve a summons with the Dutch competent authority to set up the advisory commission within 30 days after the expiration of the 120-day term. Directive 2017/1852 does not specifically include the consequences of not meeting this 30-day term. The Fiscal Arbitration Act is very clear on this: if the affected person does not serve summons within this 30-day term, the affected person will be considered inadmissible.

E.2. Appointment of the Advisory Commission

Article 4.3 of the Fiscal Arbitration Act provides that the advisory commission must be composed of:

- a chairman;
- a representative of the Dutch competent authority and a representative of the other competent authority; and
- an independent person of standing appointed by the Dutch competent authority and an independent person of standing appointed by the other competent authority.

The competent authorities may agree to increase the number of their representatives and the number of independent persons of standing to two for each of the competent authorities. The independent persons of standing are appointed from a list containing all independent persons of standing from all the Member States.

According to Article 4.3(4) Fiscal Arbitration Act, the Dutch competent authority shall agree with the other competent authority upon the rules for the appointment of the independent persons of standing (and their substitutes). If the competent authorities do not reach an agreement on the rules for the appointment of the independent persons of standing, they shall be appointed by drawing lots.

The Dutch competent authority and the other competent authority may reject the appointment of an independent person of standing for any reason agreed in advance with the concerned competent authorities or for one of the following reasons:

- that person belongs to one of the tax administrations concerned or performs functions on behalf of one of those administrations or has been in that situation at any time during the preceding three years;
- that person has or has had a large holding or voting right in an affected person at any time during the last five years preceding the date of his appointment;

23. See further in section E.2.

- that person is employed by or an adviser of an affected person, or has been so at any time during the last five years preceding the date of his appointment;
- that person does not offer sufficient guarantee of objectivity for the settlement of the dispute to be decided; or
- that person is employed by an undertaking which provides tax advice, or otherwise provides tax advice on a professional basis, or has been in that situation at any time during a period of at least three years before his appointment.[24]

The Dutch competent authority and the other competent authority can request that a person of standing or his substitute shall disclose information on any interest, relationship or other matter which might affect the independency or impartiality of that person or which might reasonably give rise to a suspicion of bias in the procedure.

Finally, an independent person who is a member of the advisory commission must not, for a period of twelve months from the date of delivery of the decision of the advisory commission, be in a situation which would have led a competent authority to object to his appointment if he had been in that situation at the time of his appointment to the advisory commission.[25]

The representatives of the competent authorities and the independent persons of standing shall appoint a chairman from the list of persons of standing provided by Article 4(4) Fiscal Arbitration Act. Article 4.3(8) Fiscal Arbitration Act provides that the chairman is a judge, unless otherwise agreed upon by the representatives of the competent authorities and the independent persons of standing. In the official Dutch explanation to the Fiscal Arbitration Act, it is explained that the representatives of the Dutch competent authority will aim to appoint a tax judge as chairman, because of the possibly complex tax issues that may be involved in settling the question in dispute.

E.3. List of Independent Persons of Standing

In accordance with Article 4.4 Fiscal Arbitration Act, the Dutch competent authority will appoint at least three persons who are qualified as well as independent and are capable of acting impartially and with integrity. The Dutch competent authority will aim to include at least one fiscal judge, who may also act as chair.

The Dutch competent authority informs the EU Commission about the names of the independent persons of standing that are appointed and also about the qualification and background of these persons, including any conflict of interest they may have. The competent authorities of the Member States can object against the appointment of persons of standing for not being sufficiently independent with the EU Commission. If a competent authority will file any such objections against an independent person of standing appointed by the Dutch competent authority, the Dutch competent authority will take all necessary measures to investigate the objections and take a decision whether to maintain the person appointed, within a period of six months. It was

24. Article 4.3(5) Fiscal Arbitration Act.
25. Article 4.3(7) Fiscal Arbitration Act.

clarified in the Dutch legislative proceedings that the affected person cannot object against the appointment of persons of standing; only the competent authorities have this right.

E.4. Alternative Dispute Resolution Commission

The Dutch competent authority and the other competent authority may agree to set up an alternative dispute resolution commission instead of an advisory commission to deliver an opinion on how to resolve the question in dispute in case the competent authorities of the Member States concerned accepted the complaint that was submitted by the affected person but failed to reach an agreement on how to resolve the question in dispute by mutual agreement within the legal term.[26] The Dutch competent authority and the other competent authority may also agree to set up an alternative dispute resolution commission in the form of a committee that is of a permanent nature (i.e., Standing Committee).

Except for the rules regarding the independence of its members, the rules on the alternative dispute resolution commission may differ from the advisory commission[27] regarding its composition and form. An alternative dispute resolution commission may apply, where appropriate, any dispute resolution processes or technique to solve the question in dispute in a binding manner.

As an alternative to the type of dispute resolution process applied by the advisory commission, any other type of dispute resolution process, including the 'final offer' arbitration process (otherwise known as 'last best offer' arbitration), can be agreed by the competent authorities of the Member States and applied by the alternative dispute resolution commission.[28]

The competent authorities of the Member States concerned shall agree on the rules of functioning. The rules concerning costs of proceedings and the information, evidence and hearings shall apply equally to the alternative dispute resolution commission unless otherwise agreed to in the rules of functioning.[29]

F. COMMON PROCEDURAL PROVISIONS

F.1. Procedural Rules of the Advisory Commission or Alternative Dispute Resolution Commission

The Dutch competent authority shall, within the 120-day period, notify the affected person with the following:[30]

26. Article 4.3(9) Fiscal Arbitration Act.
27. Article 4.3(10) Fiscal Arbitration Act.
28. Article 4.8(5) Fiscal Arbitration Act.
29. Articles 4.5 and 4.6(5) Fiscal Arbitration Act.
30. Article 4.5(2) Fiscal Arbitration Act.

- the rules of functioning for the advisory commission or alternative dispute resolution commission;
- the date by which the opinion on the resolution of the question in dispute shall be adopted;
- references to any applicable legal provisions in the national law of the Member States and to any applicable agreements or conventions.

In case the advisory commission was set up to opine on a complaint that was rejected by one but not all of the competent authorities, the rules of functioning shall provide in particular:[31]

- the description and the characteristics of the question in dispute;
- the time frame for the dispute resolution procedure;
- the composition of the advisory commission (including the number and names of the members, details of their competence and qualifications, and disclosing any conflicts of interest of the members);
- the rules governing the participation of the affected person(s) and third parties in the proceedings, exchanges of memoranda, information and evidence, the costs, the type of dispute resolution process to be used, and any other relevant procedural or organizational matters.

In all other cases, the rules of functioning shall also provide:

- the terms of reference on which the competent authorities of the Member States agree as regards the legal and factual questions to be resolved;
- the form of the dispute resolution body, which shall be either an advisory commission or an alternative dispute resolution commission, as well as the type of process for any alternative dispute resolution, if the process differs from the independent opinion process applied by an advisory commission;
- the logistical arrangements for the advisory commission's proceedings and delivery of its opinion.

The rules of functioning shall be signed between the competent authorities of the Member States involved in the dispute.

If the rules of functioning are incomplete or were not notified to the affected person, the standard rules of functioning established by the Commission shall apply.[32] The Fiscal Arbitration Act also includes certain provisions that prescribe the rules of functioning if the independent persons from standing and the chair were not able to reach an agreement on the rules of functioning.[33]

In case the complaint was rejected by one but not all of the competent authorities, the advisory commission shall adopt a decision on the acceptance of the complaint within six months from the date of its establishment. It shall notify the competent

31. Article 4.5(3) Fiscal Arbitration Act.
32. Article 4.5(5) Fiscal Arbitration Act.
33. Article 4.5(7) Fiscal Arbitration Act.

authorities of its decision within thirty days of the adoption thereof.[34] The decision whether to accept the complaint is not open for appeal.

If the advisory commission decides that all requirements for a valid complaint have been satisfied, it will inform the competent authorities about its decision and the MAP shall be initiated at the request of one of the competent authorities. When the Dutch competent authority requests to start the MAP, it shall notify the advisory commission, the other competent authority and the affected person of that request. The two-year period for the MAP to achieve shall start from the date of the notification of the decision taken by the advisory commission of the acceptance of the complaint. If none of the competent authorities has requested initiation of the MAP within sixty days of the date of the notification of the decision of the advisory commission, the advisory commission shall provide an opinion on how to resolve the question in dispute within the six-month period. In such a case, for applying the six-month period, the advisory commission shall be deemed to have been set up on the date on which that the first sixty-day period expired.

In case the competent authorities of the Member States concerned accepted the complaint that was submitted by the affected person but failed to reach an agreement on how to resolve the question in dispute by mutual agreement within the legal term, the advisory commission shall deliver an opinion on how to resolve the question in dispute, within the six-month period. The advisory commission can extend this period to another three months, if necessary.

During the Dutch legislative proceedings, many questions were asked about the procedural rules. The Dutch legislator replied that, unfortunately, the procedural rules do not provide a clear answer to all possible situations. Moreover, any affected person should realize that the procedural rules may be explained differently by the Dutch and the other competent authority. The practical application of the rules as well as the evaluation of these rules by the EC (which should take place ultimately on 30 June 2024) should provide more clarity on the application of the rules.

F.2. Costs of the Advisory Commission

The costs of the advisory commission shall be shared equally among the Member States.[35] These are the following costs:

- the expenses of the independent persons of standing, which are to be an amount equivalent to the average of the usual amount reimbursed to high-ranking civil servants of the Member States concerned; and
- the fees of the independent persons, where applicable, which are to be limited to EUR 1,000 per person per day for every day on which the advisory commission meets.

34. Article 4.7(1) Fiscal Arbitration Act.
35. Article 4.10(1) Fiscal Arbitration Act.

Costs that are incurred by the affected person shall not be borne by Member States.

In contrast with the above and provided that the Dutch competent authority and the other competent authority agree on this, the costs of the advisory commission shall be borne by the affected person, in case:

- the affected person has made a notification of withdrawal of the complaint; or
- the affected person filed a complaint that was rejected by one but not all of the competent authorities, and the advisory commission decided that the relevant competent authority was correct in rejecting the complaint.

As the Netherlands want to facilitate the possibility for affected persons to make use of the dispute resolution rules implemented in the Fiscal Arbitration Act, they will, as a starting point, not agree on charging the expenses of the advisory commission to the affected person, only in cases where the affected person abuses its rights under the Fiscal Arbitration Act. The Netherlands will also try to convince the other Member State not to pursue this possibility.

When an alternative dispute resolution commission is appointed, different rules relating to the costs may be agreed upon.

F.3. Information, Evidence and Hearings

The Dutch competent authority and the other competent authority may agree that the affected person shall provide the advisory commission with all information, evidence or documents that may be relevant for the decision or opinion.[36]

The advisory commission can also request the affected person, as well as the competent authorities of the Member States concerned, to provide all information, evidence or documents which are deemed necessary by the advisory commission to reach its decision. The Dutch competent authority may refuse to provide information to the advisory commission in any of the following cases:

- obtaining the information requires carrying out administrative measures that violate Dutch national law;
- the information cannot be obtained under the national law of the Netherlands;
- the information concerns trade secrets, business secrets, industrial secrets, professional secrets or trade processes; or
- the disclosure of the information is contrary to public policy.

Affected persons, at their request and with the consent of the competent authorities of the Member States concerned, may appear or be represented before an advisory commission.[37]

Affected persons shall appear or be represented before it upon request by the advisory commission.

36. Article 4.6(1) Fiscal Arbitration Act.
37. Article 4.6(4) Fiscal Arbitration Act.

If an alternative dispute resolution commission is appointed, different rules may be agreed upon.[38]

F.4. The Opinion of the Advisory Commission

An advisory commission shall deliver its opinion to the Dutch competent authority and the other competent authority no later than six months after the date on which it was set up.[39] If the advisory commission considers that the question in dispute is such that it would need more than six months to deliver an opinion, this period may be extended by three months. The advisory commission shall inform the competent authorities of the Member States concerned and the affected person of any such extension.

The advisory commission shall base its opinion on the provisions of the applicable agreement or convention as well as on any applicable national rules.[40]

The advisory commission shall adopt its opinion by a simple majority of its members.[41] Where a majority cannot be reached, the vote of the chair shall determine the final opinion.

The chair shall communicate the opinion of the advisory commission to the Dutch competent authority and the other competent authority.

F.5. Final Decision of the Competent Authorities

The Dutch competent authority and the other competent authority shall agree on how to resolve the question in dispute within six months of the notification of the opinion of the advisory commission.[42]

The Dutch competent authority and the other competent authority may take a decision to resolve the question in dispute that deviates from the opinion of the advisory commission.[43]

However, if they fail to reach an agreement as to how to resolve the question in dispute, they shall be bound by the opinion of the advisory commission. Either way, it will be a final decision. No appeal is possible against the final decision.

The Dutch competent authority shall notify the final decision on the resolution of the question in dispute to the affected person without delay.[44] If the affected person is a Dutch resident and will not receive the notification of the final decision within thirty days of the decision having been taken, such affected person may file a request with the preliminary relief judge of the District Court in order to obtain the final decision. The

38. Article 4.6(5) Fiscal Arbitration Act.
39. Article 4.8(1) Fiscal Arbitration Act.
40. Article 4.8(3) Fiscal Arbitration Act.
41. Article 4.8(4) Fiscal Arbitration Act.
42. Article 4.9(1) Fiscal Arbitration Act.
43. Article 4.9(2) Fiscal Arbitration Act.
44. Article 4.9(3) Fiscal Arbitration Act.

final decision of competent authorities shall be binding on the Member States concerned and shall not constitute a precedent.[45]

The final decision shall be implemented by signing a settlement agreement[46] with the affected party, which agreement will include binding and enforceable conditions on the execution of the final decision. The settlement agreement shall in any case include a confirmation from the affected person that he accepts the final decision and will not pursue any Dutch legal proceedings with respect to the question in dispute, or elements thereof. To the extent that the affected person already started any such legal proceedings, the settlement agreement will include the dissolving condition that the affected person will, within sixty days of concluding the settlement agreement, provide data and information that evidence that any such legal proceedings will be stopped.

If the final decision will not be executed by the Dutch competent authority, the affected person can enforce the execution of the final decision through the preliminary relief judge of the District Court.

F.6. Publicity

Advisory commissions and alternative dispute resolution commissions shall issue their opinions in writing.[47]

The final decisions will be published in their entirety, unless the Dutch competent authority, the other competent authority or the affected person concerned objects against this, in which case the Dutch competent authority will publish an abstract.[48] That abstract shall contain a description of the issue and the subject matter, the date, the tax periods involved, the legal basis, the industry sector, and a short description of the final outcome. It shall also include a description of the method of arbitration used. The Dutch competent authority shall send the information to be published to the affected person before its publication. No later than sixty days from the receipt of such information, the affected person may request the Dutch competent authority not to publish information that concerns any trade, business, industrial or professional secret or trade process, or that is contrary to public policy.

The Dutch competent authority shall notify the information to be published to the EU Commission without delay.[49]

F.7. Interaction with National Proceedings

The fact that a decision taken on the basis of a Dutch tax act (such as a final tax assessment) has become final shall not prevent an affected person from having recourse to the procedures provided for in the Fiscal Arbitration Act.[50] On the other

45. Article 4.9(5) Fiscal Arbitration Act.
46. As meant in Article 900, Book 7 of the Dutch Civil Code.
47. Article 7.3(1) Fiscal Arbitration Act.
48. Article 7.3(2) Fiscal Arbitration Act.
49. Article 7.3(5) Fiscal Arbitration Act.
50. Article 5.1(1) Fiscal Arbitration Act.

hand, the submission of the question in dispute to the MAP or to the dispute resolution procedure does not prevent the Netherlands from imposing administrative penalties or initiating proceedings for administrative penalties or initiating or continuing judicial proceedings in relation to the same matters.[51]

If an affected person pursuits remedies available to it under domestic law and has thus filed objections or appeal against a decision taken on the basis of the tax act (such as a final tax assessment) that relates to a question in dispute or if such an affected person started legal proceedings against a decision of a similar nature in the Member State of the other competent authority, the term within which the Dutch competent authority decides to accept a complaint and the term within which the competent authorities need to resolve a question in dispute in a MAP[52] shall commence from the date on which a judgment delivered in those proceedings has become final or on which those proceedings have otherwise been definitely concluded or where the proceedings have been suspended.

Where a final decision on a question in dispute has been rendered by the relevant court or other judicial body of an Member State, and the national law of that Member State does not allow it or derogate from the decision, that Member State may provide that:[53]

- before an agreement has been reached by the competent authorities of the Member States concerned under the MAP under Article 3.1 Fiscal Arbitration Act on that question in dispute, such mutual agreement is to be terminated as from the date of the notification to the Dutch competent authority of such final decision of the relevant court or other judicial body by the other competent authority;
- it is no longer possible to start the requested advisory commission procedure in accordance with Article 4,(1), (b) Fiscal Arbitration Act in which case the other competent authority is to inform the Dutch competent authority about the effect of the decision of the relevant court or other judicial body;
- the dispute resolution process under Article 4(1) (b) Fiscal Arbitration Act is to be terminated if the decision of the relevant court was rendered at any time after an affected person has made a request under Article 4(1) (b) Fiscal Arbitration Act but before the advisory commission or the alternative dispute resolution commission has delivered its opinion to the competent authorities of the Member States concerned. In such a case, the other competent authority is to inform the Dutch competent authority and the advisory commission or the alternative dispute resolution commission of the effect of the decision of the relevant court.

The submission of a complaint as provided under Article 2.1 Fiscal Arbitration Act shall put an end to any other ongoing proceedings under the MAP or dispute

51. Article 5.1(2) Fiscal Arbitration Act.
52. These are the terms mentioned in Articles 3(5) and 4(1) of Directive 2017/1852, implemented in Articles 2.5 and 3.1 Fiscal Arbitration Act.
53. Article 5.3 Fiscal Arbitration Act.

resolution procedure under an agreement or convention that is applied in relation to the relevant question in dispute. Such other ongoing proceedings concerning the relevant question in dispute shall come to an end with effect from the date of the first receipt of the complaint by any of the competent authorities of the Member States concerned.[54]

In accordance with Article 16 of Directive 2017/1852, the Dutch competent authority can deny an affected person access to the advisory commission in case a penalty has become irrevocable in relation to corrections of reported income or wealth as a result of a criminal offence as meant in Articles 68 and 69 of the General Taxes Act and this penalty is directly linked to the question in dispute. The Netherlands have indicated that they will use this authority reluctantly.[55] If a legal procedure is pending which may result in any such penalties, the Dutch competent authority may defer the procedure before the advisory commission, until it is clear that the affected person will indeed have access to the advisory commission. No appeal is possible against the decision to deny access to the advisory commission. Directive 2017/1852 gives the Member States also the possibility to deny access to the advisory commission if the question in dispute does not relate to double taxation. The Netherlands has not implemented this possibility in the Fiscal Arbitration Act.

G. SPECIAL PROVISIONS

G.1. Special Provisions for Individuals and Smaller Undertakings

Where the affected person is either: (i) a Dutch tax resident individual; or (ii) a corporation resident in the Netherlands, not being a large undertaking or a corporation that does form part of a large group (as defined in Directive 2013/34/EU of the European Parliament and of the Council[56]), the affected person may submit the complaints, replies to a request for additional information, withdrawals and requests (respectively 'communications'), only to the Dutch competent authority.[57]

The Dutch competent authority shall notify the other competent authority at the same time and within two months of receipt of such communications.

Once such a notification has been made, the affected person shall be deemed to have submitted the communication to all the Member States concerned as of the date of such notification.

In the case of additional information received, the Dutch competent authority shall transmit a copy to the other competent authority at the same time. Once this submission has been made, it shall be deemed that additional information has been

54. Article 2.8 Fiscal Arbitration Act.
55. Article 5.2(1) Fiscal Arbitration Act.
56. Directive 2013/34/EU of the European Parliament and of the Council of 26 June 2013 on the annual financial statements, consolidated financial statements and related reports of certain types of undertakings, amending Directive 2006/43/EC of the European Parliament and of the Council and repealing Council Directives 78/660/EEC and 83/349/EEC (OJ L 182, 29.6.2013, p. 19).
57. Article 1.2(2), Article 2.7, Article 4.1, §2 and Article 4.2(7) Fiscal Arbitration Act.

received by all the Member States concerned as at the date of such receipt of information.

G.2. Obligation of Secrecy

The domestic secrecy provision of Article 67 General Taxes Act is equally applicable with respect to all data and information received by the Dutch competent authority and its legal representatives. The Dutch competent authority will conclude an agreement with the members of an advisory commission or an alternative dispute resolution commission under which they shall be subject to obligations of secrecy in relation to information they receive in their capacity as members an advisory commission or alternative dispute resolution commission.[58]

Affected persons and, where applicable, their representatives shall undertake to treat any information (including knowledge of documents) that they receive during such proceedings as secret.[59] The affected person and his representatives shall make a declaration to this effect to the competent authorities of the Member States concerned when so requested during the proceedings. The Member States shall adopt appropriate sanctions for any breach of secrecy obligations.

H. FINAL AND TRANSITORY PROVISIONS

H.1. Entry into Force

The Fiscal Arbitration Act entered into force on 16 July 2019. It applies to any complaint filed on 1 July 2019 or later concerning disputes over revenue or capital received during a taxable period beginning on or after 1 January 2018.[60] In line with Directive 2017/1852,[61] it can also apply to complaints filed before 1 July 2019 or to complaints concerning disputes over revenue or capital received during a taxable period beginning before 1 January 2018.[62]

58. Article 7.2 Fiscal Arbitration Act.
59. Article 7.2(2) Fiscal Arbitration Act.
60. Article 8.1 Fiscal Arbitration Act.
61. Article 23, last sentence, Directive 2017/1852, implemented in Article 8.1 Fiscal Arbitration Act.
62. *See* para. 'MAP' below.

CHAPTER 10
Portugal

Pedro Vidal Matos

A. IMPLEMENTING MEASURES ADOPTED BY PORTUGAL WITH RESPECT TO DIRECTIVE 2017/1852

Directive 2017/1852 was transposed into Portuguese law by Law No. 120/2019, published in Portuguese Official Gazette No. 180 of 19 September 2019 (hereinafter 'Law No. 120/2019').

B. GENERAL PROVISIONS

B.1. Subject Matter and Scope

The scope of Law No. 120/2019 does not differ from the one provided by Directive 2017/1852. It establishes tax dispute resolution mechanisms to resolve disputes between the Competent Authorities of Portugal and other Member States when those disputes arise from the interpretation and application of Tax Treaties entered into by Portugal.[1] It also establishes the rights and obligations of the Affected Persons when such disputes arise.[2]

B.2. Definitions

Law No. 120/2019 provides the following definitions:[3]

1. Article 1(2-a) of Law No. 120/2019.
2. Article 1(2-b) of Law No. 120/2019.
3. Article 2(1) of Law No. 120/2019.

- 'National Competent Authority' means the member of the Government responsible for the area of finance, the Director General of the Portuguese Tax Authorities or their authorized representatives;
- 'Double Taxation' means the imposition by both Portugal and other Member State of taxes covered by a Tax Treaty, with respect to the same taxable income or capital, resulting in:
  an additional tax charge; or
  an increase in tax liabilities; or
  the cancellation or reduction of losses that could be used to offset taxable profits.
- 'Competent Court' means the court or other body designated by the concerned Member State;
- 'National Competent Court' means the Tax Court of First Instance with jurisdiction in the area where the Affected Person is domiciled.

In this respect, terms not defined by Law No. 120/2019 have the meaning attributed to them by the treaties that provide for the elimination of double taxation of income and are applicable on the date of receipt of the first notification of the action that has or may have given rise to the Question in Dispute, unless the context otherwise requires.[4]

In the absence of a definition provided by the relevant convention, an undefined term shall have the meaning given to it, at that specific time, by the domestic law of the Member State concerned for the purposes of the taxes to which said convention applies, taking into account that any meaning given by the applicable tax laws of that Member State prevails over the meaning given to that term by other non-tax-related laws of that Member State.[5]

C. COMPLAINT TO START A MAP

C.1. Filing of a Complaint to Start a MAP

Any Affected Person is entitled to submit a complaint on a Question in Dispute to the National Competent Authority, requesting the resolution thereof through a MAP with the Competent Authority of the other Member States involved. The Affected Person shall simultaneously submit the complaint with the same information to the Competent Authority of the other Member State concerned.[6]

The complaint must be submitted within three years from the receipt of the first notification of the action that gave rise to the Question in Dispute, regardless of whether the Affected Person has recourse to the remedies available under the domestic law of the Member States involved.[7]

4. Article 2(2) of Law No. 120/2019.
5. Article 2(3) of Law No. 120/2019.
6. Article 3(1) and 3(2) of Law No. 120/2019.
7. Article 3(3) of Law No. 120/2019.

Within two months from the date of receipt of the complaint, the National Competent Authority shall:[8]

- notify the Affected Person, acknowledging the receipt of the complaint; and
- inform the Competent Authorities of the other Member State(s) involved of the receipt of the complaint as well as about the language (or languages) it intends to use in its communications.

The complaint shall be submitted in Portuguese or in another language previously requested by the Affected Person, provided the National Competent Authority expressly admits it within ten days. The documentation enclosed with the complaint should also be in Portuguese where possible. If the supporting documentation is in another language, the National Competent Authority may require a sworn translation into Portuguese.[9]

Moreover, the complaint shall only be admitted if the Affected Person provides the following information:[10]

- the name, address, tax identification number and other information necessary for the identification of the Affected Person that filed the complaint and any other person concerned;
- the tax periods concerned;
- detailed information and supporting documents[11] regarding the facts and circumstances of the case, including details of the structure of the transaction and the relations between the Affected Person and the other parties involved in the transactions, as well as the facts recognized in good faith in a mutually binding agreement between the Affected Persons and a Competent Authority;
- detailed information and supporting documents[12] regarding the nature and the date of the action giving rise to the Question in Dispute, including, where applicable, details of the income received in the other Member State and the inclusion of such income in the taxable income in the other Member State, as well as details of the tax charged or that will be charged in relation to such income in the other Member State and the related amounts in the currencies of the Member States concerned;
- the applicable domestic provisions and Tax Treaty (where more than one agreement or convention is applicable, the Affected Person making the complaint shall specify which agreement or convention is being interpreted in relation to the relevant Question in Dispute; such agreement or convention shall be the applicable agreement or convention for the purposes of Law No. 120/2019);[13]

8. Article 3(4) of Law No. 120/2019.
9. Article 4(1) and 4(2) Law No. 120/2019.
10. Article 4(3) of Law No. 120/2019.
11. Article 4(4) of Law No. 120/2019.
12. Article 4(4) of Law No. 120/2019.
13. Article 4(5) of Law No. 120/2019.

- the following additional information together with copies of any supporting documents:[14]
  - (i) an explanation of why the Affected Person considers that there is a Question in Dispute;
  - (ii) details of any appeals and litigation initiated by the Affected Person in relation to the Question in Dispute and any court decisions concerning the Question in Dispute;
  - (iii) a declaration of commitment from the Affected Persons to answer as completely and quickly as possible to all appropriate requests of any Competent Authority and to provide the documentation requested by any Competent Authority;
  - (iv) a copy of the final tax assessment decision in the form of a final tax assessment notice, tax audit report or other equivalent document leading to the Question in Dispute and a copy of any other documents issued by the tax authorities regarding the Question in Dispute where relevant;
  - (v) information on any complaint submitted by the Affected Person under another MAP or under another dispute resolution procedure and an express commitment by the Affected Person that he will abide by the provisions of Article 22(5) and 22(6) of Law No. 120/2019;
- any specific additional information requested by the Competent Authorities, within three months from the receipt of the complaint, that is considered necessary to undertake the substantive consideration of the case.[15]

During the MAP, the National Competent Authority may request additional information where it is deemed necessary for the purposes of the case. Information requests are to be complied with within three months from the corresponding request.[16]

C.2. Withdrawal of a Complaint to Start a MAP

An Affected Person that wishes to withdraw a complaint shall simultaneously submit a written notification of withdrawal to each of the Competent Authorities of the Member States concerned.[17] Such notification shall terminate, with immediate effect, all proceedings under Law No. 120/2019.[18] Upon receipt of such notification, the National Competent Authority shall inform the other Competent Authorities of the Member States concerned of the termination of proceedings without delay.[19]

14. Article 4(4) of Law No. 120/2019.
15. Article 4(6) of Law No. 120/2019.
16. Article 4(7) and 4(8) of Law No. 120/2019.
17. Article 6(1) of Law No. 120/2019.
18. Article 6(2) of Law No. 120/2019.
19. Article 6(3) of Law No. 120/2019.

D. THE RESOLUTION OF THE QUESTION IN DISPUTE UNDER THE MAP

D.1. Decision of the Competent Authority Concerning the Complaint

The National Competent Authority shall take a decision on the complaint's formal admissibility within six months from the date of receipt of the complaint or within six months from the date of receipt of additional information requested and deemed necessary to consider the complaint. Once the National Competent Authority decided whether to admit or reject the complaint to start a MAP, it shall give timely notice to the Affected Persons and to the Competent Authorities of the other Member States involved.[20]

During the above-mentioned six-month period, the National Competent Authority may decide to resolve the Question in Dispute on a unilateral basis, without involving the Competent Authorities of the other Member States concerned. In such case, the National Competent Authority shall notify the Affected Person and the Competent Authorities of the other Member States concerned without delay, following which the proceedings under Law No. 120/2019 shall be terminated.

The complaint shall be rejected in the following cases:[21]

- the complaint does not contain the information required under Article 3 or the additional information requested by the National Competent Authority has not been transmitted within the three-month period provided;
- there is no Question in Dispute;
- the complaint was not submitted within the three-year period set out in Article 3 of Law No. 120/2019.

When rejecting a complaint, the National Competent Authority shall provide the Affected Person with the grounds for said rejection.[22]

If the National Competent Authority does not take a decision on the complaint within the above-mentioned six-month deadline, the application shall be deemed to have been admitted.[23]

D.2. MAP

If the complaint is admitted by the Portuguese National Competent Authority and the Competent Authorities of the other concerned Member State(s), such Authorities shall endeavour to settle the Question in Dispute by a MAP within two years from the date of the last notification of the decision admitting the complaint by one of the Member States. The above-mentioned two-year period can be extended by up to one year where

20. Article 5(1) and 5(2) of Law No. 120/2019.
21. Article 5(3-b) of Law No. 120/2019.
22. Article 5(5) of Law No. 120/2019.
23. Article 5(6) of Law No. 120/2019.

a reasoned written request of the National Competent Authority is submitted to the Competent Authorities of the other concerned Member States.[24]

Once the Competent Authorities of the Member States have reached an agreement as to how to resolve the Question in Dispute, the Competent Authority of each of the Member States concerned shall, without delay, notify such agreement to the Affected Person.[25] This decision is binding on the National Competent Authority and enforceable by the Affected Person, provided the Affected Person admits the decision and renounces the right to any other remedy, where applicable.[26] Where proceedings regarding such other remedies have already commenced, the decision shall only become binding and enforceable once the Affected Person has provided evidence to the Competent Authorities of the Member States concerned that action has been taken to terminate those proceedings. Such evidence shall be provided no later than sixty days from the date on which such decision was notified to the Affected Person. The decision shall then be implemented without delay, irrespective of any time limits prescribed by the domestic law of the Member States concerned.[27]

If the National Competent Authority and the Competent Authorities of the other Member States concerned do not reach an agreement within the two-year deadline (or three-year deadline in case of extension), the National Competent Authority shall inform the Affected Person of the general reasons for not reaching an agreement.[28]

D.3. Appeal of the Taxpayer Against the Decision Rejecting the Complaint

The Affected Person can file an appeal against the decision of the National Competent Authority that rejects the complaint, where all Competent Authorities of the Member States concerned have also rejected the complaint. According to Article 5(7) of Law No. 120/2019 apart from the judicial appeal referred in Directive 2017/1852, it will be possible to file an administrative appeal before the Minister of Finance.[29]

An Affected Person who exercises this appeal right shall be barred from making a request to set up an Advisory Commission and initiate a dispute resolution procedure to resolve the Question in Dispute, if:[30]

- the appeal against the rejection of the complaint is still pending under the Portuguese law or the domestic law of the other Member State concerned;
- the rejection of the complaint can be further appealed in accordance with the Portuguese law or the domestic law of the other Member State concerned; or
- the rejection decision has been confirmed by the Court of Appeal and that decision cannot be derogated from.

24. Article 8(1), 8(2) and 8(3) of Law No. 120/2019.
25. Article 8(4) of Law No. 120/2019.
26. Article 9(1) of Law No. 120/2019.
27. Article 9(2) and 9(3) of Law No. 120/2019.
28. Article 9(4) of Law No. 120/2019.
29. Article 5(8) of Law No. 120/2019.
30. Article 5(8) of Law No. 120/2019.

Where the appeal right has been exercised, the decision of such appeal shall be taken into consideration for the purposes of requesting the set-up of an Advisory Commission and initiating a dispute resolution procedure to resolve the Question in Dispute.[31]

D.4. Termination of the Dispute Resolution Procedure

If for any reason a Question in Dispute ceases to exist, the MAP or the dispute resolution procedure shall terminate with immediate effect. The National Competent Authority shall inform the Affected Person without delay of this and of the general reasons that terminated the procedures.[32]

E. DISPUTE RESOLUTION PROCEDURE

E.1. Request of Appointment of the Advisory Commission

The Affected Person can submit a request to the National Competent Authority and to the Competent Authorities of the other Member States concerned to set up an Advisory Commission and initiate a dispute resolution procedure to resolve the Question in Dispute, in the following cases:[33]

- where the complaint to start a MAP has been rejected by at least one, but not all, of the Competent Authorities of the Member States concerned. In this circumstance, the Affected Person can file a request to set up an Advisory Commission only if:
  (i) under the domestic law of the Member State in which the decision of rejection of the complaint was issued, no appeal against that decision may be filed;
  (ii) there is no pending litigation;
  (iii) the Affected Person has formally waived, in a written declaration, his right to appeal against the decision of rejection of the complaint.
- where the Competent Authorities of the Member States concerned have admitted the complaint to start a MAP but have not been able to reach an agreement on how to resolve the Question in Dispute through the MAP within two years (or three years in case of extension).

The request to set up the Advisory Commission shall be made in writing within fifty days from the receipt of the notification of:

- the decision that rejected the complaint;

31. Articles 5(9) and 10(1-a) of Law No. 120/2019.
32. Article 7 of Law No. 120/2019.
33. Article 10(1), 10(2) and 10(3) of Law No. 120/2019.

- the failure of the National Competent Authority and the Competent Authorities of the other Member States to reach an agreement;
- a favourable judicial decision of an appeal filed due to the rejection of the complaint.

Despite the above, the National Competent Authority may deny access to the dispute resolution procedure in the following cases:

- where penalties were imposed in Portugal in relation to the adjusted income or capital for tax fraud, wilful default and gross negligence (*see* Section F.1. below); or
- when the Question in Dispute does not lead to Double Taxation (*see* Section F.2. below).

E.2. Appointment of the Advisory Commission

The Advisory Commission shall be composed of:[34]

- a chairman;
- one representative of each Competent Authority of the concerned Member States (where agreed by the Competent Authorities, the number of such representatives may be increased to two for each Competent Authority);
- one independent person appointed by each Competent Authority of the concerned Member States from a specific list of independent persons of standing (where agreed by the Competent Authorities, the number of such persons appointed may be increased to two for each Competent Authority).

The representatives of the Competent Authorities and the independent persons appointed shall elect a chairman from the list of persons of standing. Unless otherwise agreed by the representatives of each Competent Authority and the independent persons of standing, the chairman shall be a judge.[35]

The Advisory Commission shall be appointed within 120 days from the receipt of the request filed by the Affected Person. Once established, its chairman shall promptly inform the Affected Person.[36]

The Advisory Commission shall:[37]

- adopt a decision on the admission of the complaint within six months from the date of its establishment; and
- notify the Competent Authorities of its decision within thirty days from the adoption thereof.

34. Article 11(1) and 11(2) of Law No. 120/2019.
35. Article 11(8) and 11(9) of Law No. 120/2019.
36. Article 13(1) of Law No. 120/2019.
37. Article 13(2) of Law No. 120/2019.

Where the Advisory Commission acknowledges that there is a Question in Dispute and that all the requirements of the complaint under Article 4 of Law No. 120/2019 have been met, the National Competent Authority may request MAP to be initiated within sixty days from the date of the notification of the decision taken by the Advisory Commission. The National Competent Authority shall notify the Advisory Commission, the Competent Authorities of the other Member States concerned and the Affected Person of that request. The period provided for in Article 4(1) shall start from the date on which the decision of admission of the complaint taken by the Advisory Commission is notified.

Where none of the Competent Authorities has requested initiation of the MAP within sixty days of the date of the notification of the decision of the Advisory Commission, the Advisory Commission shall provide an opinion on how to resolve the Question in Dispute as provided for in Article 19 of Law No. 120/2019. In such a case, for the purposes of Article 19, the Advisory Commission shall be deemed to have been set up on the date on which that sixty-day period expired.[38]

The Advisory Commission shall deliver an opinion on how to resolve the Question in Dispute in accordance with Article 19 of Law No. 120/2019.[39]

E.3. Appointment of the Advisory Commission Made by the National Competent Court

If an Advisory Commission is not set up within 120 days, within the subsequent 30 days the Affected Person can request to the National Competent Court the establishment of the said Commission, as follows:[40]

- if the National Competent Authority has failed to appoint at least one independent person of standing and one substitute, the Affected Person can request the National Competent Court to appoint an independent person of standing and a substitute from the list of independent persons of standing;
- where the National Competent Authority and the Competent Authorities of all the other Member States concerned have failed to do so, the Affected Person may request the National Competent Court to appoint two independent persons included in the list of independent persons of standing. These independent persons shall then appoint the chairman by drawing lots from the list of independent persons in accordance with Article 11(4) of Law No. 120/2019.

For this purpose, if more than one Affected Person is involved in the proceedings, only tax residents in Portugal for tax purposes may submit their request for the

38. Article 13(6) and 13(7) of Law No. 120/2019.
39. Article 13(8) of Law No. 120/2019.
40. Articles 13(1), 14(1) and 14(3) of Law No. 120/2019.

appointment of independent persons of standing and their substitutes to the National Competent Court.[41]

The Tax Court shall adopt a decision regarding the appointment of members of the Advisory Commission and shall notify it to the applicant. The procedure for the appointment of independent persons of standing and their substitutes by the National Competent Court is governed *mutatis mutandis* by the rules set out in Article 10 of the Voluntary Arbitration Law, approved by Law No. 63/2011, of 14 December 2011. The National Competent Court shall inform the National Competent Authority, which shall promptly inform the Competent Authorities of the other Member States concerned.[42]

The appointment of members of the Advisory Commission by the National Competent Court is classified as an urgent procedure and therefore the judicial decisions shall be delivered within ninety days from the date of submission of the respective requests.[43]

E.4. List of the Independent Persons of Standing

The list of independent persons of standing consists of all the independent persons of standing nominated by the Member States. For this purpose, Portugal shall appoint at least three individuals who are competent and independent and able to operate with impartiality and integrity. Portugal shall notify the EU Commission of the names of the independent persons of standing who it has nominated, as well as specify in the notification which of those persons may be appointed as chair. Portugal shall also provide the Commission with complete and up-to-date information regarding those persons' professional and academic background, their competence, their expertise and any conflicts of interest that they may have.[44]

The rules for the appointment of independent persons of standing shall be agreed between the Competent Authorities of the Member States concerned. Said rules shall include a provision regarding the appointment of a substitute for each of the independent persons of standing appointed, for cases where independent persons of standing are prevented from performing their duties. If the rules for the appointment of independent persons of standing have not been agreed, they shall be appointed by drawing lots.[45]

The independent persons appointed and their substitutes must disclose any interest, relationship or any other matter which may affect their independence or impartiality or that might reasonably create an appearance of bias in the proceedings. If based on such declaration or any other information it becomes apparent that a person who has been appointed for the list of independent persons ceases to be independent, Portugal shall put in place procedures for removing that person from the list and shall immediately notify the EU Commission of such removal. Indeed, Portugal shall

41. Article 14(2) of Law No. 120/2019.
42. Article 14(4), 14(5) and 14(6) of Law No. 120/2019.
43. Article 14(7) of Law No. 120/2019.
44. Article 12(1), 12(2), 12(3) and 12(4) of Law No. 120/2019.
45. Article 11(3) and 11(4) of Law No. 120/2019.

promptly inform the EU Commission of any changes to the list of independent persons.[46]

For a period of twelve months after the decision of the Advisory Commission was delivered, an independent person of standing who is part of the Advisory Commission shall not be in a situation that would have given cause to a Competent Authority to object to his appointment had he been in that situation at the time of appointment to that Advisory Commission.[47]

Where Portugal has reasonable cause to object to an independent person of standing remaining in the above-mentioned list for reasons of lack of independence, it shall inform the EU Commission and provide appropriate evidence to support its concern. The EU Commission shall in turn inform the Member State that nominated the person concerned of the objection and supporting evidence, which shall within six months take the necessary steps to investigate the complaint and shall decide whether to retain or remove that person from the list. The Member State in question shall then notify the EU Commission accordingly without delay.[48]

Except where the independent persons of standing are appointed by the National Competent Court or the Competent Court of one of the Member States concerned, the National Competent Authority may object to the appointment of an independent person for any reason agreed in advance with the concerned Competent Authorities or for one of the following reasons:[49]

- that person belongs to or is working on behalf of one of the tax administrations concerned or has been in that situation at any time during the previous three years;
- that person has or has had a material holding in or voting right in or is or has been an employee or adviser to the Affected Person at any time during the last five years prior to the date of the appointment;
- that person does not offer enough guarantee of objectivity for the settlement of the dispute(s) to be decided;
- that person is an employee with an enterprise that provides tax advice or otherwise gives tax advice on a professional basis or was in such a situation at any time during a period of at least three years prior to the date of the appointment.

E.5. Alternative Dispute Resolution Commission

The Competent Authorities of the Member States concerned may agree to set up:[50]

46. Articles 11(6), 12(5), 12(6) and 12(7) of Law No. 120/2019.
47. Article 11(7) of Law No. 120/2019.
48. Article 12(8), 12(9) and 12(10) of Law No. 120/2019.
49. Article 11(5) of Law No. 120/2019.
50. Article 15(1) and 15(2) of Law No. 120/2019.

- an Alternative Dispute Resolution Commission instead of an Advisory Commission to deliver an opinion on how to resolve the Question in Dispute;
- an Alternative Dispute Resolution Commission in the form of a Standing Committee that is of a permanent nature.

Instead of a dispute resolution based on an independent advice as provided for by the Advisory Commission, an Alternative Dispute Resolution Commission may apply, where appropriate, any dispute resolution processes or technique to solve the Question in Dispute in a binding manner, provided the Competent Authorities of the Member States concerned agree.[51]

Except for the rules regarding the independence of its members,[52] the Alternative Dispute Resolution Commission may differ regarding its composition and form from the Advisory Commission.[53]

The Competent Authorities of the Member States concerned shall decide on the procedural rules of the Alternative Dispute Resolution Commission. Unless otherwise agreed in those procedural rules, the provisions of Law No. 120/2019 about costs of proceedings, information, evidence and hearings shall apply to the Alternative Dispute Resolution Commission.[54]

F. COMMON PROCEDURAL PROVISIONS

F.1. Procedural Rules of the Advisory Commission or Alternative Dispute Resolution Commission

The National Competent Authority shall, within 120 days from receiving the request submitted by the Affected Person to set up an Advisory Commission, notify the Affected Person of the following:[55]

- the procedural rules of the Advisory Commission or Alternative Dispute Resolution Commission;
- the deadline by which the opinion on the resolution of the Question in Dispute shall be adopted;
- the references of the applicable domestic law provisions of the Member States and the applicable agreements or conventions.

The Competent Authorities of the concerned Member States shall define the procedural rules of the Advisory Commission or Alternative Dispute Resolution Commission. Such procedural rules shall include:[56]

- the description and characteristics of the Question in Dispute;

51. Article 15(3) of Law No. 120/2019.
52. Article 11(5) and 11(6) of Law No. 120/2019.
53. Article 15(4) of Law No. 120/2019.
54. Article 15(5) and 5(6) of Law No. 120/2019.
55. Article 16(1) of Law No. 120/2019.
56. Article 16(2) of Law No. 120/2019.

- the terms of reference on which the Competent Authorities of the Member States agree as regards the legal and factual questions to be resolved;
- the form of the dispute resolution body (i.e., the Advisory Commission or Alternative Dispute Resolution Commission), as well as the type of process for alternative dispute resolution, if the process differs from the independent opinion process applied by an Advisory Commission;
- the time frame for dispute resolution procedure;
- the composition of the Advisory Commission or Alternative Dispute Resolution Commission (including the number and names of its members, indication of their competence and qualifications and disclosure of their conflicts of interest);
- the rules governing the participation of the Affected Person and third parties in the proceedings, the exchange of memoranda, information and evidence, the costs, the type of dispute resolution process to be used, and any other relevant procedural or organizational matters;
- the logistical arrangements for the proceeding of the Advisory Commission or Alternative Dispute Resolution Commission and the delivery of their opinion.

If an Advisory Commission is set up to give an opinion when the complaint has been rejected, only the following aspects shall be defined by the Competent Authorities:[57]

- the description and characteristics of the Question in Dispute;
- the timeline of the MAP;
- the composition of the Advisory Commission or Alternative Dispute Resolution Commission (including the number and names of its members, indication of their competence and qualifications and disclosure of their conflicts of interest);
- the rules governing the participation of the Affected Person and third parties in the proceedings, the exchange of memoranda, information and evidence, the costs, the type of dispute resolution process to be used, and any other relevant procedural or organizational matters.

If the Competent Authorities do not notify the procedural rules to the Affected Person or if such notification is incomplete, the independent persons of standing and the chairman shall complete the procedural rules in accordance with the standard rules established by the EU Commission and shall send them to the Affected Person within two weeks from the date on which the Advisory Commission or Alternative Dispute Resolution Commission was set up. If the independent persons of standing and the chairman do not agree on the procedural rules, the Affected Person may apply to the National Competent Court to obtain an order for the implementation of the procedural rules.[58]

57. Article 16(3) of Law No. 120/2019.
58. Article 16(4), 16(5) and 16(6) of Law No. 120/2019.

F.2. Costs of the MAP

Unless the National Competent Authority and the Competent Authority of the other Member States concerned have agreed otherwise, the following costs shall be shared equally between the Member States:[59]

- the expenses of the independent persons of standing, which are to be an amount equivalent to the average of the usual amount reimbursed to high-ranking civil servants of the Member States concerned; and
- the fees of the independent persons, where applicable, which are to be limited to EUR 1,000 per person per day for every day on which the Advisory Commission or Alternative Dispute Resolution Commission meets.

In this regard, it is clarified that the costs incurred by the Affected Person shall not be borne by the concerned Member States.[60]

The above-mentioned costs of the MAP are borne by the Affected Person, provided the Competent Authorities of the Member States concerned agree to, in the following cases:[61]

- if the Affected Person gives a written notice of withdrawal of the MAP application; or
- if the Affected Person submits a request for setting up the Advisory Commission following a rejection of the complaint to start a MAP, and the Advisory Commission decides that the Competent Authorities were correct in rejecting the complaint.

F.3. Information, Evidence and Hearings

For the purposes of the dispute resolution procedure, where the Competent Authorities of the Member States concerned agree, the Affected Person may provide the Advisory Commission or Alternative Dispute Resolution Commission with any information, evidence or documents that may be relevant for the decision.[62]

The Affected Person and the Competent Authorities of the Member States concerned shall provide any information, evidence or documents upon request by the Advisory Commission or Alternative Dispute Resolution Commission. However, the National Competent Authority may refuse to provide information to the Advisory Commission in any of the following cases:[63]

- where obtaining the information requires carrying out administrative measures that are against national law;

59. Article 17(1) of Law No. 120/2019.
60. Article 17(2) of Law No. 120/2019.
61. Article 17(3) of Law No. 120/2019.
62. Article 18(1) of Law No. 120/2019.
63. Article 18(2) and 18(3) of Law No. 120/2019.

- where the information cannot be obtained under the national law;
- where the information concerns trade secrets, business secrets, industrial secrets, professional secrets or trade processes;
- where the disclosure of the information is contrary to public policy.

Affected Persons may appear or be represented before an Advisory Commission or an Alternative Dispute Resolution Commission:[64]

- upon request by the Advisory Commission or Alternative Dispute Resolution Commission;
- at their request and with the consent of the Competent Authorities of the Member States concerned.

The independent persons of standing or any other member of an Advisory Commission or an Alternative Dispute Resolution Commission shall be subject to obligations of professional secrecy under the national legislation in relation to information they receive in their capacity as members of said Commission.[65]

Affected Persons and, where applicable, their representatives shall undertake to treat any information and documents that they receive during such proceedings as secret. To this end, Affected Persons and their representatives shall make a declaration to the National Competent Authority.[66]

In case of breach of the above-mentioned secrecy obligations, the penalties provided for by domestic law shall apply (i.e., Articles 91 and 115 of the General Regime of Tax Infringements, approved by Law No. 15/2001, of 5 June 2001).[67] The negligent breach of such obligations is an administrative offence and is punishable with a fine ranging from EUR 75 to EUR 1,500. Conversely, where the breach of such obligations is intentional, it constitutes a crime and is punishable with imprisonment up to three years or with a fine up to 360 days.

Portugal shall notify the EU Commission of the measures adopted in order to punish the breach of secrecy obligations.[68]

F.4. The Opinion of the Advisory Commission or Alternative Dispute Resolution Commission

The Advisory Commission or Alternative Dispute Resolution Commission shall deliver its opinion in writing and shall base such opinion on the applicable national rules, as well as on the applicable Tax Treaties.[69]

The Advisory Commission or Alternative Dispute Resolution Commission shall adopt its opinion by a simple majority of its members. Where a majority cannot be

64. Article 18(4) of Law No. 120/2019.
65. Article 18(5) of Law No. 120/2019.
66. Article 18(6) of Law No. 120/2019.
67. Article 18(5) and 18(7) of Law No. 120/2019.
68. Article 18(8) of Law No. 120/2019.
69. Article 19(1) of Law No. 120/2019.

reached, the vote of the chairman shall determine the final opinion. The chairman shall communicate the opinion of the Advisory Commission or Alternative Dispute Resolution Commission to the Competent Authorities within six months from the date on which the Commission was set up.[70]

However, where the Advisory Commission or Alternative Dispute Resolution Commission considers that the Question in Dispute is such that it would need more than six months to deliver an opinion, this period may be extended by three months. The Advisory Commission or Alternative Dispute Resolution Commission shall inform the Competent Authorities of the Member States concerned and the Affected Persons of any such extension.[71]

F.5. Final Decision of the Competent Authorities

The Competent Authorities of the Member States concerned shall agree on how to resolve the Question in Dispute within six months of the notification of the opinion of the Advisory Commission or Alternative Dispute Resolution Commission. The Competent Authorities may take a decision which deviates from the opinion of the Advisory Commission or Alternative Dispute Resolution Commission. However, if they fail to reach an agreement as to how to resolve the Question in Dispute, they shall be bound by that opinion.[72]

The National Competent Authority shall notify, without delay, the final decision on the resolution of the Question in Dispute to the Affected Person. In the absence of such notification within thirty days of the decision having been taken, the Affected Persons that are resident for tax purposes in Portugal may file an administrative or judicial appeal in order to obtain the final decision.[73]

The final decision shall be binding on the Member States concerned and shall not constitute a precedent. The final decision shall be implemented subject to the Affected Person admitting the final decision and renouncing the right to any domestic remedy within sixty days from the date when the final decision was notified, where applicable.[74]

The final decision shall be implemented under the domestic law and Portugal shall amend the taxation, irrespective of any time limits prescribed by domestic law, except where the National Competent Court decides that there was lack of independence.[75] Where the final decision has not been implemented, the Affected Person may apply to the National Competent Court to implement the final decision, in order to enforce implementation thereof.[76]

70. Article 19(2) and 19(3) of Law No. 120/2019.
71. Article 19(4) and 19(5) of Law No. 120/2019.
72. Article 20(1), 20(2) and 20(3) of Law No. 120/2019.
73. Article 20(4) and 20(5) of Law No. 120/2019.
74. Article 20(6) and 20(7) of Law No. 120/2019.
75. Article 11 of Law No. 120/2019.
76. Article 20(8) and 20(9) of Law No. 120/2019.

F.6. Publicity

The National Competent Authority and the Competent Authorities of other Member States shall publish and disclose in full the decisions taken in the context of a dispute resolution procedure, subject to the consent of each of the Affected Persons.[77]

If the Competent Authorities involved or the Affected Persons do not give their consent to the full publication of a decision, the Competent Authorities shall publish a summary of the decision reporting:[78]

- the method of arbitration used;
- the Question in Dispute;
- the date and the legal basis of the decision;
- the tax periods involved and the industry sector; and
- a short description of the outcome.

Before the publication, the National Competent Authority shall provide the Affected Person with the content of the summary. Within sixty days of receipt of that information, the Affected Person may request the National Competent Authority not to disclose information relating to any trade, business, industrial or professional secret or trade process, or that is contrary to public policy.[79]

The National Competent Authority shall promptly notify the EU Commission of the information to be published, through a standard form established by Regulation of the EU Commission.[80]

F.7. Interaction with National Proceedings

The fact that the administrative act that gave rise to a Question in Dispute has become final under domestic law shall not prevent the Affected Persons from having recourse to the procedures provided for in Law No. 120/2019.[81] On the other hand, Affected Persons may have recourse to the remedies available to them under the Portuguese law.

Indeed, Law No. 120/2019 seems as a rule to point towards an Affected Person having the possibility of resorting to the domestic remedies prior to triggering the MAP, foreseeing that where an Affected Person has commenced proceedings to seek such domestic remedy, the deadlines referred to in Articles 5(1) and 8 respectively shall be computed from the date on which a judgment delivered in those proceedings has become final or on which those proceedings have otherwise been definitively concluded or where the proceedings have been suspended.[82]

77. Article 21(1) of Law No. 120/2019.
78. Article 21(2) and 21(3) of Law No. 120/2019.
79. Article 21(4) and 21(5) of Law No. 120/2019.
80. Article 21(6) and 21(7) of Law No. 120/2019.
81. Article 22(1) of Law No. 120/2019.
82. Article 22(3) of Law No. 120/2019.

However, in practice, the interaction with national proceedings may prove problematic. According to Law No. 120/2019, where a decision on a Question in Dispute has been rendered by a Portuguese Tax Court, the following proceedings shall apply, according to the moment when such decision has been issued:[83]

- if the judicial decision is rendered before an agreement has been reached by the Competent Authorities of the Member States concerned under the MAP under Article 8 on that Question in Dispute, the National Competent Authority shall notify the other Competent Authorities of the Member States concerned of the judicial decision and that the MAP is to be terminated as from the date of such notification;
- if the judicial decision is issued before the Affected Person has made a request under Article 10, this provision is not applicable if the Question in Dispute has remained unresolved during the whole of the MAP under Article 8, in which case the National Competent Authority shall inform the Competent Authorities of the other Member States concerned of the effect of the judicial decision;
- if the judicial decision is rendered at any time after the Affected Person has made a request under Article 10, the dispute resolution process is to be terminated, in which case the National Competent Authority shall inform the Competent Authorities of the other Member States concerned and the Advisory Commission or Alternative Dispute Resolution Commission of the effect of the judicial decision of the national court.

Considering the above, it is clear that once a judicial decision is issued by a Portuguese Tax Court on the Question in Dispute, the pursuit of the MAP will be blocked. This means that although an Affected Person is entitled to pursue both the MAP and the domestic remedy possibility, the latter will have to be stayed before a judicial decision is rendered. Such suspension of domestic proceedings is however not expressly foreseen in Law No. 120/2019. As such, the Affected Person will have to rely on the general rule of Article 272 of the Portuguese Civil Procedural Code, which leaves to the court's discretion the possibility of staying the procedure whenever a precedent claim is pending or if such suspension is deemed sound under another justified reason.

The submission of a complaint as provided under Article 3 shall put an end to any other ongoing proceedings under the MAP or dispute resolution procedure under an agreement or convention that is being interpreted or applied in relation to the relevant Question in Dispute. Such other ongoing proceedings concerning the relevant Question in Dispute shall come to an end with effect from the date of the first receipt of the complaint by any of the Competent Authorities of the Member States concerned.[84]

Finally, the submission of the Question in Dispute to the MAP or to the dispute resolution procedure under Article 8 or 10 of Law No. 120/2019, respectively, shall not

83. Article 22(4) of Law No. 120/2019.
84. Article 22(5) and 22(6) of Law No. 120/2019.

prevent per se Portugal from initiating or continuing judicial proceedings or proceedings for administrative and criminal penalties in relation to the same matters according to domestic law.[85]

G. SPECIAL PROVISIONS

G.1. Derogation Regarding Tax Fraud, Wilful Default and Gross Negligence

Pursuant to Article 16(6) of Directive 2017/1852, Portugal has used the prerogative to block access to the dispute resolution procedure where penalties were imposed in Portugal in relation to the adjusted income or capital for tax fraud, wilful default and gross negligence. For this purpose, the penalties for tax fraud, wilful default and gross negligence include the penalties for tax crimes and for serious misdemeanours under Article 23(3) of the General Regime of Tax Infringements, approved by Law No. 15/2001, of 5 June 2001 (i.e., infringements punishable with a maximum fine of over EUR 15,000).[86] In practice, this may constitute a real threat to the applicability of the MAP under Law No. 120/2019, given that a significant number of situations which will predictably fall under this exception.

Where judicial or administrative proceedings were commenced that could potentially lead to such penalties, and these proceedings are being conducted simultaneously with any of the proceedings referred to in Law No. 120/2019, the proceedings under this law may be suspended as from the date of admission of the complaint until the date of the outcome of those proceedings. In such a case, the National Competent Authority shall, without delay, inform the Affected Person and the Competent Authorities of the other Member States concerned of the suspension of the proceeding as well as of the reasons for said suspension.[87]

G.2. Derogation Regarding the Inexistence of Double Taxation

Pursuant to Article 16(7) of Directive 2017/1852, Portugal has used the prerogative to block access to the dispute resolution procedure, on a case-by-case basis, when the Question in Dispute does not lead to Double Taxation. For this purpose, Double Taxation shall not be deemed to exist, namely, when elements of income or capital are not subject to taxation in one of the Member States in so far as they are not included in the tax base, they are exempt from tax or they are subject to a zero rate, under the domestic legislation of that Member State.[88]

In such a case, the National Competent Authority shall inform, without delay, the Affected Person and the Competent Authorities of the other Member States concerned

85. Article 22(2) of Law No. 120/2019.
86. Article 23(1) and 23(2) of Law No. 120/2019.
87. Article 23(3) and 23(4) of Law No. 120/2019.
88. Article 24(1) and 24(2) of Law No. 120/2019.

that the access to the dispute resolution procedure is denied since the Question in Dispute does not involve Double Taxation.[89]

When the National Competent Authority considers that the Question in Dispute does not involve Double Taxation and therefore denies access to the dispute resolution procedure, the Affected Person may file an administrative or judicial appeal. If the appeal is well founded, the 120-day period[90] to request the set-up of the Advisory Commission shall only start once the decision of the administrative or judicial becomes final.[91]

G.3. Special Provisions for Individuals and Smaller Undertakings

The Affected Person may submit the complaints, replies to a request for additional information, withdrawals and requests specified in Articles 3, 4(7), 4(8), 6 and 10, by way of derogation from those provisions, only to the National Competent Authority if is resident for tax purposes in Portugal and is either:[92]

- an individual; or
- not a large undertaking[93] and does not form part of a large group[94] (both as defined in Directive No. 2013/34/EU of the European Parliament and of the Council of 26 June 2013).

The National Competent Authority shall notify the Competent Authorities of all the other Member States concerned at the same time and within two months of receipt of such communications. Once such a notification has been made, the Affected Person shall be deemed to have submitted the communication to all the Member States concerned as of the date of such notification.[95]

Upon the receipt of additional information under Article 4(6), 4(7) and 4(8), the National Competent Authority shall transmit a copy to the Competent Authorities of all the other Member States concerned at the same time. Once this submission has been made, it shall be deemed that additional information has been received by all the Member States concerned at the date of such receipt of information.[96]

89. Article 24(3) of Law No. 120/2019.
90. Article 13(1) of Law No. 120/2019.
91. Article 24(4) and 24(5) of Law No. 120/2019.
92. Article 25(1) of Law No. 120/2019.
93. Pursuant to Article 3(4) of Directive No. 2013/34/EU, large undertakings shall be undertakings which on their balance sheet dates exceed at least two of the three following criteria: (i) balance sheet total: EUR 20,000,000; (ii) net turnover: EUR 40,000,000; (iii) average number of employees during the financial year: 250.
94. Pursuant to Article 3(7) of Directive No. 2013/34/EU, large groups shall be groups consisting of parent and subsidiary undertakings to be included in a consolidation and which, on a consolidated basis, exceed the limits of at least two of the three following criteria on the balance sheet date of the parent undertaking: (i) balance sheet total: EUR 20,000,000; (ii) net turnover: EUR 40,000,000; (iii) average number of employees during the financial year: 250.
95. Article 25(2) of Law No. 120/2019.
96. Article 25(3) of Law No. 120/2019.

H. FINAL AND TRANSITORY PROVISIONS

H.1. Time Limits Applicable to the Appeals

The time limits provided for in the Portuguese Tax Procedural Code, approved by Decree-Law No. 433/99, of 26 October 1999, shall be applicable to the appeals provided for in Articles 5(7), 16(6), 20(5), 20(9) and 24(4) of Law No. 120/2019.[97]

H.2. Entry into Force

Law No. 120/2019 entered into force on 20 September 2019,[98] applying to any complaint submitted from 1 July 2019 onwards relating to Questions in Dispute relating to income or capital earned in a tax year commencing on or after 1 January 2018.

Moreover, pursuant to Article 23 of Directive 2017/1852, Portugal has used the faculty to apply the implementing measures of such Directive to Questions in Dispute related to earlier tax years than the tax period beginning on 1 January 2018. Indeed, Law No. 120/2019 contains a transitory provision according to which the rules set forth in such law will apply to any complaint which refers to the tax periods beginning on or after 1 January 2016, if such extension is made possible by the other Member States concerned having used the faculty at stake in a similar fashion.[99]

97. Article 26 of Law No. 120/2019.
98. Article 28 of Law No. 120/2019.
99. Article 27 of Law No. 120/2019.

CHAPTER 11
Spain

Joan Hortalà

A. IMPLEMENTING MEASURES ADOPTED BY SPAIN WITH RESPECT TO DIRECTIVE 2017/1852

In Spain, Directive 2017/1852 was intended to be transposed mainly through regulations, although certain law modifications were also necessary. With this purpose, on 4 February 2020, the Spanish Government passed Royal Decree-Law 3/2020, of 4 February, on urgent measures incorporating into Spanish law various EU directives in the field of public procurement in certain sectors; private insurance; pension plans and funds; taxation and tax litigation (hereinafter 'RDL 3/2020'), which partially implements Directive 2017/1852.

RDL 3/2020 introduces certain amendments to the First Additional Provision of the Non-Resident Income Tax Act, approved by Royal Legislative Decree 5/2004, of 5 March, which regulates the MAP. The main objectives of RDL 3/2020 regarding the MAPs is harmonizing the framework of dispute resolution procedures and reinforcing legal certainty. Specifically, the main legal amendments introduced as for the Directive are as follows:

- Directive 2017/1852 determines that Member States may deny access to the resolution procedure regulated in Article 6 thereof when penalties for tax fraud, deliberate default and gross negligence are imposed. In this respect, Spain, making use of this authorization, defines how these concepts should be understood for the purposes of the Spanish regulations applicable to MAPs.
- cases where the aforementioned penalties have been appealed are set as an exception to the general regime of pre-eminence of the processing of MAPs with respect to judicial and administrative review procedures.

- in addition, the Central Economic-Administrative Tribunal (TEAC)[1] is entrusted with the functions attributed by Directive 2017/1852 to national courts in the constitution and functioning of the advisory commission or alternative resolution commission.

In order to fully implement and transpose Directive 2017/1852, on 23 December 2019, it was made available for consultation the Draft Royal Decree amending the Regulations on MAPs in direct taxation matters, approved by Royal Decree 1794/2008 of November 3 (hereinafter the 'Draft Royal Decree'), which sets forth the domestic implementing measures in order to effectively put into force the provisions of Directive 2017/1852.

The Draft Royal Decree does not substantially alter the structure of the Regulation on MAPs in the field of direct taxation approved by Royal Decree 1794/2008 (hereinafter the 'Regulations on MAPs'), which continues to retain a Title I, which regulates common provisions to the MAPs developed in the aforementioned Regulation; a Title II, which regulates the MAP provided for in the double taxation treaties signed by Spain; a Title III, which develops the procedure provided for in the Arbitration Convention, and a last Title V, to date Title IV, which establishes the system for suspending the collection of the debt when a MAP has been requested.

As the main novelty, the Draft Royal Decree introduces a new Title IV in the Regulations on MAPs, which regulates the mechanisms for the resolution of disputes referred to in Directive 2017/1852. Additionally, certain amendments are made to other titles of the Regulations on MAPs in order to give consistency to the various MAPs regulated to ensure that such regulation is as uniform as possible so as to facilitate its application.

B. GENERAL PROVISIONS

B.1. Subject Matter and Scope

Directive 2017/1852 establishes a procedural framework for the resolution of tax disputes between Member State(s), provided that the disputes arise from the application of agreements and conventions designed to eliminate double taxation of income and, where appropriate, of capital (i.e., Tax Treaties and the Arbitration Convention).

The procedural framework described in Directive 2017/1852, although presenting certain novelties with respect to the existing Spanish national legislation, is not entirely original. The Regulations on MAPs already include in its wording, prior to the entry into force of the Draft Royal Decree, the possibility of appealing to an advisory commission in relation to disputes arising between Member States in the area of transfer pricing and the allocation of profits to permanent establishments, as well as,

1. National Tax Court. The Spanish tax court system is organized through Regional Tax Courts (TEAR) in every autonomous community and a National Tax Court (TEAC). Tax courts are a revision body within the tax authorities and do not form part of the Justice system but depend on the Ministry of Finance.

when so established by the respective applicable double tax treaty. Hence the novelty relates to the objective scope of the occasions in which the advisory commission can be called upon to extend them beyond transfer pricing and allocation of profits to permanent establishments to any other double tax situations unforeseen by the applicable Tax Treaty or EU legislation. This objective scope extension also includes the possibility of appealing to an advisory commission for the admission or non-admission of the procedure.

B.2. Definitions

The Draft Royal Decree does not provide for a specific section transposing the definitions provided in Article 2 of Directive 2017/1852.

The provisions regarding the 'Competent Authority' are set in Article 2 of the Regulations on MAPs which provides a different Spanish Competent Authority depending on the issue under discussion. As a rule, the Spanish Competent Authority is the General Directorate of Taxation (the so-called *Dirección General de Tributos* (DGT)). The Spanish Tax Agency (the so-called *Agencia Estatal de Administración Tributaria* (AEAT)) is responsible for specific cases, those related to transfer pricing matters, including attribution of profits to permanent establishments, for MAP under a double tax treaty, under the Arbitration Convention, or under Directive 2017/1852.

The DGT is responsible for the overall management of MAP cases, among other functions. In the event of MAP covering issues where the two Spanish competent authorities are involved, the file will be coordinated by the DGT.

RDL 2/2020 has set out that the TEAC is entrusted with the functions conferred by Directive 2017/1852 on the national courts regarding the setting up and functioning of the advisory commission or the alternative dispute resolution commission.

The term 'Double Taxation' is defined in the new Article 43 of the Regulations on MAPs, following the definition provided in Directive 2017/1852. In concrete, the referred Article 43 provides that double taxation means the taxation by two or more Member States of one of the taxes covered by a Tax Treaty in respect of the same taxable income or capital where this results in:

- an additional tax charge;
- an increase in the tax liabilities; or
- the cancellation or reduction of losses which could be used to offset taxable profits.

The terms 'Question in Dispute' and 'Affected Person' are not expressly defined but referred to in the new Article 37 of the Regulations on MAPs referred below.

C. COMPLAINT TO START A MAP

C.1. Filing of a Complaint to Start a MAP

New Article 37 of the Regulations on MAPs, as amended by the Draft Royal Decree, which regulates who can apply for a MAP under Directive 2017/1852 states that any taxpayer who meets the following requirements may request the start of a MAP under Directive 2017/1852:

- a person who is a tax resident in Spain or in any other Member State within the meaning of the relevant international convention or income tax treaty in force in Spain; and
- their taxation is directly affected by measures adopted by Spain or by one or more other Member States which involve, or may involve, taxation which is not in accordance with the provisions of international conventions or income tax treaties in force in Spain.

A request to start a MAP under Directive 2017/1852 must be filed within three years from the day following notification of the tax assessment or equivalent measure which involves or may involve taxation not in accordance with the provisions of the international conventions or income tax treaties in force in Spain.[2]

The initial request shall be made in writing and addressed simultaneously to the Spanish Competent Authority and to the other competent authorities affected, unless the taxpayer is an individual or small or medium entity. In the latter case, the request for initiation may be submitted only to the Spanish Competent Authority, which shall, within two months of the receipt of the request, send a notification to the competent authorities of the other Member State concerned.[3]

The Spanish Competent Authority shall notify to the other competent authority the language or languages which it intends to use in its communications during the relevant procedures.[4]

The initial request must include information on the taxpayer and other parties, a description of the transactions under review, and must identify the relevant foreign competent authorities when necessary. In addition, the taxpayer must identify the provisions of the Tax Treaty or convention that the taxpayer believes have been incorrectly applied, along with the taxpayer's interpretation, and state the tax periods that are affected.

The taxpayer must provide a detailed description of the facts and circumstances of the case, which shall include:

- the amounts involved and the currency of the Member State concerned;
- details of any relation, situation or structure concerning the transactions between the persons involved; and

2. Article 38 of the Regulations on MAPs.
3. Article 39(a) of the Regulations on MAPs.
4. Article 39(b) of the Regulations on MAPs.

- the nature and date of the actions which gave rise to the subject matter of the proceedings, including, where appropriate, details of the same income received in the other State concerned and of the inclusion of that income in the taxable amount in that State, and details of the tax required or to be required in respect of that income in the other State concerned. The request must also indicate whether the case or a similar one has been previously submitted to any of the competent authorities concerned and whether the matter includes any issue that may have been analysed as part of an APA or a similar procedure.[5]

The application must be accompanied by relevant documentation, which includes:

- in cases regarding transfer pricing issues, the master file, the local file, and other relevant documentation regarding the transactions under review;
- in all cases, copies of the Spanish tax authorities' assessment of the notification received by the taxpayer, or any reports issued by the tax audit teams or equivalent documents regarding the matter; and
- any documents issued by a foreign competent authority regarding the case.[6]

If the taxpayer is initiating the MAP and self-assessing tax in accordance with regulations in force, a copy of the filed tax returns must be provided.

C.2. Complaint Filed According to Tax Treaties or the Arbitration Convention

According to Article 5 of the Regulations on MAPs in the request for initiation of a MAP before the Spanish Competent Authority, the taxpayer must indicate the MAP procedure or procedures that are applicable to him or her. If, in the course of a MAP other than the MAP regulated under Directive 2017/1852 the taxpayer makes a request to initiate a procedure in accordance with the provisions of Directive 2017/1852, the prior procedure in progress shall end on the date of the receipt of the request by any of the competent authorities of the Member States concerned.

D. THE RESOLUTION OF THE QUESTION IN DISPUTE UNDER THE MAP

D.1. Decision of the Competent Authority with Reference to the Complaint

The Spanish Competent Authority has three months from the submission date to review the documentation and, as the case might be, request some clarifications. A taxpayer who receives a request to amend the application shall simultaneously send a

5. Articles 39 and 9(1) of the Regulations on MAPs.
6. Articles 39 and 9(2) of the Regulations on MAPs.

copy of his or her reply to the competent authorities of the other states concerned. However, where the taxpayer is an individual or small or medium entity, the reply may be submitted only to the Spanish Competent Authority, which, within two months of the receipt of the reply, shall send a copy of the information received to the competent authorities of the other Member States concerned.

The competent authority may reject the taxpayer's MAP request if he or she fails to respond to the request for clarification within three months from the date of the notice.[7]

The application will be considered accepted if the Spanish Competent Authority does not reply within six months after the filing of the request for the MAP, or after the taxpayer submitted responses to requested clarifications. This process protects the taxpayer's interests and is also consistent with the competent authority's obligation to expressly notify the taxpayer if the MAP application is denied.

The grounds for denying the initiation of a MAP include the following:

- no Tax Treaty or convention is applicable;
- the request for the MAP is filed after the three-year period has elapsed;
- the matter relates to a domestic issue and not a treaty issue and is therefore deemed inappropriate for a MAP;
- the matter refers to a matter previously submitted to MAP by the same taxpayer, and the competent authorities have already agreed or the taxpayer has withdrawn the case; and
- the taxpayer does not provide additional information requested by the Spanish Competent Authority.[8]

Denial of MAP requests under Directive 2017/1852 might be appealed in accordance with national rules when all competent authorities of the Member States concerned have rejected the complaint.[9]

Under the regulations of the MAP initiated under the Tax Treaties, the Spanish Competent Authority has the authority to handle the matter unilaterally when it determines that the request is reasonable and that it can provide a solution on its own. In principle, those provisions should also apply for the case of MAP initiated under Directive 2017/1852 as the regulations to the MAP under Directive 2017/1852 refer to these provisions.

D.2. MAP

When the competent authorities of the Member States concerned accept a complaint, they must endeavour to resolve the Question in Dispute by mutual agreement within two years, starting from the last notification of a decision of one of the Member States

7. Articles 39 and 10 of the Regulations on MAPs.
8. Articles 39 and 11 of the Regulations on MAPs.
9. *See* Article 5(2) of Directive 2017/1852.

on the acceptance of the complaint. Such period may be extended up to one year at the request of a competent authority if it is sufficiently justified in writing.[10]

The DGT in general, or the AEAT for cases related to transfer pricing and attributions of profits to permanent establishments, will review the background of the case and establish Spain's position in the MAP (i.e., to draft the position paper to go to the foreign competent authority). DGT will lead cases that must be dealt simultaneously by DGT and AEAT. Spanish Competent Authority might request additional documentation from the taxpayer, in which case, the taxpayer has three months to provide it. During the development of a MAP, the Spanish Competent Authority might request additional information from the taxpayer, which will have ten days, unless a different period is specified in the request, from the day following the notification of the request to provide the documentation. Failure to comply with this request may result in the termination of the MAP.[11]

If the Spanish Competent Authority requests additional information to the taxpayer, it shall answer simultaneously to all the Member States concerned. However, if the taxpayer is an individual or small or medium entity, the reply may be submitted only to the Spanish Competent Authority, which, within two months of the receipt of the reply, shall send a copy of the information received to the competent authorities of the other Member States concerned.[12]

The Spanish Competent Authority will issue and communicate to the foreign competent authority Spain's initial proposal based on its official position.

Competent authorities may exchange as many proposals as necessary to reach an agreement on the matter, although the Tax Treaty's MAP Article is a best efforts clause, not obligating competent authorities to reach an agreement. If the competent authorities fail to reach an agreement within a two-year period, the competent authority of each of the Member State concerned shall notify the affected person indicating the reasons for the failure to reach an agreement.

D.3. Appeal of the Taxpayer Against the Decision Rejecting the Complaint

When at least one of the competent authorities of the Member States concerned (but not all) has rejected the application of the MAP, the taxpayer may request the constitution of an advisory commission to the competent authorities of both Member States. However, if the taxpayer is an individual or small or medium entity, the request for the constitution of an advisory commission might be filed only to the Spanish Competent Authority.

The Member State concerned shall be deemed to have rejected the application of a MAP in the following cases: (i) where the decision of the competent authority is not open to appeal under the national law of the Member State concerned to which it

10. Article 41(1) of the Regulations on MAPs.
11. Articles 41(2) and 12 of the Regulations on MAPs.
12. Article 41(2) of the Regulations on MAPs.

belongs; or (ii) where a final administrative or judicial decision confirming the competent authority's rejection is taken.[13]

A request for the constitution of an advisory commission may be made only if the following conditions are met:

- no appeal can be made against the decision rejecting the application of the MAP;
- no appeal is pending;
- the taxpayer has formally renounced his right of appeal; and
- if the initiation has been refused by a final administrative or judicial decision confirming the competent authority's refusal, that decision is not binding on the competent authority.[14]

The taxpayer must request the constitution of an advisory commission in writing not later than 50 calendar days from the date of receipt of the last notification rejecting the complaint. The advisory commission must be established not later than 120 days from the receipt of the request.[15]

When the advisory commission is set up, it must decide on the acceptance of the complaint within six months from the date of its establishment. The advisory commission must notify its decision within thirty calendar days of its adoption.[16] If the advisory commission accepts the complaint, a MAP is subsequently initiated at the request of one of the competent authorities. However, if a MAP is not initiated within sixty days of the advisory commission's notice, the advisory commission shall deliver an opinion on how to resolve the dispute.[17]

E. DISPUTE RESOLUTION PROCEDURE

E.1. Request to Appointment of the Advisory Commission

When the competent authorities of the Member States concerned have not reached an agreement on how to resolve the Question in Dispute within the two-year period, the taxpayer may request the competent authority to establish an advisory commission.

The taxpayer must request the advisory commission in writing not later than 50 days from the date of receipt of the notification stating that the competent authorities have not reached an agreement. The advisory commission must be established not later than 120 days from the receipt of the request.[18]

The Spanish Competent Authority will deny the establishment of an advisory commission if the taxpayers concerned have been sanctioned with serious tax penalties or criminal tax offences, or, on a case-by-case basis, where question under dispute does

13. Article 40(1) of the Regulations on MAPs.
14. Article 40(2) of the Regulations on MAPs.
15. Article 40(3) of the Regulations on MAPs.
16. Article 40(5) of the Regulations on MAPs.
17. Article 40(6) of the Regulations on MAPs.
18. Article 42 of the Regulations on MAPs.

not give rise to double taxation. In that case, the competent authority shall inform the taxpayer and the competent authorities of the other Member States concerned without delay.[19]

E.2. Appointment of the Advisory Commission

The advisory commission shall be appointed within 120 days from the receipt of the request filed by the taxpayer. Once established, its chairman shall promptly inform the taxpayer.

The advisory commission will have the following composition:

- one chair;
- one representative of each competent authority concerned. If the competent authorities agree, two additional representatives may be selected for each competent authority;
- one independent person of standing, appointed by each competent authority of the Member States concerned among the persons designated in the list of independent persons referred in section E.4. below. If the competent authorities agree, two additional persons may be appointed for each competent authority.

After the appointment of the independent persons, an alternate shall be appointed for each of them, in case the latter are unable to perform their duties.[20]

The competent authority shall agree with the competent authorities of the Member States concerned on the rules for the designation of the independent persons. Where the competent authorities do not agree upon the rules for the designation of the independent persons, the appointment of such persons shall be by lot.[21]

The competent authority may oppose the appointment of any independent person when:

- the appointed person belongs to or works on behalf of one of the tax administrations concerned (or has done so at any time during the previous three years);
- where the appointed person has participated, been employed, or advised in the taxpayer in the last five years;
- where the person does not provide sufficient guarantee of objectivity for the resolution of the question under dispute, or
- where that person is an employee of a company providing tax advice or otherwise providing tax advice on a professional basis, or was in that situation at any time for at least three years before the date of his appointment.[22]

19. Article 43(1) of the Regulations on MAPs.
20. Article 45(1) of the Regulations on MAPs.
21. Article 45(2) of the Regulations on MAPs.
22. Article 45(4) of the Regulations on MAPs.

The representatives of the competent authorities and the independent persons appointed elect a chairman from the list of independent persons.[23]

E.3. Appointment of the Advisory Commission Made by a Competent Court

If the advisory commission is not set up within the 120-day period, the taxpayer may request the Central-Economic Administrative Tribunal (TEAC) to set up the advisory commission.

If none of the competent authorities of the Member States concerned has appointed at least one independent person, the taxable person may request the TEAC to appoint the two independent persons from the list of independent persons referred in section E.4. below. Those independent persons shall draw lots to appoint the chairman from that list of independent persons.[24]

The appointment of the independent persons and their substitutes by the TEAC shall be made within thirty calendar days of the end of the period of 120 days period to set up the advisory commission by the competent authorities.

The TEAC shall take a decision and inform the affected person, and the Spanish Competent Authority, which shall in turn inform without delay the competent authority of the other Member States concerned.[25]

E.4. List of the Independent Persons of Standing

The list of independent persons shall include all independent persons appointed by the Member States.

In Spain, the DGT and the AEAT shall by mutual agreement choose at least three competent, independent persons capable of acting impartially and with integrity to be included in the list of independent persons. In the event that, after their appointment, any of these persons should incur in any cause of ineligibility, the DGT and the AEAT shall decide by mutual agreement on their replacement.[26]

The DGT shall communicate to the EU Commission the names of the independent persons chosen, providing complete and updated information on their academic and professional background, competencies, technical knowledge and conflicts of interest. The communication shall specify which of the persons nominated may be appointed chairman. The DGT shall promptly inform the EU Commission of any changes in the list of independent persons.[27]

Where, for reasons of lack of independence, the DGT, in agreement with the AEAT, objects to a person remaining on the list of independent persons, it shall inform the Commission thereof by providing appropriate evidence of lack of independence. The Commission shall in turn inform the Member State which appointed that person of

23. Article 45(7) of the Regulations on MAPs.
24. Article 47(1) of the Regulations on MAPs.
25. Article 47(2) of the Regulations on MAPs.
26. Article 46(2) of the Regulations on MAPs.
27. Article 46(3) of the Regulations on MAPs.

the objection and of the evidence in support thereof. On the basis of such opposition and evidence, that Member State shall within six months take the necessary measures to investigate the complaint and to decide whether or not to maintain that person on the list, and shall inform the Commission thereof without delay.[28]

E.5. Alternative Dispute Resolution Commission

Alternatively to the advisory commission, in accordance with Article 10 of Directive 2017/1852, the competent authorities of the Member States concerned may agree to set up an alternative dispute resolution commission instead of an advisory commission to deliver an opinion on how to resolve the Question in Dispute. The alternative dispute resolution commission can be in the form of a permanent standing committee. An alternative dispute resolution commission may apply, where appropriate, any dispute resolution processes or techniques to solve the Question in Dispute in a binding manner. The alternative dispute resolution commission must deliver its opinion within the six-month period.[29]

F. COMMON PROCEDURAL PROVISION

F.1. Rules of Functioning for the Advisory Commission or Alternative Dispute Resolution Commission

Within the period of 120 days to set up the advisory commission or the alternative dispute resolution commission, the Spanish Competent Authority shall notify the taxpayer of the rules of functioning for the advisory commission; the date by which the opinion on the resolution of the Question in Dispute shall be adopted; and the Articles of the Tax Treaty and any internal rules that might be applicable.[30]

The competent authority shall agree with the competent authorities of the other Member States concerned on the functioning rules which shall include, in particular:

- the description and characteristics of the subject matter of the procedure;
- the legal and factual issues to be resolved as agreed between the competent authorities of the Member States concerned;
- the form of the dispute resolution body, which shall be either an advisory commission or an alternative resolution commission, as well as the type of procedure for the alternative resolution if this differs from the independent opinion procedure applied by an advisory commission;
- the time limits for the procedure;
- the composition of the respective commission (including the number and names of members, details of their powers and qualifications, and disclosure of members' conflicts of interest);

28. Article 46(5) of the Regulations on MAPs.
29. Article 48 of the Regulations on MAPs.
30. Article 49(1) of the Regulations on MAPs.

- the rules governing the participation of the taxable person and third parties in the proceedings, exchanges of notes, information and evidence, costs and any other procedural or organizational aspects;
- the logistical aspects of the proceedings of the advisory commission and the manner according to which it will disclose its position.[31]

Where an advisory commission is set up to give an opinion when the complaint has been rejected, only the following aspects shall be defined by the competent authorities:

- the description and characteristics of the subject matter of the procedure;
- the time limits for the procedure;
- the composition of the advisory commission or the alternative dispute resolution commission (including the number and names of its members, indication of their competence and qualifications and disclosure of their conflicts of interest);
- the rules governing the participation of the affected person and third parties in the procedure, the exchange of briefs, information and evidence, costs, the type of dispute resolution procedure to be used and other relevant procedural or organizational matters.

Where the competent authorities have not notified the functioning rules to the affected persons, the independent persons and the chairman shall complete the functioning rules as laid down for that purpose by the EU Commission and send them to the taxable person within two weeks of the establishment of the respective commission. Where the independent persons and the chairman disagree on the functioning rules or do not notify the taxable person, the latter may apply to the TEAC for an order for the application of the operating rules.[32]

Once the advisory commission has been set up, as long as the competent authorities of the Member States concerned agree so, the taxpayer may provide the advisory commission with any information, evidence or documents which might be relevant to the decision. Likewise, the advisory commission may ask the taxpayer and the competent authority for any information, evidence or documents. However, the competent authority may refuse to provide such information in any of the following cases:

- where obtaining the information requires administrative measures that are contrary to domestic law;
- where the information cannot be obtained under domestic law;
- where the information relates to commercial, business, industrial or professional secrets or commercial procedures;
- where the disclosure of the information is contrary to public policy.[33]

31. Article 49(2) of the Regulations on MAPs.
32. Article 49(3) of the Regulations on MAPs.
33. Article 44(1) of the Regulations on MAPs.

Taxpayers may, if they previously request it and with the consent of the competent authorities of the Member States concerned, attend or be represented before the advisory commission, and must do so if the advisory commission so requests.[34]

F.2. Costs of the MAP

Pursuant to Article 50 of the Regulations on MAPs, unless the concerned Member States of the competent authorities have agreed otherwise, the following costs shall be shared equally between the Member States:

- expenditure incurred by independent persons of standing, which must be equivalent to the average of the amount usually reimbursed to senior officials of the concerned Member States; and
- the fees of the independent persons, where applicable, which are to be limited to EUR 1,000 per person per day for every day on which the advisory commission or alternative dispute resolution commission meets.

Under no circumstances will the costs incurred by the taxpayer be borne by the Spanish State.[35]

If the taxable person: (i) withdraws from the MAP, or (ii) requests the setting up of the advisory commission because the competent authorities denied the access to the MAP, and the advisory commission decides that the competent authority concerned has correctly rejected the MAP, all the costs of the MAP referred in previous paragraph shall be borne by the taxable person if the competent authorities of the Member States concerned agree so.[36]

F.3. The Opinion of the Advisory Commission or the Alternative Dispute Resolution Commission

An advisory commission or alternative dispute resolution commission must deliver its opinion to the competent authorities no later than six months from the date it was established. This period might be extended in three additional months, in which case the respective committee shall inform the competent authorities of the Member States concerned and the taxpayers of such extension.[37]

The advisory commission or alternative dispute resolution commission shall base its resolution on the provisions of the applicable international convention or Tax Treaty and on the domestic tax laws of the Member States concerned, where applicable.[38]

34. Article 44(2) of the Regulations on MAPs.
35. Article 50(1) of the Regulations on MAPs.
36. Article 50(2) of the Regulations on MAPs.
37. Article 51(1) of the Regulations on MAPs.
38. Article 51(2) of the Regulations on MAPs.

The Commission shall adopt its opinion by a simple majority of its members. If no majority is reached, the chairman shall have the casting vote for the adoption of the final opinion. The chairman shall forward the opinion to the competent authorities.[39]

The opinion of the advisory commission or alternative dispute resolution commission shall be given in writing.[40]

F.4. Final Decision of the Competent Authorities

The competent authorities concerned have six months from the date on which they receive the opinion to agree on how to resolve the Question in Dispute. The competent authorities may take a decision which deviates from the opinion; however, if they fail to reach an agreement, they are bound by that opinion.[41]

The Spanish Competent Authority shall notify the taxpayer within thirty days of the agreement reached, who may accept it or reject it.[42]

The final decision is binding on all the Member States concerned[43] but does not constitute a precedent.[44] The final decision is implemented subject to the affected person submitting a written statement in which he or she agrees to the mutual agreement and to waive his or her right to all outstanding appeals or claims relating to the same issues discussed in the MAP, or abandons any pending appeals that he or she may have concerning the elements of the tax liability that are the subject of the MAP.

F.5. End of a MAP

The MAP under Directive 2017/1852, in addition to those situations where the competent authorities reach an agreement, might be terminated by any of the following circumstances:

- by the taxpayer withdrawal;
- on the grounds that the matter which is the subject of the proceedings does not exist or has disappeared;
- due to repeated miss attention by the taxpayer to additional information requests during the MAP made by any of the competent authorities of any of the States concerned, after consultation with the competent authorities of the other State;
- by a final judgment of a Spanish court, or by any equivalent decision of a court of another State concerned, provided that such judgment relates to the elements of the tax obligation that were the object of the MAP, and provided

39. Article 51(3) of the Regulations on MAPs.
40. Article 51(4) of the Regulations on MAPs.
41. Article 54(2) of the Regulations on MAPs.
42. Article 54(3) of the Regulations on MAPs.
43. Article 54(4) of the Regulations on MAPs.
44. Article 54(5) of the Regulations on MAPs.

that under the national law of the other State whose courts have given the judgment, the competent authority is bound by that decision.[45]

F.6. Withdrawal

A taxpayer may withdraw from a MAP under Directive 2017/1852 at any time. This decision should be communicated to all the competent authorities concerned. This communication shall immediately end the MAP. However, where the taxpayer is an individual or small or medium entity, the communication to withdraw the MAP might be filed only to the Spanish Competent Authority.

The withdrawal of the MAP will prevent the possibility to reopen the case in the future, as one of the grounds for rejecting a MAP request is the fact that the case has been previously reviewed or withdrawn.[46]

F.7. Enforcement of Decisions Taken under the MAP or Dispute Resolution Procedures

Once the MAP decision is final, the Spanish tax authorities should be notified within one month. This shall be understood as an official notification to the AEAT team in charge of issuing the final assessment deriving from the MAP. The fact that a representative of the AEAT has been involved in the case from the start should theoretically ease the process.[47]

However, in practice, taxpayers should not expect to receive tax refunds immediately after the end of the MAP. For this reason, the MAP decision may be implemented ex officio or at the request of the taxpayer, who will be interested in monitoring the process and following up with the tax authorities.

A MAP decision is implemented in Spain through a new assessment of each of the taxable years concerned, taking into account the regulations in force in each taxable year. If the case concerns a tax not based on taxable years but accrued and declared on a transaction-by-transaction basis, a new assessment will be issued upon the adoption of the MAP decision based on the relevant regulations applicable at the moment of accrual of each tax event included in the MAP.[48]

However, the implementation of the MAP decision may be carried out through a single assessment document including or adding up the result of all the assessments for each taxable year or taxable event analysed within the MAP. If the MAP refers to a previous assessment of the Spanish tax authorities, the contents of the MAP decision and its execution will legally modify it (or declare it null, when needed).[49]

45. Article 52 of the Regulations on MAPs.
46. Article 53 of the Regulations on MAPs.
47. Articles 56 and 17(1) of the Regulations on MAPs.
48. Articles 56 and 17(3) of the Regulations on MAPs.
49. Articles 56 and 17(4) of the Regulations on MAPs.

The new assessment resulting from the MAP decision shall include interest for late payment corresponding to the outstanding tax liability derived therefrom.[50]

F.8. Publicity

Competent authorities can agree to publish and disclose in full the decisions taken in the context of a dispute resolution procedure pursuant to Article 55 of the Regulations on MAPs, subject to the consent of each of the affected persons.

The competent authority shall forward the information to be published to the taxpayer before publication. The taxpayer may, within sixty calendar days of receiving that information, request that any information relating to commercial, business, industrial or professional secrets or commercial procedures, or which is contrary to public policy, not to be published.

If the competent authorities involved or the affected persons did not give their consent to the full publication of a decision, the competent authorities shall publish a summary of the decision containing a description of the problem identified and of the object, date and periods of settlement, legal basis, industry, and a brief summary of the final result and description of the method of arbitration used, if any. In these cases, the competent authorities shall notify the EU Commission without delay of the information to be published.

G. FINAL AND TRANSITORY PROVISIONS

G.1. Entry into Force

The Draft Royal Decree shall enter into force the following date of its publication in the Spanish Official Gazette (BOE).

MAPs initiated before the date of entry into force of the Draft Royal Decree will not be eligible for this regulation, hence shall be governed by the regulations in force prior to that date until their final conclusion.

50. Articles 56 and 17(5) of the Regulations on MAPs.

APPENDIX: EU Council Directive 2017/1852

Article 1
Subject matter and scope

This Directive lays down rules on a mechanism to resolve disputes between Member States when those disputes arise from the interpretation and application of agreements and conventions that provide for the elimination of double taxation of income and, where applicable, capital. It also lays down the rights and obligations of the affected persons when such disputes arise. For the purposes of this Directive, the matter giving rise to such disputes is referred to as a 'question in dispute'.

Article 2
Definitions

1. For the purposes of this Directive, the following definitions apply:
   (a) 'competent authority' means the authority of a Member State which has been designated as such by the Member State concerned;
   (b) 'competent court' means the court, tribunal or other body of a Member State which has been designated as such by the Member State concerned;
   (c) 'double taxation' means the imposition by two or more Member States of taxes covered by an agreement or convention referred to in Article 1 in respect of the same taxable income or capital when it gives rise to either: (i) an additional tax charge; (ii) an increase in tax liabilities; or (iii) the cancellation or reduction of losses that could be used to offset taxable profits;
   (d) 'affected person' means any person, including an individual, that is a resident of a Member State for tax purposes, and whose taxation is directly affected by a question in dispute.
2. Any term not defined in this Directive shall, unless the context requires otherwise, have the meaning that it has at that time under the relevant agreement or convention referred to in Article 1 that applies on the date of receipt of the first notification of the action that resulted in, or that will result

in, a question in dispute. In the absence of a definition under such agreement or convention, an undefined term shall have the meaning that it had at that time under the law of the Member State concerned for the purposes of the taxes to which the said agreement or convention applies, any meaning under the applicable tax laws of that Member State prevailing over a meaning given to the term under other laws of that Member State.

Article 3
Complaint

1. Any affected person shall be entitled to submit a complaint on a question in dispute to each of the competent authorities of each of the Member States concerned, requesting the resolution thereof. The complaint shall be submitted within 3 years from the receipt of the first notification of the action resulting in, or that will result in, the question in dispute, regardless of whether the affected person has recourse to the remedies available under the national law of any of the Member States concerned. The affected person shall simultaneously submit the complaint with the same information to each competent authority, and shall indicate in the complaint which other Member States are concerned. The affected person shall ensure that each Member State concerned receives the complaint in at least one of the following languages:
   (a) one of that Member State's official languages in accordance with national law; or
   (b) any other language that such a Member State accepts for this purpose.
2. Each competent authority shall acknowledge receipt of the complaint within 2 months from the receipt of the complaint. Each competent authority shall also inform the competent authorities of the other Member States concerned of the receipt of the complaint within 2 months of such receipt. The competent authorities shall inform each other at that time also about the language or languages they intend to use for their communications during the relevant proceedings.
3. The complaint shall only be accepted if, as a first step, the affected person making the complaint provides the competent authorities of each of the Member States concerned with the following information:
   (a) the name(s), address(es), tax identification number(s) and any other information necessary for identification of the affected person(s) who presented the complaint to the competent authorities and of any other person concerned;
   (b) the tax periods concerned;
   (c) details of the relevant facts and circumstances of the case (including details of structure of the transaction and of the relationship between the affected person and the other parties to the relevant transactions, as well as any facts determined in good faith in a mutually binding agreement between the affected person and the tax administration, where

applicable) and more specifically, the nature and the date of the actions giving rise to the question in dispute (including, where applicable, details of same income received in the other Member State and of inclusion of such income in the taxable income in the other Member State, and details of the tax charged or that will be charged in relation to such income in the other Member State), as well as the related amounts in the currencies of the Member States concerned, with a copy of any supporting documents;

(d) reference to the applicable national rules and to the agreement or convention referred to in Article 1; where more than one agreement or convention is applicable, the affected person making the complaint shall specify which agreement or convention is being interpreted in relation to the relevant question in dispute. Such agreement or convention shall be the applicable agreement or convention for the purposes of this Directive;

(e) the following information provided by the affected person who presented the complaint to the competent authorities, together with copies of any supporting documents:

  (i) an explanation of why the affected person considers that there is a question in dispute;

  (ii) the details of any appeals and litigation initiated by the affected person regarding the relevant transactions and of any court decisions concerning the question in dispute;

  (iii) a commitment by the affected person to respond as completely and quickly as possible to all appropriate requests made by a competent authority and to provide any documentation at the request of the competent authorities;

  (iv) a copy of the final tax assessment decision in the form of a final tax assessment notice, tax audit report or other equivalent document leading to the question in dispute and a copy of any other documents issued by the tax authorities with regard to the question in dispute where relevant;

  (v) information on any complaint submitted by the affected person under another mutual agreement procedure or under another dispute resolution procedure as defined in Article 16(5) and an express commitment by the affected person that he will abide by the provisions of Article 16(5), if applicable;

(f) any specific additional information requested by the competent authorities that is considered necessary to undertake the substantive consideration of the particular case.

4. The competent authorities of each of the Member States concerned may request the information referred to in point (f) of paragraph 3 within 3 months from the receipt of the complaint. Further requests for information may be made during the mutual agreement procedure under Article 4 if the competent authorities consider this to be necessary. National laws regarding the protection of information and the protection of trade, business, industrial or professional secret or trade processes shall apply. An affected person that

receives a request in accordance with point (f) of paragraph 3 shall reply within 3 months of receiving the request. A copy of this reply shall also be sent simultaneously to the competent authorities of the other Member States concerned.

5. The competent authorities of each of the Member States concerned shall take a decision on the acceptance or rejection of the complaint within 6 months of the receipt thereof or within 6 months of the receipt of the information referred to in point (f) of paragraph 3, whichever is later. The competent authorities shall inform the affected person and the competent authorities of the other Member States of their decision without delay.

   Within the period of 6 months from the receipt of a complaint, or within 6 months of the receipt of the information referred to in point (f) of paragraph 3, whichever is later, a competent authority may decide to resolve the question in dispute on a unilateral basis, without involving the other competent authorities of the Member States concerned. In such case, the relevant competent authority shall notify the affected person and the other competent authorities of the Member States concerned without delay, following which the proceedings under this Directive shall be terminated.

6. An affected person that wishes to withdraw a complaint shall simultaneously submit a written notification of withdrawal to each of the competent authorities of the Member States concerned. Such notification shall terminate all proceedings under this Directive with immediate effect. Competent authorities of the Members States who receive such a notification shall inform the other competent authorities of the Member States concerned of the termination of proceedings without delay.

   If for any reason a question in dispute ceases to exist, all proceedings under this Directive shall terminate with immediate effect, and the competent authorities of the Member States concerned shall inform the affected person of this state of affairs and of the general reasons therefore without delay.

Article 4
Mutual agreement procedure

1. Where the competent authorities of the Member States concerned accept a complaint, they shall endeavour to resolve the question in dispute by mutual agreement within 2 years, starting from the last notification of a decision of one of the Member States on the acceptance of the complaint.

   The period of 2 years referred to in the first subparagraph may be extended by up to 1 year at the request of a competent authority of a Member State concerned to all of the other competent authorities of the Member States concerned, if the requesting competent authority provides written justification.

2. Once the competent authorities of the Member States have reached an agreement as to how to resolve the question in dispute within the period

provided for in paragraph 1, the competent authority of each of the Member States concerned shall, without delay, notify this agreement to the affected person, as a decision that is binding on the authority and enforceable by the affected person, subject to the affected person accepting the decision and renouncing the right to any other remedy, where applicable. Where proceedings regarding such other remedies have already commenced, the decision shall only become binding and enforceable once the affected person has provided evidence to the competent authorities of the Member States concerned that action has been taken to terminate those proceedings. Such evidence shall be provided not later than 60 days from the date on which such decision was notified to the affected person. The decision shall then be implemented without delay, irrespective of any time limits prescribed by the national law of the Member States concerned.

3. Where the competent authorities of the Member States concerned have not reached an agreement on how to resolve the question in dispute within the period provided for in paragraph 1, the competent authority of each of the Member States concerned shall inform the affected person indicating the general reasons for the failure to reach agreement.

Article 5
Competent authority decision concerning the complaint

1. The competent authority of a Member State concerned may decide to reject a complaint within the period provided for in Article 3(5) if:
   (a) the complaint lacks information required under Article 3(3) (including any information requested under Article 3(3)(f) that was not submitted within the deadline specified in Article 3(4));
   (b) there is no question in dispute; or
   (c) the complaint was not submitted within the 3-year period set out in Article 3(1).

   When informing the affected person in accordance with the provisions of Article 3(5), the competent authority shall provide the general reasons for its rejection.
2. Where a competent authority of a Member State concerned has not taken a decision on the complaint within the time provided for in Article 3(5), the complaint shall be deemed to be accepted by that competent authority.
3. The affected person shall be entitled to appeal against the decision of the competent authorities of the Member States concerned in accordance with national rules where all competent authorities of the Member States concerned have rejected the complaint. An affected person who exercises this appeal right shall be barred from making a request under Article 6(1)(a):
   (a) while the decision is still under appeal according to the laws of the Member State concerned;

(b) where the rejection decision can still be further appealed under the appeal procedure of the Member States concerned; or

(c) when a rejection decision has been confirmed under the appeal procedure in point (a) but it is not possible to derogate from the decision of the relevant court or other judicial bodies in any of the Member States concerned.

Where the appeal right has been exercised, the decision of the relevant court or other judicial body shall be considered for the purposes of Article 6(1)(a).

Article 6
Dispute resolution by the Advisory Commission

1. Upon a request made by the affected person to the competent authorities of the Member States concerned, an advisory commission (an 'Advisory Commission') shall be set up by such competent authorities in accordance with Article 8 where:
   (a) the complaint submitted by such affected person was rejected under Article 5(1) by at least one, but not all of the competent authorities of Member States concerned; or
   (b) the competent authorities of the Member States concerned had accepted the complaint that was submitted by the affected person but failed to reach an agreement on how to resolve the question in dispute by mutual agreement within the time limit provided for in Article 4(1).

   The affected person may only make such a request if, in accordance with any applicable national rules against a rejection referred to in Article 5(1): no appeal can be made; no appeal is pending; or the affected person has formally renounced his right of appeal. The request shall include a declaration to this effect.

   The affected person shall make the request to set up an Advisory Commission in writing, not later than 50 days from the date of receipt of the notification under Articles 3(5) or 4(3) or 50 days from the date of delivery of the decision by the relevant court or judicial body under Article 5(3), as the case may be. The Advisory Commission shall be set up not later than 120 days from the receipt of such request, and once set up, its chair shall inform the affected person thereof without delay.
2. The Advisory Commission set up in the case of point (a) of paragraph 1 shall adopt a decision on the acceptance of the complaint within 6 months from the date of its establishment. It shall notify the competent authorities of its decision within 30 days of the adoption thereof.

   Where the Advisory Commission has confirmed that all of the requirements under Article 3 have been satisfied, the mutual agreement procedure provided for in Article 4 shall be initiated at the request of one of the competent authorities. The competent authority concerned shall notify the

Advisory Commission, the other competent authorities concerned and the affected person of that request. The period provided for in Article 4(1) shall start from the date of the notification of the decision taken by the Advisory Commission of the acceptance of the complaint.

Where none of the competent authorities has requested initiation of the mutual agreement procedure within 60 days of the date of the notification of the decision of the Advisory Commission, the Advisory Commission shall provide an opinion on how to resolve the question in dispute as provided for in Article 14(1). In such a case, for the purposes of Article 14(1), the Advisory Commission shall be deemed to have been set up on the date on which that 60-day period expired.

3. In the case of point (b) of the first subparagraph of paragraph (1) of this Article, the Advisory Commission shall deliver an opinion on how to resolve the question in dispute in accordance with Article 14(1).

Article 7

Appointments by competent courts or national appointing body

1. If an Advisory Commission is not set up within the period provided for in Article 6(1), Member States shall provide that the relevant affected person may apply to a competent court or to any other body or person designated in their national law for the carrying out of such function (national appointing body) to set up the Advisory Commission.

   Where the competent authority of a Member State has failed to appoint at least one independent person of standing and a substitute, the affected person may request the competent court or national appointing body in that Member State to appoint an independent person of standing and a substitute from the list referred to in Article 9.

   If the competent authorities of all Member States concerned have failed to do so, the affected person may request the competent courts or national appointing body of each Member State to appoint the two independent persons of standing from the list referred to in Article 9. Those independent persons of standing shall appoint the chair by drawing lots from the list of independent persons according to Article 8(3).

   Affected persons shall submit their referral to appoint the independent persons of standing and their substitutes to each of their respective states of residence, if more than one affected person is involved in the proceedings, or to the Member States whose competent authorities have failed to appoint at least one independent person of standing and a substitute if only one affected person is involved.
2. The appointment of the independent persons and their substitutes under paragraph 1 of this Article shall be referred to a competent court of a Member State or national appointing body only after the end of the 120-day period referred to in Article 6(1), and within 30 days after the end of that period.

3. The competent court or national appointing body shall adopt a decision under paragraph 1 and notify it to the applicant. The applicable procedure for the competent court to appoint the independent persons, when the Member States fail to appoint them, shall be the same as the procedure under national rules in matters of civil and commercial arbitration that applies when courts or national appointing bodies appoint arbitrators because parties have failed to agree in this respect. The competent court or national appointing body of the Member State shall inform the competent authority of that Member State, which shall in turn inform the competent authority of the other Member States concerned without delay. The competent authority of the Member State that initially failed to appoint the independent person of standing and the substitute shall be entitled to appeal the decision of the court, or national appointing body in that Member State, provided that the competent authority has the right to do so under national law. In case of rejection, the applicant shall be entitled to appeal against the decision of the court in accordance with national procedural rules.

Article 8
The Advisory Commission

1. The Advisory Commission referred to in Article 6 shall have the following composition:
   (a) one chair;
   (b) one representative of each competent authority concerned. If the competent authorities agree, the number of such representatives may be increased to two for each competent authority;
   (c) one independent person of standing, who shall be appointed by each competent authority of the Member States concerned from the list referred to in Article 9. If the competent authorities agree, the number of such persons appointed may be increased to two for each competent authority.
2. The rules for the appointment of the independent persons of standing shall be agreed between the competent authorities of the Member States concerned. Following the appointment of the independent persons of standing, a substitute shall be appointed for each of them according to the rules for the appointment of the independent persons in cases where the independent persons are prevented from carrying out their duties.
3. Where the rules for the appointment of independent persons of standing have not been agreed in accordance with paragraph 2, the appointment of such persons shall be carried out by drawing lots.
4. Except where the independent persons of standing have been appointed by the competent court or national appointing body as provided in Article 7(1), the competent authority of any of the Member States concerned may object to the appointment of any particular independent person of standing for any reason

agreed in advance between the competent authorities concerned or for any of the following reasons:

(a) that person belongs to or is working on behalf of one of the tax administrations concerned or was in such a situation at any time during the previous 3 years;

(b) that person has, or has had, a material holding in or voting right in or is or has been an employee of or adviser, at any time during the last 5 years prior to the date of his appointment, to any affected person concerned;

(c) that person does not offer a sufficient guarantee of objectivity for the settlement of the dispute or disputes to be decided;

(d) that person is an employee with an enterprise that provides tax advice or otherwise gives tax advice on a professional basis, or was in such a situation at any time during a period of at least 3 years prior to the date of his appointment.

5. Any competent authority of a Member State concerned may request that a person of standing who has been appointed in accordance with paragraph 2 or 3, or his substitute, shall disclose any interest, relationship or any other matter that is likely to affect that person's independence or impartiality or that might reasonably create an appearance of bias in the proceedings.

   For a period of 12 months after the decision of the Advisory Commission was delivered, an independent person of standing who is part of the Advisory Commission shall not be in a situation that would have given cause to a competent authority to object to his appointment as provided for in this paragraph had he been in that situation at the time of appointment to that Advisory Commission.

6. The representatives of the competent authorities and the independent persons of standing appointed in accordance with paragraph 1 of this Article shall elect a chair from the list of persons referred to in Article 9. Unless the representatives of each competent authority and independent persons of standing agree otherwise, the chair shall be a judge.

Article 9
The list of independent persons of standing

1. The list of independent persons of standing shall consist of all the independent persons of standing nominated by the Member States. For this purpose, each Member State shall nominate at least three individuals who are competent and independent, and who can act with impartiality and integrity.

2. Each Member State shall notify the Commission of the names of the independent persons of standing who it has nominated. Each Member State shall also provide the Commission with complete and up-to-date information regarding those persons' professional and academic background, their competence, their expertise and any conflicts of interest that they may have. Member States may specify in the notification which of those persons may be appointed as a chair.

3. Member States shall inform the Commission of any changes to the list of independent persons without delay.

   Each Member State shall put in place procedures for removing any person whom it has appointed from the list of independent persons of standing if that person ceases to be independent.

   Where, taking into consideration the relevant provisions of this Article, a Member State has reasonable cause to object to an independent person of standing remaining in the abovementioned list for reasons of lack of independence, it shall inform the Commission and provide appropriate evidence to support its concern. The Commission shall in turn inform the Member State that nominated such person of the objection and supporting evidence. On the basis of such objection and supporting evidence, the latter Member State shall within 6 months take the necessary steps to investigate the complaint, and shall decide whether to retain or remove that person from the list. The Member State shall then notify the Commission accordingly without delay.

Article 10
The Alternative Dispute Resolution Commission

1. The competent authorities of the Member States concerned may agree to set up an alternative dispute resolution commission (an 'Alternative Dispute Resolution Commission') instead of an Advisory Commission to deliver an opinion on how to resolve the question in dispute in accordance with Article 14. The competent authorities of the Member States may also agree to set up an Alternative Dispute Resolution Commission in the form of a committee that is of a permanent nature (a 'Standing Committee').
2. Except for the rules regarding the independence of its members set out in Article 8(4) and 8(5), the Alternative Dispute Resolution Commission may differ regarding its composition and form from the Advisory Commission. An Alternative Dispute Resolution Commission may apply, where appropriate, any dispute resolution processes or technique to solve the question in dispute in a binding manner. As an alternative to the type of dispute resolution process applied by the Advisory Commission under Article 8, i.e. the independent opinion process, any other type of dispute resolution process, including the 'final offer' arbitration process (otherwise known as 'last best offer' arbitration), can be agreed by the competent authorities of the Member States concerned under this Article and applied by the Alternative Dispute Resolution Commission.
3. The competent authorities of the Member States concerned shall agree on the Rules of Functioning in accordance with Article 11.
4. Articles 12 and 13 shall apply to the Alternative Dispute Resolution Commission unless otherwise agreed to in the Rules of Functioning referred to in Article 11.

Article 11
Rules of Functioning

1. Member States shall provide that, within the 120-day period provided for in Article 6(1), the competent authority of each of the Member States concerned shall notify the affected person with the following:
   (a) the Rules of Functioning for the Advisory Commission or Alternative Dispute Resolution Commission;
   (b) the date by which the opinion on the resolution of the question in dispute shall be adopted;
   (c) references to any applicable legal provisions in national law of the Member States and to any applicable agreements or conventions.
2. The Rules of Functioning shall be signed between the competent authorities of the Member States involved in the dispute. The Rules of Functioning shall provide in particular:
   (a) the description and the characteristics of the question in dispute;
   (b) the terms of reference on which the competent authorities of the Member States agree as regards the legal and factual questions to be resolved;
   (c) the form of the dispute resolution body, which shall be either an Advisory Commission or an Alternative Dispute Resolution Commission, as well as the type of process for any Alternative Dispute Resolution, if the process differs from the independent opinion process applied by an Advisory Commission;
   (d) the time frame for the dispute resolution procedure;
   (e) the composition of the Advisory Commission or Alternative Dispute Resolution Commission (including the number and names of the members, details of their competence and qualifications, and disclosing any conflicts of interest of the members);
   (f) the rules governing the participation of the affected person(s) and third parties in the proceedings, exchanges of memoranda, information and evidence, the costs, the type of dispute resolution process to be used, and any other relevant procedural or organisational matters;
   (g) the logistical arrangements for the Advisory Commission's proceedings and delivery of its opinion.

   If an Advisory Commission is set up to deliver an opinion under point (a) of the first subparagraph of Article 6(1), only the information referred to points (a), (d), (e) and (f) of the second subparagraph of Article 11(2) shall be set out in the Rules of Functioning.
3. The Commission shall establish standard Rules of Functioning on the basis of the provisions of the second subparagraph of paragraph 2 of this Article by means of implementing acts. Such standard Rules of Functioning shall apply in cases where the Rules of Functioning are incomplete or were not notified to the affected person. Those implementing acts shall be adopted in accordance with the procedure referred to in Article 20(2).

4. Where the competent authorities have not notified the Rules of Functioning to the affected person in accordance with paragraphs 1 and 2, the independent persons of standing and the chair shall complete the Rules of Functioning on the basis of the standard form provided for under paragraph 3 and shall send them to the affected person within two weeks from the date that the Advisory Commission or Alternative Dispute Resolution Commission was set up. Where the independent persons and the Chair have not agreed on the Rules of Functioning or have not notified them to the affected person, the affected person or affected persons may apply to a competent court in one of the Member States concerned in order to obtain an order for the implementation of the Rules of Functioning.

Article 12

Costs of proceedings

1. Except as provided in paragraph 2, and unless the competent authorities of the Member States concerned have agreed otherwise, the following costs shall be shared equally among the Member States:
   (a) the expenses of the independent persons of standing, which are to be an amount equivalent to the average of the usual amount reimbursed to high ranking civil servants of the Member States concerned; and
   (b) the fees of the independent persons, where applicable, which are to be limited to Euro 1,000 per person per day for every day on which the Advisory Commission or Alternative Dispute Resolution Commission meets. Costs that are incurred by the affected person shall not be borne by Member States.
2. Where the affected person has made:
   (a) a notification of withdrawal of complaint under Article 3(6); or
   (b) a request under the provisions of Article 6(1) following a rejection made under Article 5(1) and the Advisory Commission has decided that the relevant competent authorities were correct in rejecting the complaint;

   and, where the competent authorities of the Member States concerned agree, all the costs referred to in paragraphs 1(a) and (b) shall be borne by the affected person.

Article 13

Information, evidence and hearings

1. For the purposes of the procedure referred to in Article 6, where the competent authorities of the Member States concerned agree, the affected person(s) concerned may provide the Advisory Commission or Alternative Dispute Resolution Commission with any information, evidence or documents that may be relevant for the decision. The affected person(s) and the competent authorities of the Member States concerned shall provide any information,

evidence or documents upon request by the Advisory Commission or Alternative Dispute Resolution Commission. However, those competent authorities may refuse to provide information to the Advisory Commission in any of the following cases:

(a) obtaining the information requires carrying out administrative measures that are against national law;
(b) the information cannot be obtained under the national law of the Member State concerned;
(c) the information concerns trade secrets, business secrets, industrial secrets, professional secrets or trade processes;
(d) the disclosure of the information is contrary to public policy.

2. Affected persons may, at their request and with the consent of the competent authorities of the Member States concerned, appear or be represented before an Advisory Commission or Alternative Dispute Resolution Commission. Affected persons shall appear or be represented before it upon request by the Advisory Commission or Alternative Dispute Resolution Commission.
3. The independent persons of standing or any other member shall be subject to obligations of professional secrecy under the national legislation of each of the Member States concerned in relation to information they receive in their capacity as members an Advisory Commission or Alternative Dispute Resolution Commission. Affected persons, and where applicable, their representatives, shall undertake to treat any information (including knowledge of documents) that they receive during such proceedings as secret. The affected person and his representatives shall make a declaration to this effect to the competent authorities of the Member States concerned when so requested during the proceedings. The Member States shall adopt appropriate sanctions for any breach of secrecy obligations.

Article 14
The opinion of the Advisory Commission or Alternative Dispute Resolution Commission

1. An Advisory Commission or Alternative Dispute Resolution Commission shall deliver its opinion to the competent authorities of the Member States concerned no later than 6 months after the date on which it was set up. Where the Advisory Commission or Alternative Dispute Resolution Commission considers that the question in dispute is such that it would need more than 6 months to deliver an opinion, this period may be extended by 3 months. The Advisory Commission or Alternative Dispute Resolution Commission shall inform the competent authorities of the Member States concerned and the affected persons of any such extension.
2. The Advisory Commission or Alternative Dispute Resolution Commission shall base its opinion on the provisions of the applicable agreement or convention referred to in Article 1 as well as on any applicable national rules.

3. The Advisory Commission or Alternative Dispute Resolution Commission shall adopt its opinion by a simple majority of its members. Where a majority cannot be reached, the vote of the chair shall determine the final opinion. The chair shall communicate the opinion of the Advisory Commission or Alternative Dispute Resolution Commission to the competent authorities.

Article 15
Final decision

1. The competent authorities concerned shall agree on how to resolve the question in dispute within 6 months of the notification of the opinion of the Advisory Commission or Alternative Dispute Resolution Commission.
2. The competent authorities may take a decision which deviates from the opinion of the Advisory Commission or Alternative Dispute Resolution Commission. However, if they fail to reach an agreement as to how to resolve the question in dispute, they shall be bound by that opinion.
3. Each Member State shall provide that its competent authority shall notify the final decision on the resolution of the question in dispute to the affected person without delay. In the absence of such notification within 30 days of the decision having been taken, the affected person may appeal in its Member State of residence in accordance with the applicable national rules in order to obtain the final decision.
4. The final decision shall be binding on the Member States concerned and shall not constitute a precedent. The final decision shall be implemented subject to the affected person(s) accepting the final decision and renouncing the right to any domestic remedy within 60 days from the date when the final decision was notified, where applicable.

   Except where the relevant court or other judicial body of a Member State concerned decides according to its applicable national rules on remedies and applying the criteria under Article 8 that there was lack of independence, the final decision shall be implemented under the national law of the Member States concerned which as a result of the final decision shall amend their taxation, irrespective of any time limits prescribed by the national law. Where the final decision has not been implemented, the affected person may apply to the competent court of the Member State that failed to implement the final decision, in order to enforce implementation thereof.

Article 16
Interaction with national proceedings and derogations

1. The fact that the action of a Member State that gave rise to a question in dispute has become final under national law shall not prevent the affected persons from having recourse to the procedures provided for in this Directive.

2. The submission of the question in dispute to the mutual agreement procedure or to the dispute resolution procedure under Articles 4 and 6 respectively shall not prevent a Member State from initiating or continuing judicial proceedings or proceedings for administrative and criminal penalties in relation to the same matters.
3. Affected persons may have recourse to the remedies available to them under the national law of the Member States concerned. However, where the affected person has commenced proceedings to seek such a remedy, the terms of periods referred to in Articles 3(5) and 4(1) respectively shall commence from the date on which a judgement delivered in those proceedings has become final or on which those proceedings have otherwise been definitively concluded or where the proceedings have been suspended.
4. Where a decision on a question in dispute has been rendered by the relevant court or other judicial body of a Member State, and the national law of that Member State does not allow it to derogate from the decision, that Member State may provide that:
   (a) before an agreement has been reached by the competent authorities of the Member States concerned under the mutual agreement procedure under Article 4 on that question in dispute, the competent authority of such Member State is to notify the other competent authorities of the Member States concerned of the decision of the relevant court or other judicial body and that that procedure is to be terminated as from the date of such notification;
   (b) before the affected person has made a request under Article 6(1), the provisions of Article 6(1) do not apply if the question in dispute had remained unresolved during the whole of the mutual agreement procedure under Article 4, in which case the competent authority of that Member State is to inform the other competent authorities of the Member States concerned of the effect of the decision of the relevant court or other judicial body;
   (c) the dispute resolution process under Article 6 is to be terminated if the decision of the relevant court or other judicial body was rendered at any time after an affected person has made a request under Article 6(1) but before the Advisory Commission or the Alternative Dispute Resolution Commission has delivered its opinion to the competent authorities of the Member States concerned in accordance with Article 14, in which case the competent authority of the relevant Member State concerned is to inform the other competent authorities of the Member States concerned and the Advisory Commission or the Alternative Dispute Resolution Commission of the effect of the decision of the relevant court or other judicial body.
5. The submission of a complaint as provided under Article 3 shall put an end to any other ongoing proceedings under the mutual agreement procedure or dispute resolution procedure under an agreement or convention that is being interpreted or applied in relation to the relevant question in dispute. Such other ongoing proceedings concerning the relevant question in dispute shall

come to an end with effect from the date of the first receipt of the complaint by any of the competent authorities of the Member States concerned.

6. By way of derogation from Article 6, a Member State concerned may deny access to the dispute resolution procedure under that Article in cases where penalties were imposed in that Member State in relation to the adjusted income or capital for tax fraud, wilful default and gross negligence. Where judicial or administrative proceedings were commenced that could potentially lead to such penalties, and these proceedings are being conducted simultaneously with any of the proceedings referred to in this Directive, a competent authority may stay the proceedings under this Directive as from the date of acceptance of the complaint until the date of the final outcome of those proceedings.
7. A Member State may deny access to the dispute resolution procedure under Article 6 on a case-by-case basis where a question in dispute does not involve double taxation. In such a case, the competent authority of the said Member State shall inform the affected person and the competent authorities of the other Member States concerned without delay.

Article 17
Special provisions for individuals and smaller undertakings

Where the affected person is either:

(a) an individual; or
(b) not a large undertaking and does not form part of a large group (both as defined in Directive 2013/34/EU of the European Parliament and of the Council,[1]

the affected person may submit the complaints, replies to a request for additional information, withdrawals and requests specified in Articles 3(1), 3(4), 3(6) and 6(1), respectively ('communications'), by way of derogation from those provisions, only to the competent authority of the Member State in which the affected person is resident. The competent authority of that Member State shall notify the competent authorities of all the other Member States concerned at the same time and within 2 months of receipt of such communications. Once such a notification has been made, the affected person shall be deemed to have submitted the communication to all the Member States concerned as of the date of such notification.

In the case of additional information received under Article 3(4), the competent authority of the Member State that received the additional information shall transmit a copy to the competent authorities of all the other Member States concerned at the same

1. Directive 2013/34/EU of the European Parliament and of the Council of 26 June 2013 on the annual financial statements, consolidated financial statements and related reports of certain types of undertakings, amending Directive 2006/43/EC of the European Parliament and of the Council and repealing Council Directives 78/660/EEC and 83/349/EEC (OJ L 182, 29.6.2013, p. 19).

time. Once this submission has been made, it shall be deemed that additional information has been received by all Member States concerned as at the date of such receipt of information.

Article 18

Publicity

1. Advisory Commissions and Alternative Dispute Resolution Commissions shall issue their opinions in writing.
2. The competent authorities may agree to publish the final decisions referred to in Article 15 in their entirety, subject to consent of each of the affected person concerned.
3. Where the competent authorities or affected person concerned do not consent to publishing the final decision in its entirety, the competent authorities shall publish an abstract of the final decision. That abstract shall contain a description of the issue and the subject matter, the date, the tax periods involved, the legal basis, the industry sector, and a short description of the final outcome. It shall also include a description of the method of arbitration used. The competent authorities shall send the information to be published in accordance with the first subparagraph to the affected person before its publication. No later than 60 days from the receipt of such information, the affected person may request the competent authorities not to publish information that concerns any trade, business, industrial or professional secret or trade process, or that is contrary to public policy.
4. The Commission shall establish standard forms for the communication of the information referred to in paragraphs 2 and 3 of this Article by means of implementing acts. Those implementing acts shall be adopted in accordance with the procedure referred to in Article 20(2).
5. The competent authorities shall notify the information to be published in accordance with paragraph 3 to the Commission without delay.

Article 19

Role of the Commission and administrative support

1. The Commission shall keep the list of the competent authorities and the list of the independent persons of standing referred to in Article 8(4) up to date and shall make them available online. That list shall contain only the names of those persons.
2. Member States shall inform the Commission of the measures they have taken in order to penalise any breach of secrecy obligation provided for in Article 13. The Commission shall inform the other Member States thereof.
3. The Commission shall maintain a central repository in which the information that is published in accordance with Articles 18(2) and (3) is archived and made available online.

Article 20
Committee procedure

1. The Commission shall be assisted by the Committee on Dispute Resolution. That Committee shall be a committee within the meaning of Regulation (EU) No 182/2011.
2. Where reference is made to this paragraph, Article 5 of Regulation (EU) No 182/2011 shall apply.

Article 21
Review

By 30 June 2024, the Commission shall evaluate the implementation of this Directive and shall present a report to the Council. That report shall, if appropriate, be accompanied by a legislative proposal.

Article 22
Transposition

1. Member States shall bring into force the laws, regulations and administrative provisions necessary to comply with this Directive by 30 June 2019 at the latest. They shall forthwith communicate to the Commission the text thereof. When Member States adopt those provisions, they shall contain a reference to this Directive or be accompanied by such a reference on the occasion of their official publication. Member States shall determine how such reference is to be made.
2. Member States shall communicate to the Commission the text of the main provisions of national law which they adopt in the field covered by this Directive.

Article 23
Entry into force

This Directive shall enter into force on the twentieth day following that of its publication in the *Official Journal of the European Union.*

It shall apply to any complaint submitted from 1 July 2019 onwards relating to questions of dispute relating to income or capital earned in a tax year commencing on or after 1 January 2018. Competent authorities of Member States concerned may however agree to apply this Directive with regard to any complaint that was submitted prior to that day or to earlier tax years.

Article 24
Addressees

This Directive is addressed to the Member States. Done at Luxembourg, 10 October 2017.

Glossary

ACD	Luxembourg competent authority (‘*Administration des contributions directes*’)
Affected Person	Any natural or legal person that is a resident of a Member State for tax purposes and whose taxation is directly affected by a Question in Dispute, as defined below
Arbitration Convention	Convention 90/463/EEC of 23 July 1990
Austrian EU-TDRA	Austrian law BGBl. I Nr. 62/2019, Austrian EU-TDRA (‘*EU-Besteuerungsstreitbeilegungsgesetz*’)
Competent Authority	The authority which has been designated as such by the Member State concerned
Contracting State	The State party to the Tax Treaty, as defined below
Circular 21/2012	Circular No. 21 of 5 June 2012 issued by the Italian Revenue Agency
Decree	Italian Legislative Decree No. 49 of 10 June 2020
Decree 546/1992	Italian Legislative Decree No. 546 of 31 December 1992
Directive 2017/1852	Council Directive 10 (EU) 2017/1852 of 10 October 2017
Double Taxation	the imposition of taxes covered by a Tax Treaty (as defined below) by two or more Member States (as defined below) in respect of the same taxable income or capital when it gives rise to either: (i) an additional tax charge; (ii) an increase in tax liabilities; or (iii) the cancellation or reduction of losses that could be used to offset taxable profits
Draft Royal Decree	The Spanish Draft Royal Decree amending the Regulations on MAPs in direct taxation matters, approved by Royal Decree 1794/2008 of November 3, available on 23 December 2019
Fiscal Arbitration Act	Dutch Law implementing Directive 2017/1852 of 10 July 2019

FFC	The Austrian Federal Fiscal Code
FFCA	The Austrian Federal Finance Court Act
FPC	The French Procedural Code
General Taxes Act	Dutch Law (*'Algemene Wet inzake Rijksbelastingen'*)
General Time Limits Act	Dutch Law which provides for generally applicable rules on legal terms (*'Algemene termijnenwet'*)
Implementation Act	Danish act No. 1726 of 27 December 2018
Implementing Decree	French Decree No. 2019-616 of 21 June 2019
IRA	The Italian revenue agency (*'Agenzia delle Entrate'*)
Law of 2 May 2019	Belgian Law implementing Directive 2017/1852 of 2 May 2019
Law of 20 December 2019	Law implementing Directive 2017/1852 in the Luxembourg domestic tax system
Law No. 117	Italian Law No. 117/2019 published in Italian Official Gazette No. 245 of 18 October 2019 (the so-called *legge di delegazione europea*)
Law No. 120/2019	Portuguese Law No. 120/2019, published in Portuguese Official Gazette No. 180 of 19 September 2019
Member States	Member States of the European Union
MAP	Mutual agreement procedure
MLI	The Multilateral Convention to Implement Tax Treaty-Related Measures to Prevent Base Erosion and Profit Shifting
OECD Model Convention	Model Tax Convention on Income and on Capital published by the OECD
Procedure 31-*quater*	The procedure referred to in Article 31-*quater*(1)(c) of Italian Presidential Decree No. 600 of 29 September 1973
Question in Dispute	A matter giving rise to disputes arising from the interpretation and application of a Tax Treaty as defined below
Regulations	The EU (Tax Dispute Resolution Mechanisms) Regulations 2019 (S.I. No. 306/2019) adopted by Ireland
Regulations on MAPs	the Spanish Regulation on MAPs in the field of direct taxation approved by Royal Decree 1794/2008
RDL 3/2020	Spanish Royal Decree-Law 3/2020 of 4 February 2020
Revenue Commissioners	The Irish Revenue Commissioners
Tax Courts	Italian Provincial and Regional Tax Courts
Tax Treaties	Bilateral treaties against double taxation in force between the various States

TDRM Law	The German Law implementing Directive 2017/1852 of 10 December 2019 ('Gesetz zur Umsetzung der Richtlinie (EU) 2017/1852 des Rates vom 10. Oktober 2017 über Verfahren zur Beilegung von Besteuerungsstreitigkeiten in der Europäischen Union')
UGB	The Austrian Commercial Code

Index

C

D

Q

R

S

T

www.ingramcontent.com/pod-product-compliance
Lightning Source LLC
Chambersburg PA
CBHW071242230926
51849CB00001B/197
9789403523606